WILDLIFE

of East Africa | A PHOTOGRAPHIC GUIDE

Dave Richards

Published by Struik Nature
(an imprint of Penguin Random House
South Africa (Pty) Ltd)
Reg. No. 1953/000441/07
The Estuaries No. 4, Oxbow Crescent,
Century Avenue, Century City
PO Box 1144, Cape Town, 8000 South Africa

Visit **www.struiknature.co.za** and join
the Struik Nature Club for updates, news, events,
and special offers

First published in 2013

10 9 8 7

Publisher: Pippa Parker
Managing editor: Helen de Villiers
Editor: Lesley Hay-Whitton
Project manager: Colette Alves
Design director: Janice Evans
Layout: Neil Bester
Proofreader: Emsie du Plessis

Reproduction by Hirt & Carter Cape (Pty) Ltd
Printed and bound in China by Toppan Leefung Packaging
and Printing (Dongguan) Co., Ltd

MIX
Paper from
responsible sources
FSC
www.fsc.org   FSC® C104723

Front cover: (top) Reticulated Giraffe – Dave Richards; (bottom, left to right) Dark Blue Pansy – Dave Richards; Velvety-green Night Adder – Steve Spawls; Kedong Dracaena, Grey-headed Kingfisher, Mountain Gladiolus – Dave Richards; **Back cover:** (top to bottom) Grey Crowned Crane, Lion, Painted Lady – Dave Richards; Olive Sand Snake – Johan Marais; Flame Lily – Dave Richards; **Page 1:** Collared Sunbird – Dave Richards; **Page 3:** Zanzibar Red Colobus – Paolo Torchio; Woodland Kingfisher – Dave Richards; Galam White-lipped Frog – Alan Channing; Migratory Butterfly, Red-leaved Rock Fig, Desert Rose – Dave Richards

ACKNOWLEDGEMENTS

First of all, I have to thank my wife, Val, for her help, patience and support throughout the many months while I was writing this guidebook and, especially, when I was away for long periods in the bush.

The following people (not in any particular order) have given me help and advice in various ways, and I apologise to anyone I have inadvertently left out.

Dr Geoffrey Mwachala, Dr Itambo Malombe, the late Tim Noad, Gordon Boy, Karen Maclean, Harrison Kinyanku Nampaso, Patrick Reynolds, Dino Martins, Wilson Lolpapit, Brian Finch, Steve Collins, Paul Oliver, Will Knocker, Bruce Patterson, Paolo Torchio, Sue Allan, Wendy and Alan McKittrick, Amedeo Buonajuti, David Elsworthy, Don Turner, Brian Williams, Patrick Beresford, Lis Farrell, Ben Mgambi, Marcell Claassen, Musa Lekwale and Charles Mwangi Gitau. A special thanks also to all the staff and, particularly, the guides of Governors' Camps, for all their help.

Last but not least, I have to thank Pippa Parker of Penguin Random House for her tireless support and encouragement and her team in Cape Town, including Colette Alves, Colette Stott and Lesley Hay-Whitton, for all their care taken in helping me to complete this, my latest guidebook.

CONTENTS

Lesser Flamingos on Lake Magadi, Kenya

INTRODUCTION

East Africa – an area that comprises Kenya, Tanzania, Uganda, Burundi and Rwanda – is one of the most wildlife-rich regions in Africa. This region is intersected by several major biomes, with the result that its vegetation is very diverse. It is bisected by two rift valleys, running north to south, which contain numerous lakes, both fresh water and soda. It also has a number of isolated mountains, with their own varied habitats. These include the ice- and snow-covered Kilimanjaro (the highest mountain in Africa), montane forests, tropical rain forests, semi-desert, savanna, mangrove forests and a palm-fringed coastline, with its many lagoons and estuaries. This diversity of vegetation and animal life makes this the premier wildlife viewing region in Africa.

The mountains in the west are home to the rare and endangered Mountain Gorilla, which occurs both in Rwanda and Uganda. Chimpanzees are also found in Rwanda, Uganda and Tanzania. One of the world's largest migrations of mammals takes place between Tanzania and Kenya, with over one million Wildebeest, accompanied by approximately 200 000 Zebra and thousands of Gazelle, moving to better grazing areas.

The economic benefits that result from the conservation of the region's wildlife have now been realised, and wildlife tourism has become a major source of revenue and employment. There has been a huge upsurge of interest in Africa and its wildlife. Viewing wildlife in natural surroundings is a satisfying experience, and there is arguably no better way to relax from the stresses and strains of modern life. However, most visitors would benefit more if they had information on the wildlife they were watching.

The aim of this compact guidebook is to help visitors to the region's national parks, national reserves and other wildlife areas enjoy the wildlife even more. It does not claim to be a comprehensive field guide, but is an introduction to the more noticeable and interesting mammals, birds, reptiles, frogs, trees, flowers and insects (including butterflies) that can be seen on safari. Comprehensive guides are available for each group, with the exception, perhaps, of butterflies. Anyone who would like more detailed information should consult the list of recommended reading matter in the bibliography on page 162.

This book illustrates and describes a carefully selected range of species, with notes on their identification, habitat, status, size and, if applicable, the best locations in which to see them. Chapters are arranged in such a way that similar or related species are placed together for comparison, but this means that the sequence more typical of comprehensive reference books has not always been followed.

GEOGRAPHY AND CLIMATE

The East African topography is a study of contrasts. Features range from snow-capped mountains and deserts, sandy coastlines and fresh-water lakes, to savanna grasslands, fertile agricultural plantations, extinct volcanoes and coral reefs.

The surface relief of East Africa is more varied than most other parts of the continent.

Areas below 500 m are confined to the coast and parts of interior eastern Tanzania, eastern Kenya and the Lake Turkana area in northern Kenya. Most of the remaining region is plateau country (between 500 and 1 500 m), with highland areas in northern Rwanda, southwestern Uganda, western and central Kenya, and much of interior Tanzania.

The region is bisected by two rift valleys. In the west is the Central African Rift Valley, which runs from the Sudan in the north down to Malawi in the south, and roughly forms the political borders of the DRC with Uganda, Rwanda and Burundi. This valley contains a number of fresh-water lakes, which all vary in altitude above sea level, from Lake Albert (612 m), Lake Edward and Lake George (both 913 m), to Lake Kivu (1 460 m). Lake Tanganyika, the world's second-deepest lake, with a depth of 1 435 m, is also located in this Rift Valley, 773 m above sea level.

In the east is the better-known East African Rift Valley or The Great Rift Valley, which runs from the Red Sea across Ethiopia, through Kenya and Tanzania. This also has a chain of lakes, some of which are alkaline, and again all at varying altitudes. In northern Kenya is Lake Turkana (375 m), and, to the south, Lake Baringo (972 m), Lake Nakuru (1 753 m), Lake Naivasha (1 890 m) and Lake Magadi (579 m). Across the border in Tanzania are Lake Natron (610 m), Lake Manyara (960 m) and Lake Eyasi (1 030 m). A feature of these eastern Rift Valley lakes is that none have outlets, or at least no obvious ones.

Almost in the middle of East Africa is the world's second-largest fresh-water lake, Lake Victoria (at an altitude of 1 133 m), which covers 69 000 km² and fills up a shallow depression between the two Rift Valleys. At its deepest it is only 84 m. To the east of Lake Victoria are the famous Serengeti plains, which are dotted with ancient koppies. Surprisingly, East Africa has mountains with permanent ice: in Tanzania, the well-known Kilimanjaro (5 895 m high) in Kenya, Mount Kenya (5 199 m) and, straddling the Uganda/DRC border, the Rwenzori Mountains (5 119 m). Other high mountains include Meru (4 565 m) in Tanzania, Elgon (4 321 m), which straddles the Uganda/Kenya border and Muhabura (4 192 m), the highest of the Virungas, which straddles the Uganda/Rwanda border.

Apart from the north and east, most parts of East Africa receive between 60 and 150 cm of rainfall per annum. The seasons vary across the region and from year to year. In the north rain mostly falls between March and November. The long rains fall between March and May in much of Kenya and southern Uganda, and the short rains in October and November. Most of the rain in southern and western Tanzania, Rwanda and Burundi falls between October and May. There are many local variations, depending on the altitude and proximity to the coast or Lake Victoria.

African Elephants in Amboseli National Park, Kenya

Daryl & Sharna Balfour/IOA

IDENTIFYING AND WATCHING WILDLIFE

Although the region's fast-rising human population means that wildlife is increasingly being confined to protected areas, it is perhaps surprising that it is still possible to see wildlife almost anywhere in East Africa. In city parks and gardens, monkeys, Tree Hyrax and Greater Galagos can still be seen. Nairobi is unique in being the only city in the world with a national park within its city limits.

East Africa is blessed with abundant wildlife areas: with over 100 national parks, national reserves and other wildlife areas, it can quite rightly be called the home of the safari. In fact, the word 'safari' is a Kiswahili word for 'a journey'.

Over the past few years safaris have evolved. These days, the tourist is not confined to a vehicle for wildlife viewing; many wildlife areas now offer walks with armed guides, horse-riding safaris, camel safaris, bird walks and visits to cultural villages and schools. Another recent development is the creation of regional airlines, with more and more tourists flying to their safari destination. For instance, Air Kenya now has three flights each day to the Masai Mara and at times makes use of 40-seat aircraft. While flying to a destination is far quicker than driving, which leaves more time to view the wildlife, in the process tourists miss out on seeing and experiencing much of the country they are visiting. So, a flight from Nairobi to the Masai Mara takes only 40 to 45 minutes, compared with a drive of five to six hours, but on the drive the visitor crosses the Great Rift Valley, with its spectacular scenery and glimpses of wildlife, and has the opportunity to see the Maasai people, their cattle and villages. Apart from a modern road, little has changed in this area for hundreds of years.

On arrival by air, you will be met by a safari guide, who will brief you on the area and its wildlife. Most, if not all, safari guides will have wildlife guidebooks on mammals and birds (sometimes even trees and wildflowers) in their safari vehicle. It is recommended that visitors have their own pair of binoculars. Even though much of the wildlife can be seen up close, there are sometimes interesting things to see that are further off; it is frustrating having to wait to borrow binoculars.

Watching wildlife requires patience: by all means tell your guide which animals you would most like to see but don't expect to see them immediately. Most visitors want to see Lions, particularly a male, but at certain times of the year, especially when the grass is long, even such large animals can be difficult to find. When on safari, it is essential to get up early as most animals, and particularly the cats, are best seen in the cooler hours of the day. Another good time is late afternoon and, in some private wildlife areas, night-viewing drives are possible.

Silence is considered good etiquette while watching wildlife. Of course, you can speak quietly to your guide to ask him questions, but consideration for the wildlife is critical and they should never be disturbed or threatened in any way. Although much of the wildlife is accustomed to tourists, it is disrespectful to shout at animals. Lions are often sleeping when spotted by tour groups: although we all want to photograph them while they are active, do not try to wake them. In most wildlife areas the wildlife has become almost immune to tourists and, as they have come to feel safe, their habits have changed. Cheetahs now often jump onto tourist vehicles and use them as lookout posts. Lions may ignore you entirely. Leopards can often be seen hunting during the day and elephants can be found lying on their sides sleeping, something almost unheard of just a few years ago. Of course, tourism also does have negative effects. A good example is that of Cheetahs: because they are so often followed closely by tourist vehicles, more of their hunts end in failure. Some Cheetahs now hunt during the hot midday hours, when the tourists are back at their lodge or camp enjoying their lunch. This is far from ideal for Cheetahs, as they can suffer severely from overheating when hunting at this time of the day.

One final word: do not be tempted to feed wildlife, particularly monkeys and mongooses, as they can give a severe bite.

NATIONAL PARKS AND OTHER PROTECTED AREAS

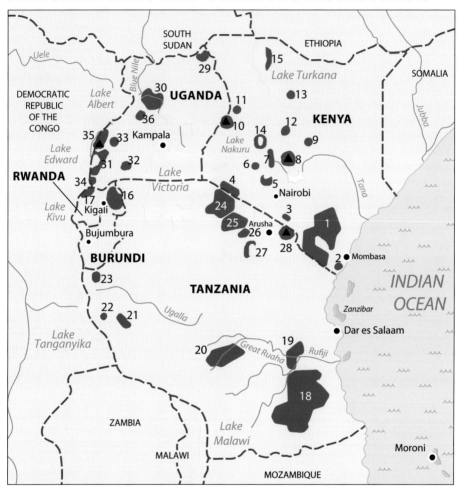

1 Tsavo	13 Marsabit	25 Ngorongoro
2 Shimba Hills	14 Lake Bogoria	26 Lake Manyara
3 Amboseli	15 Sibiloi (Lake Turkana)	27 Tarangire
4 Masai Mara	16 Akagera	28 Kilimanjaro
5 Nairobi	17 Virunga (+ Mgahinga)	29 Kidepo Valley
6 Hell's Gate	18 Selous	30 Murchison Falls
7 Aberdares	19 Mikumi	31 Queen Elizabeth
8 Mt Kenya	20 Ruaha	32 Lake Mburo
9 Meru	21 Katavi	33 Kibale Forest
10 Mt Elgon	22 Mahale Mountains	34 Bwindi Impenetrable
11 Saiwa Swamp	23 Gombe Stream	35 Rwenzori Mountains
12 Samburu	24 Serengeti	36 Budongo Forest

VEGETATION ZONES IN EAST AFRICA

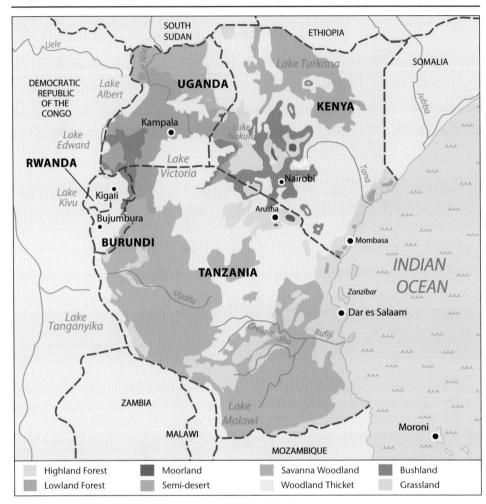

Highland Forest	Moorland	Savanna Woodland	Bushland
Lowland Forest	Semi-desert	Woodland Thicket	Grassland

Vegetation zones are areas that have distinct types of plants, soil and weather patterns. The types of plant species that grow in a region are influenced by the climate, soil, rainfall and the ability of the soil to hold water.

Highland Forest

HIGHLAND FOREST resembles lowland forest, although different tree species are involved and it does not grow as tall and dense. It is mostly broad-leaved, but *Juniperus* and *Podocarpus* are dominant in many drier types. Bamboo grows in patches or belts up to 15 m high, typically at higher altitudes than forest, but also as low as 1 600 m. Unforested areas, both above and below the timber-line, are usually dominated by bushy growth, with ericaceous shrubs and giant lobelias and senecios at high altitudes.

LOWLAND FOREST is typically confined to areas with at least 150 cm of rain evenly distributed throughout the year. In its primary condition, this forest is richer in biomass and plant species than any other vegetation type in Africa. It forms a dense stand of trees of one or more storeys, with an interlaced upper canopy, often between 20 and 30 m above ground. Taller trees emerge from the canopy but rarely exceed 60 m in height. The ground cover of this and other forest types is dominated by herbs and shrubs. In East Africa, lowland forest is mainly fragmented, having been greatly modified by human activities.

Lowland Forest

MOORLAND occurs above the timber-line. The ground is often boggy, with tussock grasses, rushes and spectacular giant rosette plants (*Lobelia* and *Senecio* species).

SEMI-DESERT has some of the characteristics of a desert but receives more annual rain, varying from 0–200 mm. The mean monthly temperatures range from 27–33°C, although 50°C was recorded at Lake Turkana. These areas have shallow, stony soils that support sparse annual grassland, dry stunted thorny shrubs and acacia thickets along dry river courses.

Moorland

SAVANNA WOODLANDS are stands of trees (mainly deciduous) up to 18 m high, sometimes with shrubs interspersed, with an open or continuous but not thickly interlaced canopy, providing cover of more than 20 per cent. Grasses and herbs dominate the ground cover. This widespread, varied habitat needs more than 30 cm of rain per annum. Many of the trees have a thick corky bark, which protects them from fire in the severe dry season.

Semi-desert

WOODLAND THICKET is where woody plants form a closed stand through which man or the larger ungulates can pass only with extreme difficulty. Trees of the genus *Isoberlinia* predominate in higher-rainfall areas north of the equator (mainly Uganda), while *Brachystegia* and *Julbernardia* species are dominant in the vast tracts of miombo woodland characteristic of plateau country in much of southern and western Tanzania.

BUSHLAND, often forming thickets, consists of woody plants with a shrub canopy of less than 6 m in height, and a canopy cover of more than 20 per cent.

Savanna Woodland

Woodland Thicket

Bushland

Grassland

Soda Lake

Bushland (especially thicket) in areas formerly forested is often moist and evergreen. The extensive thicket area near Itigi in central Tanzania is unique in East Africa. In this type of deciduous thicket, shrubs grow to 5 m in height, interlaced overhead to form a dense canopy that is sometimes pierced by trees between 8 and 11 m high. Areas of bushland and woodland are often intermixed, particularly in drier areas. *Acacia* and *Commiphora* species are dominant in these drier areas, mainly in the north and east, with numerous Baobabs (*Adansonia digitata*) at lower altitudes. Semi-arid conditions characterised by *Acacia-Commiphora* bushland and woodland extend to the Rukwa Valley and parts of eastern Mbeya in the southwest, virtually separating the miombo woodlands of southeastern and western Tanzania.

GRASSLANDS are areas dominated by grasses and occasionally other herbs, sometimes with widely scattered or grouped trees and shrubs, the canopy cover of which does not exceed two per cent. These often extensive areas are usually subject to periodic burning. Most large tracts of grassland in East Africa are on free-draining land and dominated by short perennial grasses, usually less than 50 cm. Seasonally inundated areas on floodplains and poorly drained soils are included here. In some areas the trees and shrubs scattered over grasslands are of a dwarf type (shrubs are < 1 m and trees are > 2 m in height). Dwarf-tree grasslands with *Acacia drepanolobium* are characteristic of the Athi Plains in central Kenya. In arid regions, with erratic rainfall of less than 30 cm per annum, bushed and wooded grasslands of dwarf types often predominate, though grass cover is sometimes of limited duration in these often barren or denuded areas.

WETLANDS, FRESH-WATER AND SODA LAKES are a feature of the two Rift Valleys, with Lake Victoria situated roughly between them. The Rift Valley lakes are varied: some fresh, some soda. Soda lakes are essentially alkaline because they have no outlets, and have been filled by drainage from lava rocks. Lakes Baringo and Naivasha are fresh, with no obvious outlets, although they must have subterranean outlets. Lake Tanganyika, at 1 400 m deep, is the deepest fresh-water lake in Africa. Soda lakes have varying alkalinity: for example, the three Momella lakes in Tanzania vary from fresh water to alkaline, and life in each is different. For example, Lesser Flamingos feeding on blue-green algae can be found on one lake, while Greater Flamingos, which feed on crustaceans, feed on a slightly fresher lake nearby.

PHOTOGRAPHING WILDLIFE

Nowadays almost all tourists or visitors carry digital cameras, ranging from small entry-level 'point-and-shoot' models to those with large lenses. One of the advantages of digital photography is that the camera uses a memory card and is therefore able to store hundreds of photographs (depending on the size of the card). Conveniently, memory cards are generally widely available at most camps and lodges.

When you're on safari, always have your camera ready, not shut up inside a bag. As dust is unavoidable on safari, always keep your camera covered. A good solution is to buy a kikoi (a colourful cotton wrap traditionally worn by men) and use this to cover your camera. When taking pictures, keep as steady as possible and don't be shy to ask fellow travellers to keep still in the vehicle. If you are using a large lens, rest your camera on the windowsill or roof of the vehicle. Shoot from as low as possible, which produces more dramatic photographs. If you have a camera with interchangeable lenses, be very careful when changing them. Always make sure your camera is switched off: a digital camera has a sensor that is electrically charged when the camera is on. Any dust on the camera body will be attracted to the sensor; it may be invisible to the eye but will show up on photographs as a dark mark or smudge. Even if your camera is switched off when you change a lens, it is still possible to get dust inside the camera body, which will eventually find its way onto the sensor. Some cameras have built-in sensor cleaners, but even so, large particles of dust can still adhere to the sensor.

An ideal lens for safaris is a 100 to 300 or 400 mm lens. A smaller zoom lens, such as 28 to 85 mm, is useful for photographing people and scenery. If possible, have these lenses mounted on two separate camera bodies; if you don't have to change lenses, dust can't get into your camera. If you are keen on bird photography, a 500 or even a 600 mm lens is very useful. If you want to photograph local people, please ask their permission first. At most cultural villages the price of admission usually entitles you to take photographs.

CONSERVATION OF WILDLIFE

'The survival of our wildlife is a matter of grave concern to all of us in Africa. These wild creatures amid wild places they inhabit are not only important as a source of wonder and inspiration but are an integral part of our national resources and our future livelihood and well-being.'

Julius Nyerere, Tanzania's first President

East African organisations for protection of wildlife:
- Kenya Wildlife Service (KWS): **www.kws.org**
- Tanzania National Parks (TANAPA): **www.tanzaniaparks.com**
- Uganda Wildlife Authority: **www.ugandawildlife.org**
- Rwanda Office of Tourism and National Parks (responsible for nature conservation and tourism): **www.rwandatourism.com**

ABBREVIATIONS

NP = National Park	Kinyarwanda (Rwa)
NR = National Reserve	Kiswahili (Swa)
GR = Game Reserve	Luganda (Lug)
CA = Conservation Area	Luo (Luo)
Arusha (Aru)	Maasai (Maa)
Chagga (Chag)	Samburu (Sam)
Kamba (Kam)	Teso (Teso)
Kikuyu (Kik)	Turkana (Turk)

MAMMALS

East Africa's plains are home to the last great herds of wildlife in Africa. There are almost 100 species of grazers, compared with Europe's 13 and North America's 11. These species, together with a large variety of predators and scavengers, make East Africa the last Eden. Overall, there are an impressive 1 116 species of mammal in the region. This book illustrates 116 of these species, most of which can be seen in the region's national parks, national reserves and other wildlife areas. Although it is rarely seen, the Naked Mole Rat, which lives underground, has been included in this book because its distinctive, volcano-shaped 'erupting' heaps are a feature of the countryside where it occurs.

With the huge rise in the human population, wildlife is increasingly being confined to protected areas, particularly the larger mammal species. Elephant numbers have grown so much in some areas that many are being translocated to protected areas that are not surrounded by large human populations. At the same time, in other areas more elephants are being killed than ever before for their ivory. Poaching is another threat – large numbers of mammals are snared for bush meat to feed the human populations near the protected areas. Wildlife is further threatened by the wide use of the cheap and easily available chemical Furadan to poison animals. In most cases local farmers use it to kill problem animals such as Leopard and Hyaena. These are not the only animals affected by this practice: other mammals and birds, such as vultures, die after feeding on poisoned carcasses. The serious knock-on effects of Furadan poisoning are illustrated by the following incident. A Hippopotamus in a national reserve died of Furadan poisoning. Its carcass was fed upon by several Lion, Hyaena and Jackal, which all died. Even more disturbing is that, because the presence of vultures often betrays the presence of poachers to rangers, there is evidence that poachers poisoned the animal with Furadan so that all the vultures in the area would die.

But there is hope. In northern Kenya the local people are slowly realising the value of the wildlife and the potential it offers for ecotourism on their land. The Northern Rangelands Trust has been set up and now employs over 1 500 people in conservation projects. This is a whole new economy that previously did not exist. Their biggest project at the moment is the re-establishment of the Black Rhino in northern Kenya. Since the Black Rhino population in protected areas is increasing at five per cent each year, new safe areas for Rhino are needed, and northern Kenya has the perfect habitat. This is a big challenge, given the high price of rhino horn.

The names used here largely follow *The Kingdon Field Guide to African Mammals* by Jonathan Kingdon (Academic Press, 1997). Where relevant, the Kiswahili (Swa), Maasai (Maa), Samburu (Sam) or Kinyarwanda (Rwa) names are also included.

The measurements given are height (foot to shoulder) and length (nose to tip of the tail). In some cases, the length of the tail or horns or the wingspan is included. The weight of the mammal, its habitat, its status and the best place to see it are also given. Most of the photographs are of adult males, but the text describes the females if they differ.

COMMON CHIMPANZEE
Pan troglodytes   sokwe mtu (Swa)

Habitat: forests and savanna woodland **Standing height:** 100–170 cm **Weight:** 40–55 kg (♂); 30 kg (♀) **Status:** endangered

Tailless ape with long, black hair and large, protruding ears. Lives in large social groups, 15–120 strong, within territories that are defended by both sexes but usually by males. Active mostly early morning and evening; each evening, adults build a nest to sleep in. Feeds on fruit, leaves, bark, birds' eggs and nestlings; adult males also hunt monkeys. Uses tools, such as grass stems to extract termites from their nests, and stones to break nuts.

BEST VIEWING: Tanzania: Gombe Stream, Mahale Mountains NPs; **Uganda:** Budongo Forest, Bwindi Impenetrable, Queen Elizabeth, Murchison Falls, Semuliki, Kibale Forest NPs; **Rwanda:** Nyungwe NP

MOUNTAIN GORILLA
Gorilla gorilla beringei   makaku (Swa)

Habitat: mountain forests **Standing height:** 140–185 cm (♂); 140–150 cm (♀) **Weight:** 160–210 kg (♂); 68–114 kg (♀) **Status:** endangered

A large, tailless ape, covered with dense black hair. Older male has a prominent, high crown, a heavy brow ridge and a grey-white mantle. Lives in small family groups, with one dominant male. Female gives birth, on average, once every four years and gives the young continuous care. Feeds on a variety of plants, wild celery, bamboo, thistles and even stinging nettles. Builds nest on the ground or low in trees to sleep in at night. Lives 50–60 years.

BEST VIEWING: Uganda: Bwindi Impenetrable, Mgahinga Gorilla NPs; **Rwanda:** Volcanoes NP

ZANZIBAR RED COLOBUS
Piliocolobus kirkii   kima punju (Swa)

Habitat: relict forest patches and scrub forest growing on waterless coral rag **Length:** 45–70 cm (♂); 45–62 cm (♀) **Tail:** 42–80 cm **Weight:** 9–13 kg (♂); 7–9 kg (♀) **Status:** endangered due to habitat destruction

Large, pot-bellied monkey with a long tail and arched back. Distinctive, red, black and white coloration. Nose and lips pink, contrasting with black face. Tufts of long hair on the crown and cheeks characteristic. A specialised leaf-eater with a four-chambered stomach to break down cellulose; observed eating charcoal, which is thought to aid digestion of toxin-containing leaves. One of Africa's rarest and most endangered primates.

BEST VIEWING: Tanzania: Jozani Forest, Zanzibar

Paolo Torchio

ANGOLAN BLACK AND WHITE COLOBUS
Colobus angolensis   mbega, kuluzu (Swa)

Habitat: coastal forests, lowland forests **Length:** 50–67 cm (♂); 50–61 cm (♀) **Tail:** 63–90 cm **Weight:** 9–20 kg **Status:** vulnerable as they occur in isolated populations

A distinctive, mainly black monkey with long white epaulettes and whiskers contrasting with its black face. The long tail is black, turning white towards the tip. Young are completely white for their first month, slowly darkening as they mature. Occurs in family groups. Feeds mostly on leaves, but also on seeds and fruit.

BEST VIEWING: Kenya: Diani Forest; **Tanzania:** Saadani, Serengeti NPs, Grumeti River; **Rwanda:** Nyungwe NP

EASTERN BLACK AND WHITE COLOBUS
Colobus guereza　　mbega mweupe (Swa); ol-koroi (Maa)

Habitat: highland forests **Length:** 54–75 cm (♂); 45–65 cm (♀)
Tail: 65–90 cm **Weight:** 10–23 kg **Status:** abundant in national
parks and forest reserves, but declining elsewhere

A distinctive, black-and-white forest monkey with long, thick
black fur, contrasting white cape and whiskers, and bushy white
beard and tail. Newborns are completely white, slowly darkening
until they resemble adults at around three months. Occurs in
family groups high (35–40 m) in the treetops. Often seen making
huge leaps from tree to tree; rarely descends to the ground.

BEST VIEWING: Kenya: Aberdare, Mount Kenya NPs; **Tanzania:** Arusha
NP, Ngorongoro CA; **Uganda:** Mgahinga Gorilla, Bwindi Impenetrable,
Queen Elizabeth, Semuliki, Kibale, Murchison Falls NPs

OLIVE BABOON
Papio anubis　　nyani (Swa); ol-otim (Maa)

Habitat: variety of habitats from open plains (with nearby trees
or rocky outcrops) to savanna and woodland **Length:** 127–142 cm
Tail: 45–68 cm **Weight:** 22–50 kg (♂); 11–30 kg (♀)
Status: widespread and common

Male is heavy, thickset, olive-green, with a well-developed mane.
Holds tail in an upright, curved position when walking. Female is
smaller; carries newborn under the belly. Young are black when
born. At about six weeks, they ride on their mother's back. Lives in
large troops of 40–80, consisting of family groups of females, their
young and a number of mature males. Feeds on grass, seeds, flowers,
seedpods and roots. Males occasionally hunt and eat young gazelles.

BEST VIEWING: most wildlife areas in the region

YELLOW BABOON
Papio cynocephalus　　nyani (Swa)

Habitat: bush country, woodland and rocky outcrops
Length: 116–137 cm **Tail:** 45–50 cm **Weight:** 22–30 kg (♂);
11–15 kg (♀) **Status:** common

Much lighter coloured than Olive Baboon. Smaller, slimmer build,
with longer legs. Male lacks mane, female is smaller. Both sexes have
white cheeks, contrasting with dark, bare skin on muzzle. Lives in
troops of 30–80 members, consisting of family groups of females,
their young and a number of mature males. Like all baboons, has a
varied diet, but prefers seeds and fruits of *Acacia*, *Albizia* and mopane
trees. Males occasionally hunt and eat young gazelles.

BEST VIEWING: Kenya: Amboseli, Tsavo East, Tsavo West NPs;
Tanzania: Ruaha, Tarangire NPs, Selous GR

PATAS MONKEY
Cercopithecus patas (*Erythrocebus patas*)　　kima punju (Swa)

Habitat: open grassland, *Acacia* and dry woodland **Length:** 49–75 cm
Tail: 50–74 cm **Weight:** 10–25 kg (♂); 7–14 kg (♀) **Status:** under threat
where land cleared for farming, but adapting

Long-legged, bright ginger-red above with contrasting white belly.
Young are straw-coloured. Mainly terrestrial, only using trees and
termite mounds as lookouts. Lives in small troops, consisting of a
male and up to 12 females, with their young. Feeds on grass, seeds,
fruits, flowers and gum from trees.

BEST VIEWING: Kenya: Laikipia area; **Tanzania:** Serengeti NP;
Uganda: Murchison Falls, Kidepo Valley NPs

Juniors Tierbildarchiv/Photoshot

VERVET MONKEY
Cercopithecus aethiops pygerythrus **tumbili (Swa)**

Habitat: *Acacia* woodland **Length:** 50–65 cm (♂); 38–62 cm (♀)
Tail: 48–75 cm **Weight:** 4–8 kg (♂); 3.5–5 kg (♀) **Status:** widespread

Black face with white brow and cheeks. Body greyish, with yellowish-olive tinge, paler belly, hands and feet darker. Long tail is held almost horizontally when walking, with the tip curving downwards. Lives in troops of 10–50 with a core of mature females, their young and a number of mature males. Newborns are black with a pink face; after about 3–4 months they reach adult coloration. Young males leave the troop and join neighbouring troops. Feeds on bark, flowers, fruit, grass seeds, birds' eggs and nestlings.
BEST VIEWING: common in most national parks and reserves

COPPERY-TAILED (WHITE-NOSED) MONKEY
Cercopithecus ascanius **nyani mwenye mkia mwekundu (Swa)**

Habitat: lowland western forests **Length:** 34–63 cm **Tail:** 22–37 cm
Weight: 3–6 kg (♂); 1.8–4 kg (♀) **Status:** uncommon; threatened by forest clearance

Dark brown, with a distinctive, white nose, bright blue eyes and a long, coppery tail. Common in forests of western Uganda and western Kenya. Troops of up to 20 normally consist of a dominant male with females and young. Eats fruit, insects and leaves. Often associates with Blue Monkey.
BEST VIEWING: Kenya: Kakamega Forest, Masai Mara NR;
Uganda: Mahale Mountains NP; **Tanzania:** Bwindi Impenetrable, Queen Elizabeth, Kibale NPs; **Rwanda:** Nyungwe NP

BLUE MONKEY
Cercopithecus mitis stuhlmanni **kima rufiji (Swa)**

Habitat: lowland forests **Length:** 49–66 cm **Tail:** 55–109 cm
Weight: 7.4 kg (♂); 4.2 kg (♀) **Status:** not endangered

Grizzled, blue-grey back, black arms and cap, pale grizzled brow. The tail is blue-grey with a black tip. Most have distinctive, dense, forward-facing bristles on the forehead. On the ground has a distinctive, trotting gait, with the tail high and curved. Groups consist of a dominant male, with up to 40 females and young. Feeds mostly on fruits and seeds, occasionally leaves and buds.
BEST VIEWING: Kenya: Kakamega Forest, Masai Mara NR;
Tanzania: Lake Manyara NP, Ngorongoro CA; **Uganda:** Bwindi Impenetrable, Queen Elizabeth, Kibale NPs

SYKES'S MONKEY
Cercopithecus mitis kolbi **kima (Swa)**

Habitat: highland and coastal forests **Length:** 49–66 cm
Tail: 55–109 cm **Weight:** 5.5–12 kg (♂); 3.5–5.5 kg (♀)
Status: mostly restricted to protected areas

Greyish, with a broad, white collar (absent in coastal dwellers) and black shoulders, back tinged rufous. In the highlands, their hair is longer and thicker, making them appear bigger. Groups consist of a dominant male, with up to 40 females and young. Feeds mostly on fruits and seeds, occasionally leaves and buds. Its chirping and trilling sounds could be mistaken for bird calls. Male has a loud coughing call and a distinctive, deep boom.
BEST VIEWING: Kenya: Aberdare, Mount Kenya NPs, coastal strip;
Tanzania: coastal strip

GOLDEN MONKEY

Cercopithecus mitis kandti   inkende, inkima (Rwa)

Habitat: high-altitude bamboo forest **Length:** 48–67 cm (♂);
46–53 cm (♀) **Weight:** 4.5–12 kg (♂); 3.5–4.5 kg (♀)
Status: endangered, locally common

A beautiful monkey with bright rufous-red on the back, cheeks
and tail. Has black legs, crown and tip of the tail; pale patch
around the nose and mouth. Female is brighter. Lives in groups
of 30–100, led by a dominant male. Other males leave the group
and return when the females are in oestrus. The females defend
the group's territory. Eats mainly bamboo, but also a variety of
leaves, fruits and invertebrates. Endemic to the Albertine Rift,
found mostly in the bamboo zone.

BEST VIEWING: Uganda: Mgahinga Gorilla NP; **Rwanda:** Volcanoes NP

L'HOEST'S (MOUNTAIN) MONKEY

Cercopithecus l'hoesti

Habitat: montane forests up to 2 500 m **Length:** 54–70 cm (♂);
45–55 cm (♀) **Tail:** 48–80 cm **Weight:** 6–10 kg (♂); 3–4.5 kg (♀)
Status: locally common

Striking, large, long-legged, dark species with a distinctive, white
'beard'. Its back has a saddle of russet, bordered with grizzled grey.
Lives in troops 10–17 strong, with one male and a number of
females and their young. Mostly terrestrial, feeds on a variety of
fruits and young leaves. When disturbed, flees over the ground.

BEST VIEWING: Uganda: Bwindi Impenetrable Forest NP;
Rwanda: Nyungwe NP

GREATER GALAGO/THICK-TAILED BUSHBABY

Otolemur crassicaudatus   komba ya miombo (Swa)

Habitat: dense vegetation **Length:** 32–35 cm **Tail:** 36–45 cm
Weight: 567 g–2 kg **Status:** common and widespread in dense
highland forest and coastal woodland

Dense fur, long bushy tail and large oval ears. Colour variable,
from light grey, brown to all black. Nocturnal primate, usually
found high in trees, where it has a leafy nest. Occasionally seen
on the ground; hops kangaroo-like with hindquarters and tail
elevated. Eats flowers, seeds, fruits, insects, reptiles and small
birds. Very noisy at night, with childlike wails and screams.

BEST VIEWING: Kenya: Governors' Camp and Intrepids Camp,
Masai Mara NR; **Tanzania:** Arusha, Lake Manyara NPs, Selous GR;
Rwanda: Nyungwe NP

LESSER GALAGO (BUSHBABY)

Galago senegalensis   komba (Swa)

Habitat: coastal bush and *Acacia* woodland **Length:** 17 cm **Tail:** 23 cm
Weight: 100–300 g **Status:** not threatened

A tiny, sand-coloured primate with a large, round face and large
eyes. Nocturnal; very vocal at night, with loud, shrill cries that
can sound very like a human baby. Occurs in small family groups,
marking its routes with urine. Feeds on insects, blossoms, flowers,
fruit, resins, young birds, lizards and mice. Remarkably agile,
often leaping as far as 7 m from bush to bush, covering long
distances in a series of leaps.

BEST VIEWING: on night game drives, in private wildlife areas

David Elsworthy

STRAW-COLOURED FRUIT BAT/FLYING FOX
Eidolon helvum   **popo** (Swa)

Habitat: western coastal and inland forests **Length:** 15–19.5 cm
Tail: 1.3 cm **Wingspan:** 76 cm **Weight:** 250–311 g **Status:** locally
common but killed for food and as a pest in some areas

Large, pale yellowish bat with a tawny tinge on the foreneck and
blackish wings. Large eyes and a good sense of smell are important
in locating food. Gregarious, sometimes occurring in tens of
thousands, roosting together in open trees, often in towns.
BEST VIEWING: coastal districts of Kenya and Tanzania but also towns,
especially in Uganda

EAST AFRICAN EPAULETTED FRUIT BAT
Epomophorus minimus   **popo** (Swa)

Habitat: dry savanna and rocky areas **Length:** 14–28 cm
Wingspan: 50 cm **Weight:** 40–120 g **Status:** common and widespread

Small brown bat with distinctive, white tufts at the base of
the ears. Male has white epaulettes. At night, the high-pitched
chinking call is a feature of areas where it occurs. Feeds on fruits,
flowers, nectar and pollen. Often found roosting under leaves in
palms and other trees.
BEST VIEWING: safari camps throughout the region

YELLOW-WINGED BAT
Lavia frons   **popo** (Swa)

Habitat: *Acacia* woodland **Length:** 6–8 cm **Wingspan:** 38 cm
Weight: 28–36 g **Status:** widespread and not uncommon

A colourful bat with a yellow leaf-shaped nose, wings and long
ears; grey body and large black eyes. Perhaps the most commonly
seen bat on safari, often disturbed during daylight hours. Roosts
singly or in twos and threes in the light shade of *Acacia* trees and
bushes. Feeds mostly on insects, but occasionally on small reptiles.
Has been recorded chasing other bat species.
BEST VIEWING: most wildlife areas in the region

AFRICAN PIPISTRELLE/BANANA BAT
Pipistrellus nanus   **popo** (Swa)

Habitat: almost all habitats **Length:** 7.5 cm **Tail:** 2.5 cm
Wingspan: 22.5 cm **Weight:** 4–9 g **Status:** widespread

A dark-coloured bat with black wings. The most commonly
seen bat in East Africa, often spotted flying out well before
sunset. Feeds on insects. Roosts singly or in small groups in
tree holes and buildings.
BEST VIEWING: most wildlife areas in the region

Chris & Mathilde Stuart

David Elsworthy

AFRICAN HEDGEHOG
Atelerix albiventris kalunguyeye (Swa)

Habitat: dry highland forests and open, dry, overgrazed areas
Length: 13–30 cm **Weight:** 250 g–1.6 kg **Status:** widely distributed
and mostly uncommon

A small, long-snouted hedgehog covered in brown, white-tipped spines; white on the forehead, sides of face and underparts. Nocturnal, sleeping most of the day. Hibernates during cool weather, especially in the highlands.

BEST VIEWING: occasionally seen crossing roads at night, otherwise rarely seen

Albert Visage/FLPA

GOLDEN-RUMPED ELEPHANT SHREW
Rhynchocyon chrysopygus njule ya gedi (Swa)

Habitat: dry evergreen thickets **Length:** 23.5–31.5 cm **Tail:** 19–26.3 cm
Weight: 408–440 g **Status:** endangered; often killed by village dogs

A large, dark-bodied shrew with a distinctive, golden rump; forehead and face tawny. Feeds on a variety of insects, ants, earthworms and termites. It is thought by researchers that the status of this shrew is an indicator of the health and status of the coastal forests where it occurs.

BEST VIEWING: Kenya: Gedi Ruins, Arabuko-Sokoke Forest Reserve (near Malindi)

CAPE HARE
Lepus capensis sungura (Swa); en-kitejo (Maa)

Habitat: open ground and sparse bush and woodland in arid areas
Length: 40–55 cm **Weight:** 1–3.5 kg **Status:** not endangered

Coloration variable within the region but generally light brown, buff or grey. Underparts pale, separated from upperparts by a buff-coloured band. Nocturnal, spending the day hidden in long grass or under bushes, ears laid flat. Mostly solitary; young are born above ground with fur and their eyes open (compared with rabbits, which are born underground, naked, eyes shut). Feeds on coarse vegetation, cropped close to the ground, leaves, roots, berries and bark.

BEST VIEWING: often disturbed during the day on game drives in wildlife areas; more easily seen on night drives in private reserves

AFRICAN SAVANNA HARE
Lepus microtis sungura (Swa)

Habitat: grassy areas within woodland and highland grasslands
Length: 40–49 cm **Weight:** 1.5–4.5 kg **Status:** not endangered

Darker than Cape Hare, with all-white underparts and well-defined white facial markings. Mostly nocturnal and solitary. Feeds on rank grass, not cropped close to the ground. When disturbed, runs in a zigzag pattern for cover, does not run and freeze motionless as Cape Hare tends to do.

BEST VIEWING: often disturbed during the day on game drives in wildlife areas; more easily seen on night drives in private reserves

STRIPED GROUND SQUIRREL
Xerus erythropus   kidiri (Swa)

Habitat: open woodland, dry savanna and sandy bush country
Length: 30–46 cm **Tail:** 18.5–27 cm **Weight:** 500 g–1 kg
Status: common and widespread

Body grizzled-brown with a short, pale whitish side stripe. Tail is long and faintly banded. Terrestrial, living in burrows. Feeds on roots, grass seeds, fruit and *Acacia* pods.

BEST VIEWING: Kenya: Meru, Tsavo East, Tsavo West NPs;
Tanzania: Lake Manyara, Mikumi, Tarangire NPs;
Uganda: Kidepo Valley, Murchison Falls, Queen Elizabeth NPs

Lanz von Horsten/IOA

UNSTRIPED GROUND SQUIRREL
Xerus rutilus   kidiri (Swa)

Habitat: semi-desert **Length:** 20–26 cm **Tail:** 18–23 cm
Weight: 300–335 g **Status:** widespread

Body pale brown with white underparts. Tail similar colour but often tinged reddish from soil. Lives in burrows and termite mounds and feeds on roots, seedpods, seeds, fruit and leaves.

BEST VIEWING: Kenya: Amboseli, Marsabit, Tsavo East, Tsavo West NPs, Samburu, Buffalo Springs NRs

BUSH (TREE) SQUIRREL
Paraxerus ochraceus   kindi (Swa)

Habitat: bush country and savanna woodland **Length:** 16–37 cm
Tail: 12–22 cm **Weight:** 76–265 g **Status:** common and widespread

East Africa's most common squirrel. Lives in pairs and small family groups. Yellow-brown, with underparts ranging from dark olive to pale brown, feet yellowish. Feeds on fruits, leaves, nuts, insects, young birds and eggs, mostly in trees but will also forage on the ground.

BEST VIEWING: almost everywhere

RED-LEGGED SUN SQUIRREL
Heliosciurus rufobrachium

Habitat: low- and medium-altitude forests **Length:** 20–27 cm
Tail: 18–30 cm **Weight:** 250–400 g **Status:** not endangered

The back and top of head grizzled-brown, gradually turning to reddish on the limbs. The underside is pale cream. The tail is barred with 18 black and 18 white bands. Its loud calls and habit of flicking its tail very noticeable.

BEST VIEWING: Kenya: Kakamega Forest, Meru NP; **Tanzania:** Semiliki, Mahale Mountains NPs; **Uganda:** Bwindi Impenetrable, Queen Elizabeth, Lake Mburo, Semliki NPs; **Rwanda:** Nyungwe NP

Gerard Lacz/FLPA

Vicky & Adam Kennedy

GIANT FOREST SQUIRREL
Protoxerus stangeri

Habitat: rain and swamp forests **Length:** 22–40 cm **Tail:** 24–36 cm
Weight: 540 g–1 kg **Status:** not endangered

A large, mostly brown squirrel with a large, rounded, grey head.
Has a long black-and-white tail. Feeds on fruits, seeds and nuts.
BEST VIEWING: Kenya: Kakamega Forest NR; **Tanzania:** Mahale
Mountains NP; **Uganda:** Bwindi Impenetrable, Queen Elizabeth,
Kibale, Murchison Falls NPs; **Rwanda:** Nyungwe NP

Chris & Mathilde Stuart

EAST AFRICAN SPRINGHARE
Pedetes surdaster　　　　**kamendegere (Swa); en-kipuldiany (Maa)**

Habitat: sandy plains and dry lake shores **Length:** 35–43 cm
Tail: 34–49 cm **Weight:** 3–4 kg **Status:** common and widespread
but hunted in some areas for food and as a pest

A very distinctive, long-tailed rodent with large eyes. Body pale
brown with a bushy, black-tipped tail. Hops, kangaroo-like,
holding its short front legs tucked tightly to its body. The long,
sharp front claws are used for digging. Nocturnal, spending the
days in burrows. Lives in small groups of 30–40. Feeds at night
on grass, fruits and herbs.
BEST VIEWING: seen on night game drives on private reserves in
the region

Chris & Mathilde Stuart

EAST AFRICAN PYGMY DORMOUSE
Graphiurus murinus

Habitat: occurs in almost all habitats **Length:** 7.5–15 cm **Tail:** 5–11 cm
Weight: 18–85 g **Status:** common but displaced by rats in villages

A small grey rodent with white underparts, a dark mask around
the eyes and a distinctive, bushy, darker, white-tipped tail.
Nocturnal, feeding on beetles, crickets and other small insects.
It has a curious taste for soap in safari camps.
BEST VIEWING: at night, particularly in safari camps

NAKED MOLE RAT
Heterocephalus glaber

Habitat: dry savanna and open woodland **Length:** 8–10 cm
Tail: 2–5 cm **Weight:** 30–80 g **Status:** widespread

A small, naked, short-legged rodent with prominent, long,
protruding teeth. Lives completely underground, in large colonies,
with one dominant female, attended by workers. Feeds on tree
roots, bulbs and tubers. Rarely seen but its volcano-shaped spoil
heaps betray its presence, especially on sandy tracks.
BEST VIEWING: Kenya: Samburu, Buffalo Springs NRs

CRESTED PORCUPINE
Hystrix cristata   **nnungu (Swa); o-yoyai (Maa)**

Habitat: savanna, woodlands and rocky country **Length:** 60–100 cm
Tail: 8–17 cm **Weight:** 12–27 kg **Status:** not endangered; considered
a pest in some areas

A large, distinctive, stout rodent with small eyes. Has long black-
and-white spines on the back and a crest of spiny hairs from
the head to shoulders. Mainly nocturnal. Lives in small family
groups in burrows or caves; usually forages for food alone at
night. Feeds on roots, fruit, bones and dried animal remains.
Gnawed bones often found outside dens. Contrary to popular
belief, porcupines cannot shoot out quills.

BEST VIEWING: mostly only seen at night on game drives on private
reserves in the region

GIANT POUCHED RAT
Cricetomys gambianus   **panya (Swa)**

Habitat: varied **Length:** 28–45 cm **Tail:** 36–46 cm **Weight:** 1–1.4 kg
Status: not endangered, but killed for food by some people

A large brown rat with large ears and a very long tail, half of which
is white. Nocturnal, usually solitary, feeding on fruits, seeds and
roots, which it collects in its cheek pouches. Lives in burrows;
temporary burrows may be dug near abundant food source.

BEST VIEWING: rarely seen

Chris & Mathilde Stuart

ACACIA RAT
Thallomys paedulcus   **panya (Swa)**

Habitat: *Acacia* woodland **Length:** 12–17 cm **Tail:** 13–21 cm
Weight: 63–100 g **Status:** little known

A brownish-grey rat with whitish underparts and a black mask
around the eyes. Has a long, slightly hairy tail, large ears and sharp
curved claws. Arboreal, often building a covered 'nest' on branches.
Feeds on leaves, seeds and gum.

BEST VIEWING: not often seen

Karl Switak/NHPA/Photoshot

STRIATED GRASS MOUSE
Lemniscomys striatus   **panya (Swa)**

Habitat: grasslands **Length:** 9–14 cm **Tail:** 9.5–15 cm
Weight: 18–70 g **Status:** locally common

A distinctive, small, brown mouse with dark stripes along the body
and a black line running along the centre of its back. Often seen
foraging for food in the early morning and late afternoon. Feeds
on seeds, fruits, earthworms and insects.

BEST VIEWING: almost anywhere in suitable habitat

GOLDEN JACKAL
Canis aureus bweha wa mbuga (Swa)

Habitat: arid grasslands and savanna **Length:** 86 cm
Height: 65–105 cm **Tail:** 18–27 cm **Weight:** 6–15 kg
Status: not endangered in most protected areas

Has a shaggy, coarse, yellowish-grey coat, no saddle markings
(unlike Silver-backed Jackal) and a black-tipped tail. Almost always
seen in pairs, sometimes with offspring. Sub-adult offspring often
help parents rear young. Feeds on small mammals up to the size
of small gazelles, insects, beetles, berries and fruit, when available.
Will scavenge from other predator kills; able to go without water
for long periods.

BEST VIEWING: Kenya: Amboseli NP; **Tanzania:** Serengeti NP

SIDE-STRIPED JACKAL
Canis adustus bweha miraba (Swa)

Habitat: moist savanna, forest edges and swamps
Length: 86–96 cm **Height:** 70–80 cm **Tail:** 35–45 cm
Weight: 7.3–20 kg **Status:** not endangered

Coat usually darker than that of other jackals, with black-and-
white stripes along its flanks and a distinctive white tip to its tail.
Mainly nocturnal but is also active at dawn and dusk. Mostly
seen singly; feeds on almost anything from insects and
stranded fish to young gazelles. Rarely scavenges.

BEST VIEWING: in just about all wildlife areas in the region

SILVER-BACKED (BLACK-BACKED) JACKAL
Canis mesomelas bweha nyekundu (Swa); em-barie (Maa)

Habitat: *Acacia* savanna and light woodland **Length:** 86–96 cm
Height: 70–100 cm **Tail:** 30–35 cm **Weight:** 6.5–13.5 kg
Status: not endangered

A striking-looking, rufous-tan jackal with a distinctive, black-
and-silver saddle. Usually seen in pairs but often assisted by older
offspring in rearing latest young. Pairs often hunt young and
sick gazelles together. Omnivorous, often seen hanging about
kills of other predators, such as Lion and Cheetah. If hungry,
becomes very daring, snatching small pieces of the prey away
from the predator.

BEST VIEWING: common, seen in most wildlife areas

BAT-EARED FOX
Otocyon megalotis bweha masigio (Swa); i-siro (Maa)

Habitat: *Acacia* savanna, open plains and grasslands
Length: 81 cm **Height:** 47–66 cm **Tail:** 23–34 cm **Weight:** 3–5.3 kg
Status: not endangered in the area

Unmistakable, with very large ears and a black face mask. Body
buff-grey with black legs and a black-tipped tail. Nocturnal but often
seen in early morning and late evening in pairs or family groups,
close to the den. Its large ears are specialised to detect insects such as
harvester ants and dung beetles at night. Has 45–50 sharp teeth, the
largest number of any African land mammal.

BEST VIEWING: Kenya: Masai Mara, Samburu, Buffalo Springs NRs;
Tanzania Serengeti NP; **Uganda:** Kidepo Valley NP

WILD DOG
Lycaon pictus mbwa mwitu (Swa); o-suyai (Maa)

Habitat: open plains, savanna **Length:** 121–127 cm **Height:** 76–112 cm
Tail: 30–41 cm **Weight:** 18–36 kg **Status:** endangered

A large, lanky dog with large round ears and a white-tipped tail.
Body consists of black, white and brown blotches, which differ
from individual to individual. Occurs in packs of eight or more
adults. Only the dominant pair breeds but all the pack feed the
offspring. Hunts mostly in the cool morning, running prey down
with speeds of up to 48 km/h. Mostly preys on small antelopes
but large packs will hunt Wildebeest, Zebra and even Eland.
BEST VIEWING: Kenya: Laikipia Wildlife Conservancy, Samburu NR;
Tanzania: Ruaha NP, Selous GR; **Uganda:** Kidepo Valley NP

RATEL/ HONEY BADGER
Mellivora capensis nyegere (Swa); enk-owuaru oo naishi (Maa)

Habitat: occurs in most habitats but prefers open woodland
Length: 60–77 cm **Tail:** 16–30 cm **Weight:** 7–16 kg
Status: uncommon; persecuted in some areas

A stout, stocky animal with short legs, a bushy tail and conspicuous
colouring: black below and white back, sometimes washed light
grey. Mostly nocturnal, generally solitary but occasionally seen
in pairs, not necessarily mates. A specialist feeder, excavates mice,
insects, dung beetles and scorpions from their hiding places. It also
eats reptiles and birds. Better known for its habit of following the
Greater Honeyguide to beehives. Has a bow-legged, lumbering gait,
probably because of the large, long claws on its forelegs.
BEST VIEWING: Tanzania: Serengeti NP, early morning

AFRICAN CLAWLESS OTTER
Aonyx capensis fisi maji kubwa (Swa)

Habitat: rivers, streams, lakes and marshes **Length:** 72–92 cm
Tail: 40–71 cm **Weight:** 12–34 kg **Status:** although widespread,
under threat from man and dogs in most areas

A very large otter with a broad head, thick neck and unwebbed
fingers and toes. Colour varies but is mostly dark chocolate-
brown, with a white chest, chin and cheeks. Feeds on fresh-water
crabs, crayfish (an introduced species), fish, small mammals,
birds and molluscs. Mostly occurs singly or a female with
young, and mainy active at night.
BEST VIEWING: very shy and rarely seen; usually the only sign of its
presence is its distinctive, smelly scats

Roger de la Harpe/IOA

SPOTTED-NECKED OTTER
Lutra maculicollis fisi maji mdogo (Swa)

Habitat: rivers and lakes with clear water **Length:** 60–65 cm
Tail: 35–40 cm **Weight:** 4–6.5 kg **Status:** locally common but
hunted in some areas as a pest or for its pelt

A sleek, slender, pale brown otter with webbed feet. Brown-and-
white blotching on the throat and underparts, which varies
from individual to individual. Emits a distinctive, high-pitched
whistle. Found in groups of up to 20 individuals. Feeds on fish,
frogs, fresh-water crabs, aquatic insects and larvae, mostly for
2–3 hours after dawn and again in the late afternoon. Has been
observed feeding in moonlight.
BEST VIEWING: Kenya: Lake Victoria, where it has become accustomed
to tourist boats

Chris & Mathilde Stuart

LARGE GREY (EGYPTIAN) MONGOOSE
Herpestes ichneumon   nguchiro (Swa)

Habitat: floodplains, lake shores and moist savanna; water-dependent **Length:** 45–60 cm **Tail:** 33–54 cm **Weight:** 2.2–4.1 kg **Status:** not endangered

A very large, pale grey-brown mongoose with a small, slender head and a long tail, which ends in a conspicuous black tassel. A grizzled coat and long coarse hair, which often conceals its legs. Mainly nocturnal, seen singly or in small family parties, walking one behind the other, resembling a snake. Feeds on reptiles, frogs, birds and stranded fish.

BEST VIEWING: very shy, so not often seen

SLENDER (BLACK-TIPPED) MONGOOSE
Galerella sanguinea   nguchiro (Swa)

Habitat: forest, thickets and forest swamps **Length:** 26–34 cm **Tail:** 23–31 cm **Weight:** 350–800 g **Status:** common but localised

Brown, very long-bodied, short-legged, with a long, black-tipped tail. When it walks, its long tail curves downwards, then upwards, with the tip curling over; when it runs, the tail is held high. Mostly diurnal, usually occurring singly or in pairs, or a female with up to three young. Feeds on rodents, insects, and birds and their eggs and young. Climbs trees readily, using holes and crevices for shelter.

BEST VIEWING: most wildlife areas

DWARF MONGOOSE
Helogale parvula   kitafe (Swa)

Habitat: dry savanna and woodlands, especially where there are termite mounds **Length:** 18–28 cm **Tail:** 14–19 cm **Weight:** 210–350 g **Status:** common in suitable habitats

Small, yellowish-brown, with a short snout. Very social, living in packs of 8–20, with a dominant pair, led by the dominant female. Young are cared for by non-breeding adults of both sexes. Forages as a group, feeding on insects, grasshoppers, termites, scorpions, rodents, snakes and lizards. Has been observed associating with Eastern Yellow-billed Hornbill.

BEST VIEWING: Kenya: Samburu, Buffalo Springs NRs, Tsavo East, Tsavo West NPs; **Tanzania:** Tarangire NP, Selous GR; **Uganda:** Lake Mburo, Kidepo Valley NPs

BANDED MONGOOSE
Mungos mungo   nkuchiro (Swa)

Habitat: savanna and light woodland **Length:** 30–35 cm **Tail:** 15–30 cm **Weight:** 1.5–2.25 kg **Status:** not endangered

Stout, with a brown-grey, coarse, conspicuously striped coat and a short tapering tail. Its long, sharp claws are visible at close range. Lives in groups of 15–20, sometimes larger, led by a dominant male and several females. Diurnal, foraging in loose formations, keeping in touch with others with 'twitters' and 'churs'. Feeds on termites, beetles, birds' eggs, small rodents, berries and fruit (not snakes). Growls and spits like a cat when threatened.

BEST VIEWING: Kenya: Masai Mara NR; **Tanzania:** Serengeti NP; **Uganda:** Queen Elizabeth NP

MARSH (WATER) MONGOOSE
Atilax paludinosus   nguchiro wa maji (Swa)

Habitat: rivers and lake shores, papyrus swamps **Length:** 46–64 cm
Tail: 32–53 cm **Weight:** 2.2–5 kg **Status:** widespread and common

Dark-coloured, with distinctive, thick, shaggy fur and a shortish,
bushy tail. Nocturnal, except in drought times. Mostly forages
singly for frogs, crabs, fish, small reptiles, including crocodile eggs
and young, and rodents. An excellent swimmer. Has long, sensitive
'fingers', which it uses to find its prey in turbid water.

BEST VIEWING: not often observed because of its nocturnal habits

Chris & Mathilde Stuart

WHITE-TAILED MONGOOSE
Ichneumia albicauda   karambago (Swa); en-kishiren (Maa)

Habitat: savanna, woodland, cultivated land and the suburbs of
villages and towns **Length:** 47–71 cm **Tail:** 35–50 cm **Weight:** 2–5.2 kg
Status: not endangered, but persecuted as a pest in some areas

Large, slender, long-legged, with a pointed head and long, shaggy
coat. General colour grizzled-grey, with black legs and a bushy
white tail. Melanistic individuals occur in some areas (Masai Mara
NR and in Uganda). Solitary and mostly nocturnal. Feeds on
rodents, reptiles, insects, grubs, fruit and berries.

BEST VIEWING: often seen on night drives in private reserves

STRIPED HYAENA
Hyaena hyaena   fisi (Swa)

Habitat: dry *Acacia* country **Length:** 100–120 cm **Tail:** 25–35 cm
Weight: 25–55 kg **Status:** near threatened

Smallish, with a large head, a long, thick neck and long, pointed
ears. Has a distinctive sloping back, a large bushy tail and a
dorsal crest, which can be raised when it is excited or alarmed.
Coat buff-coloured, long and shaggy, legs and body striped.
Mostly nocturnal and solitary. Feeds almost entirely on carrion,
but will hunt small rodents, hares and foxes, and sick larger
animals, as well as tortoises, insects and fruits. Eats cucurbits for
their water content.

BEST VIEWING: Kenya: Amboseli NP; **Tanzania:** Serengeti NP;
Uganda: Kidepo Valley NP

SPOTTED HYAENA
Crocuta crocuta   fisi, nyangao (Swa); ol-ng'ojine (Maa)

Habitat: *Acacia* savanna, *Acacia* woodland, grasslands and
forests **Length:** 100–180 cm **Tail:** 25–36 cm **Weight:** 40–90 kg
Status: threatened outside protected wildlife areas

Large and powerfully built. Tail short and bushy, with a dark tip.
Colour varies from pale buff to dull grey, marked with irregular
spots, which become fainter with age. Lives in clans of related
females and unrelated males, centred on a den. Female larger than
male – up to 6 kg heavier. Cubs, up to four, are born black and can
be suckled for up to 18 months. Known for scavenging, but they are
skilful hunters, killing Wildebeest calves and occasionally even Topi.

BEST VIEWING: Kenya: Amboseli NP, Masai Mara NR;
Tanzania: Serengeti NP, Ngorongoro CA; **Uganda:** Queen Elizabeth NP

Chris & Mathilde Stuart

AARDWOLF
Proteles cristata   fisi ya nkole (Swa)

Habitat: grasslands, savanna and sandy plains where harvester ants occur **Length:** 55–80 cm **Tail:** 20–30 cm **Weight:** 8–12 kg
Status: threatened outside protected wildlife areas

Often confused with Striped Hyaena but much smaller. Tawny with well-spaced, narrow dark stripes, brown feet and tip of tail. Has a long crest along the neck and back, which can be raised when it is excited or alarmed. Individuals can be seen at night or on dull, late evenings, foraging for termites. Pairs are territorial but always forage alone and spend the day in separate burrows; both care for their young during their early months.

BEST VIEWING: rarely seen except in areas where night game drives take place

Chris & Mathilde Stuart

COMMON GENET
Genetta genetta   kanu (Swa)

Habitat: wide ranging in drier habitats **Length:** 40–55 cm
Tail: 40–51 cm **Weight:** 1.3–2.25 kg **Status:** not endangered

Long-legged, with a coarse coat and a well-developed crest running along its spine. Body is sandy-coloured, covered in small dark spots. Its long, tapered tail has 9–11 rings. Nocturnal and forages solitarily for insects, small rodents and birds.

BEST VIEWING: rarely seen except in areas where night drives take place or at safari camps, where they eat insects attracted to lights

LARGE-SPOTTED (BLOTCHED) GENET
Genetta maculata   kanu (Swa)

Habitat: bush, woodlands, forests and suburbia **Length:** 40–55 cm
Tail: 40–54 cm **Weight:** 1.2–3.1 kg **Status:** not endangered

Short-legged, with a soft coat and a distinct dorsal line. Body colour variable, mostly sandy, covered in dark blotches, its tail has 8–9 rings and a wide, dark tip. Like the Common Genet, it is nocturnal and forages solitarily, mostly for rodents and insects and, occasionally, fruit.

BEST VIEWING: rarely seen except in areas where night drives take place or at safari camps where it eats insects attracted to lights

Nigel Dennis/IOA

AFRICAN CIVET
Civettictis civetta   fungo (Swa)

Habitat: dry, open country where there is dense cover
Length: 68–95 cm **Tail:** 40–53 cm **Weight:** 7–20 kg
Status: widely distributed

Large, stocky, shaggy-coated, long-legged. Body buff with bands and blotches, arranged in longitudinal rows; the tail is banded. Distinctive markings on the head, with a pale forehead and a whitish muzzle separated by a black mask, which extends to the throat. Nocturnal and usually solitary, foraging for lizards, snakes, large insects and birds and their eggs. Also eats fruit, grass and leaves and will raid gardens for potatoes.

BEST VIEWING: Kenya: Amboseli, Tsavo East, Tsavo West NPs;
Tanzania: Serengeti NP; **Uganda:** Murchison Falls NP

AFRICAN WILD CAT
Felis silvestris lybica **paka mwitu (Swa); em-barie (Maa)**

Habitat: open savanna **Length:** 45–73 cm **Tail:** 20–38 cm
Weight: 3–6.5 kg **Status:** widespread

Resembles a house cat but generally paler with longer legs; the
backs of the ears are gingery. Upperparts of limbs are marked
with dark bands. Usually solitary, except when females are
followed by young. Feeds on mice, rats and small mammals
as large as a hare, birds (francolins, small bustards) and,
occasionally, insects, frogs and reptiles.

BEST VIEWING: Tanzania: Serengeti NP

SERVAL
Leptailurus serval (*Felis serval*) **mondo (Swa); e-seperua (Maa)**

Habitat: grasslands, forests, moorlands, reed beds and marshes
Length: 67–100 cm **Tail:** 24–35 cm **Weight:** 10–18 kg (♂); 6–12.5 kg (♀)
Status: widespread and not uncommon

A tall, long-legged cat with a small head, large oval ears and a rather
short tail. Body buff, heavily marked with spots and bands, tail
banded. Backs of ears are black with distinctive, white marks. In the
highlands all-black specimens are common. Solitary and mostly
crepuscular, occasionally hunts by day. Hunts by sound and sight in
long grass, pouncing with high leaps onto prey. Feeds mostly on rats
and mice, small mammals, birds, reptiles and large insects.

BEST VIEWING: Kenya: Masai Mara NR; **Tanzania:** Serengeti NP;
Uganda: Murchison Falls, Queen Elizabeth NPs

CARACAL
Caracal caracal (*Felis caracal*) **simba mangu (Swa)**

Habitat: dry savanna, woodlands and rocky country
Length: 62–91 cm **Tail:** 18–34 cm **Weight:** 12–19 kg (♂); 8–13 kg (♀)
Status: not endangered

A large, reddish-fawn-coloured cat with distinctive, large, pointed
ears and a long tassel of black hair. Mostly solitary and nocturnal.
Feeds on small antelopes, hares, hyraxes, rodents and birds such
as guineafowl and doves. Even eagles and ostriches have been
recorded as prey. Well known for prodigiously long and high
leaps in the air when capturing prey.

BEST VIEWING: Kenya: Masai Mara, Shaba NRs; **Tanzania:** Serengeti NP;
Uganda: Kidepo Valley NP

Nigel Dennis/IOA

LEOPARD
Panthera pardus **chui (Swa); ol-owuaru (Maa)**

Habitat: highland forests, woodlands and rocky country
Length: 130–190 cm (♂); 104–140 cm (♀) **Tail:** 60–110 cm
Weight: 35–90 kg (♂); 28–60 kg (♀) **Status:** now quite common

Large and powerful-looking, with a long, white-tipped tail. General
colour tan, with black-and-brown rosettes (not spots) on back and
sides, and spots on face and lower limbs. Melanistic individuals
occur, especially in highlands. Mostly nocturnal and solitary, except
when a female has young. An opportunistic hunter, hunts by day if
prey is available. Feeds on gazelles, impala, warthogs, hares, baboons,
monkeys and birds. Often carries prey high into trees to feed.

BEST VIEWING: Kenya: Masai Mara NR, Lake Nakuru NP;
Tanzania: Serengeti, Tarangire NPs; **Uganda:** Murchison Falls NP

LION
Panthera leo   simba (Swa); ol-ng'atuny (Maa)

Habitat: grasslands and arid areas, mostly avoiding forests
Length: 172–250 cm (♂); 158–192 cm (♀) **Tail:** 60–100 cm
Weight: 150–260 kg (♂); 122–182 kg (♀) **Status:** numbers
reducing especially outside protected areas

The largest cat. Males develop thick woolly manes on neck and
shoulder at about 2 years, the colour varying from tan to black.
Female is smaller and more lightly built. Cubs have rosette
markings, which slowly disappear as they mature. Lives in prides of
related females, their young and 1–3 unrelated males. Mostly hunts
at night, feeding on Wildebeest, Zebra, Buffalo and Warthog.

BEST VIEWING: Kenya: Masai Mara NR; **Tanzania:** Serengeti NP;
Uganda: Queen Elizabeth NP

CHEETAH
Acinonyx jubatus   duma (Swa); ol-kinyalasho (Maa)

Habitat: open plains **Length:** 110–150 cm **Tail:** 65–90 cm
Weight: 35–65 kg **Status:** vulnerable; in tourist areas often
disturbed by safari vehicles when hunting

Slender, with long, thin legs, a small head and a long, white-tipped
tail. Tawny-buff, covered in evenly spaced black spots, belly paler.
Face distinctive, with characteristic teardrop markings from eye
to mouth. Cubs smoky-grey, with long woolly hair. Diurnal and
mostly found singly. Young accompany female for about a year.
Hunts gazelles, small antelope and hares but male coalitions (of
2–6 individuals) hunt larger prey (Wildebeest, Zebra and Ostrich).

BEST VIEWING: Kenya: Masai Mara NR; **Tanzania:** Serengeti NP;
Uganda: Kidepo Valley NP

Jenny Hartree

GROUND PANGOLIN
Manis temminckii   kakakuona (Swa)

Habitat: sandy soils in woodlands and savanna, within reach of water
Length: 69–107 cm **Tail:** 31–50 cm **Weight:** 7–18 kg **Status:** threatened

Unmistakable: upper surface of body and long, broad, prehensile
tail are covered in scales. The tip of the tail is bare and highly
sensitive. A small head with a black face and a naked, pointed
muzzle. Front feet have long claws, used to excavate ant heaps
and termite mounds. Extremely long sticky tongue, for feeding
on ants and termites. Mostly nocturnal and solitary; uses burrows
dug by other mammals as daytime resting place. Will roll up into
a ball when threatened.

BEST VIEWING: Kenya: Tsavo East NP; **Uganda:** Murchison Falls,
Kidepo Valley NPs

Nigel Dennis/IOA

AARDVARK
Orycteropus afer   muhanga, kukukifuku (Swa)

Habitat: dry savanna and open country where there are termites
Length: 100–158 cm **Tail:** 44–63 cm **Height:** 58–66 cm
Weight: 40–82 kg **Status:** vulnerable outside protected areas

A large, pig-like mammal (its name means 'earth pig' in Afrikaans).
Unmistakable, with a long nose, a large arched body, short,
strong-looking limbs and a tapered tail. Shy and nocturnal, lives
in burrows that it easily digs. Feeds almost exclusively on termites
and ants, which it digs out of the earth with strong claws. Uses its
long, sticky tongue to catch insects as they try to escape.

BEST VIEWING: rarely seen because of its nocturnal habits; **Kenya:** Lewa
Wildlife Conservancy; **Tanzania:** Selous GR; **Uganda:** Queen Elizabeth NP

ROCK HYRAX
Procavia johnstoni   pimbi (Swa); en-deer (Maa)

Habitat: rocky outcrops and koppies **Length:** 38–60 cm
Weight: 1.8–5.5 kg **Status:** numerous

Small and stocky, with a short brown coat, with a lighter dorsal patch. Highly social, lives among rocks and boulders in large colonies consisting of family groups of a male, up to 20 females and their young. Each family group is territorial. Feeds mainly on grass but also on shrubs and trees. When feeding, a group will face outwards in a circle, watching for predators. Usually seen sunning itself on rocks but always on the alert; if a predator is seen, leaps up quickly and runs to safety.

BEST VIEWING: common in almost all wildlife areas where there are rocks; **Tanzania:** Seronera Lodge, Serengeti NP

BUSH HYRAX
Heterohyrax brucei   perere mawe (Swa)

Habitat: rocky escarpments and outcrops where there are trees
Length: 32–57 cm **Weight:** 2–3.5 kg **Status:** widespread and abundant

Very similar to Rock Hyrax but smaller, with a more pointed nose. A conspicuous white mark above the eye, underside paler and the dorsal patch is whitish or sometimes yellowish. Lives in colonies, sometimes alongside Rock Hyrax, but they do not interbreed. Feeds on leaves, particularly *Acacia tortilis*, but also on fruits, twigs and bark.

BEST VIEWING: in most wildlife areas with suitable habitats; **Tanzania:** Serengeti NP

TREE HYRAX
Dendrohyrax arboreus   perere (Swa); en-deerin (Maa)

Habitat: montane forests **Length:** 32–60 cm **Mass:** 1.5–4.5 kg
Status: not endangered but outside protected areas at risk to logging and snaring for meat and fur

Large, generally darker in colour and more densely furred than the other two hyraxes. Dorsal spot usually white or yellow. Nocturnal; lives in holes in trees or hidden in dense foliage; in the mountains they live among rocks. Occurs mostly in pairs; in larger groups in mountainous areas. Feeds on leaves, fruits, twigs and grass. Very territorial; their loud territorial calls consist of a series of cries, which gradually become louder, climaxing in a shriek or choking scream.

BEST VIEWING: Kenya: Aberdares, Mt Kenya NPs; **Tanzania:** Kilimanjaro NP; **Uganda:** Mgahinga Gorilla, Rwenzori, Queen Elizabeth NPs

AFRICAN ELEPHANT
Loxodonta africana   ndovu, tembo (Swa); ol-tome (Maa)

Habitat: forested savanna, mountain forests and sub-desert if water available **Height:** 3–4 m (♂); 2.4–3.4 m (♀) **Length:** 7–9 m
Weight: 4 000–6 300 kg (♂); 2 200–3 500 kg (♀) **Status:** vulnerable

Long trunk and large ears. Males larger than females, with a much larger, rounded head. Male's tusks are usually larger and thicker than female's. Female unique in herbivores in having two teats located between the front legs. Gregarious, living in herds, consisting of related females and their young, led by a matriarch. Young males of 12–15 years are usually expelled from the herd. Spends most of the day feeding on grass, leaves, bark, fruit and seedpods.

BEST VIEWING: Kenya: Amboseli NP, Samburu NR; **Tanzania:** Tarangire NP, Ngorongoro CA; **Uganda:** Queen Elizabeth, Murchison Falls NPs

COMMON (PLAINS) ZEBRA
Equus quagga boehmi punda milia (Swa); ol-oitiko (Maa)

Habitat: grassland, savanna and light woodland **Height:** 127–140 cm
Length: 217–246 cm **Weight:** 220–322 kg (♂); 175–250 kg (♀)
Status: common in most wildlife areas

Black-and-white, with a stiff, erect mane. Lives in family groups of
about seven, consisting of a stallion, 2–4 mares and their young.
Males usually leave the group between 1–4 years, joining all-
male groups; females are usually abducted by other stallions on
maturity. Dominant female leads the group; stallion follows or walks
alongside. Seasonal migratory herds of tens of thousands in the
Serengeti/Masai Mara consist of family groups and bachelor groups.
BEST VIEWING: Kenya: Amboseli NP, Masai Mara NR;
Tanzania: Serengeti, Tarangire NPs; **Uganda:** Lake Mburo, Kidepo Valley NPs

GREVY'S ZEBRA
Equus grevyi punda milia somali (Swa); ioitiko (Sam)

Habitat: arid open grasslands and *Acacia* savanna **Height:** 140–160 cm
Length: 250–300 cm **Weight:** 380–450 kg (♂); 350–400 kg (♀)
Status: endangered, as they wander widely outside protected areas

Long-legged with large ears and narrow, black stripes, which do
not reach the belly. Does not form stable herds or migrate. Mature
stallions occupy individual territories; other males form bachelor
groups; females form loose groups of adults and foals. Female and
bachelor groups wander widely, passing through stallions' territories.
Stallions stay in their territories even when food is scarce. When
mating, male has distinctive loud bray, followed by strangled squeak.
BEST VIEWING: Kenya: Samburu, Buffalo Springs NRs, Lewa Wildlife
Conservancy

BLACK RHINOCEROS
Diceros bicornis faru (Swa)

Habitat: dry bush country with scrub and highland moorlands
Height: 137–180 cm **Length:** 290–375 cm **Weight:** 700–1 400 kg
Status: critically endangered

Unmistakable, skin grey, can look brown or white after wallowing
in mud and dust bathing. Both sexes have horns, the front one
usually longer. Poor eyesight but good hearing. Generally solitary,
except when a female has young. Calf walks alongside or behind
its mother. An odd-toed ungulate with three toes on each foot. A
browser, differs from White Rhino in having a pointed, prehensile
upper lip. Eats a variety of leaves, buds, shoots of bushes and trees.
BEST VIEWING: Kenya: Lake Nakuru, Nairobi NPs, Lewa Wildlife
Conservancy; **Tanzania:** Ngorongoro CA

WHITE RHINOCEROS
Ceratotherium simum kiaru ya majani (Swa)

Habitat: grasslands and savanna with scrub **Height:** 170–185 cm
Length: 360–420 cm **Weight:** 2 000–3 600 kg (♂); 1 400–2 000 kg (♀)
Status: near threatened; an introduced species

Larger and bulkier than Black Rhino, with a distinctive hump on the
neck. Both sexes have horns, the front one usually longer. Its skin
colour is similar to that of Black Rhino. The name is a corruption
of the Dutch word *weit* ('wide'), referring to its mouth, which is
adapted for grazing. Not as solitary as Black Rhino; often in small
groups. Calves walk ahead of their mothers. An odd-toed ungulate
with three toes on each foot. Far less aggressive than Black Rhino.
BEST VIEWING: Kenya: Lake Nakuru NP, Lewa Wildlife Conservancy;
Uganda: Ziwa Rhino Sanctuary (four were moved from Kenya)

HIPPOPOTAMUS
Hippopotamus amphibius kiboko (Swa); ol-makau (Maa)

Habitat: rivers and lakes **Height**: 130–165 cm **Length**: 320–420 cm
Weight: 650–3 200 kg (♂); 510–2 500 kg (♀) **Status**: vulnerable

Unmistakable, large and round-bodied, with large head and short,
stumpy legs. Male is larger, with larger head and jaws. Spends its
days in water, coming out each evening to graze. Gregarious, living
in groups as large as 15 individuals but, in times of drought, larger
numbers will congregate. Groups are made up mainly of females,
their young and a number of males. Dominant males occupy areas
of water and shoreline, which they defend aggressively.

BEST VIEWING: Kenya: Tsavo West, Amboseli NPs, Masai Mara NR;
Tanzania: Lake Manyara NP, Ngorongoro Crater; **Uganda**: Murchison Falls,
Queen Elizabeth NPs

BUSHPIG
Potamochoerus larvatus nguruwe (Swa)

Habitat: dense vegetation in forests and woodland **Height**: 55–100 cm
Length: 100–177 cm **Weight**: 45–150 kg **Status**: threatened outside
protected areas

Short-legged, with an elongated face. Colour variable, from
bright rufous to dark brown, becoming darker with age. Mane
and whiskers white and ear tips tufted. Mostly solitary and, in
areas where not hunted, can be quite common, but rarely seen
as it is mostly nocturnal and extremely shy. Can be very
destructive to crops.

BEST VIEWING: Kenya: night-viewing lodges, Aberdare, Mount
Kenya NPs

Nigel Dennis/IOA

GIANT FOREST HOG
Hylochoerus meinertzhageni nguruwe nyeusi (Swa)

Habitat: mostly in highland forest areas, 1 500–3 000 m above sea
level, but occurs in open bush in Queen Elizabeth NP, Uganda
Height: 80–100 cm **Length**: 130–210 cm **Weight**: 140–275 kg (♂);
100–200 kg (♀) **Status**: vulnerable, as it is hunted by humans

Very large, unmistakable, heavily built, with coarse, bristly black
hair, a large head, and an elongated, flattened snout. Male has
large swellings below the eyes and short thick tusks. Older males
are usually solitary, while young males live in small groups.
Females live in family groups, which are made up of a female
and up to three generations of young. Mostly nocturnal but, in
protected areas, seen during daytime.

BEST VIEWING: Kenya: Aberdare NP; **Uganda**: Queen Elizabeth NP

COMMON WARTHOG
Phacochoerus africanus ngiri (Swa); ol-bitir (Maa)

Habitat: open plains and grasslands **Height**: 55–85 cm
Length: 105–152 cm **Weight**: 60–150 kg (♂); 45–75 kg (♀)
Status: common in protected areas

Long-legged, grey and naked, with distinctive, large wart-like
growths on side of face and prominent curved tusks. Has long,
black bristles down the back and shoulders. When running, has a
distinctive, jaunty trot and a habit of holding its tail straight up.
Often feeds on its knees. Occasionally observed chewing on old
animal carcasses. Has been observed chasing a Cheetah off its kill
(gazelle) and then eating the kill (pers. obs.). Usually gregarious in
family groups but old males often solitary.

BEST VIEWING: in most national parks and reserves

DESERT WARTHOG
Phacochoerus aethiopicus   **ngiri ya somalia (Swa)**

Habitat: arid areas **Height:** 50–75 cm **Length:** 105–152 cm
Weight: 45–100 kg **Status:** safe in protected areas but vulnerable
in other areas

Very similar to Common Warthog but head is shorter and broader
and lacks front incisors. Occurs in much more arid habitats than
Common Warthog and is very difficult to identify for sure.

BEST VIEWING: Kenya: Tsavo East NP, Buffalo Springs, Samburu,
Shaba NRs

MASAI GIRAFFE
Giraffa camelopardalis tippelskirchi   **twiga (Swa) ol-meut (Maa)**

Habitat: *Acacia* savanna and open woodlands **Height:** 3.9–5.2 m (♂);
3.5–4.7 m (♀) **Length:** 3.5–4.8 m **Tail:** 76–110 cm **Weight:** 1 800–
1 930 kg (♂); 450–1 180 kg (♀) **Status:** common in protected areas

Fawn-coloured with variable star-shaped, blotched markings, which
darken with age. Male larger than female, with two thick horns,
which are bald at the tips, and a smaller horn on forehead. Female's
horns are covered by long hair. Live in loose associations. Young live
in nursery groups, often away from adults and very vulnerable; only
25% survive their first year. Uses its prehensile lip and 45 cm-long
tongue to browse on leaves and twigs 6 m above ground.

BEST VIEWING: Kenya: Amboseli, Tsavo East, Tsavo West NPs, Masai
Mara NR; **Tanzania:** Arusha, Lake Manyara, Serengeti NPs

RETICULATED GIRAFFE
Giraffa camelopardalis reticulata   **twiga (Swa); imaraa (Sam)**

Habitat: dry *Acacia* woodland and desert bush country
Height: 4.5–5 m **Length:** 3.5–4.8 cm **Tail:** 76–110 cm
Weight: 1 800–1 930 kg (♂); 450–1 180 kg (♀)
Status: common in protected areas

Handsome giraffe with dark, chestnut-coloured square patches,
outlined with fine white lines. Like other species, males spar
(sometimes called 'necking') with one another, for dominance.
Males stand shoulder to shoulder and swing their heads at one
another like a club. Occasionally, they lift one another off their
feet and sometimes cause serious injuries.

BEST VIEWING: Kenya: Samburu, Buffalo Springs NRs, Lewa
Wildlife Conservancy

ROTHSCHILD'S GIRAFFE
Giraffa camelopardalis rothschildi   **twiga (Swa)**

Habitat: *Acacia* savanna and open woodlands **Height:** 4.5–5.5 m
Length: 3.5–4.8 m **Tail:** 76–110 cm **Weight:** 1 800–1 930 kg (♂);
450–1 180 kg (♀) **Status:** most endangered giraffe but a population
introduced into Lake Nakuru NP is thriving

Similar to Reticulated Giraffe but chestnut patches separated by
buff-coloured lines and no markings below the knees. Male also
differs in having five horns, rather than three. Giraffe 'horns' are
not true horns but fused protuberances fused to the skull. Giraffe
are not mute, as is generally thought, but make grunts and
braying distress calls. They defend themselves and their young
by kicking with their forelegs.

BEST VIEWING: Kenya: Lake Nakuru NP; **Uganda:** Murchison Falls NP

AFRICAN BUFFALO
Syncerus caffer   nyati, mbogo (Swa); ol-osowuan (Maa)

Habitat: variety of habitats, savanna, montane forests and near lakes and rivers **Height:** 100–170 cm **Length:** 170–340 cm **Horns:** 100 cm **Weight:** 250–850 kg **Status:** not endangered

Male's horns are widely curved, with a spread of up to 1 m wide, the base joined by a heavy boss. Female's are shorter and thinner, without a boss. Body brownish-black, covered in coarse hair, which becomes sparse with age. Lives in large herds of several hundred. Within the herds are family groups made up of a number of females, their young and one or two males. Old bulls tend to stay together, keeping on the outer edges of the herd.

BEST VIEWING: Kenya: Amboseli NP, Masai Mara NR; **Tanzania:** Serengeti, Katave NPs; **Uganda:** Queen Elizabeth, Murchison Falls NPs

FOREST BUFFALO
Syncerus caffer nanus   nyati (Swa)

Habitat: grassy forest glades **Height:** 100–120 cm **Length:** 180–220 cm **Horns:** 30–40 cm **Weight:** 170–320 kg **Status:** not endangered but interbreeding with African buffalo

Smaller than African Buffalo and reddish. Lives in small groups of up to 12, made up mainly of females, their young and one or more males. Occurs in the Ishasha area of Queen Elizabeth NP, where two vegetation types – the west African rain forest and eastern African savanna – meet. Forest and African Buffalo interbreed, so one can never be sure if they are pure Forest Buffalo.

BEST VIEWING: Uganda: Queen Elizabeth NP

BUSHBUCK
Tragelaphus scriptus   pongo, mbawala (Swa); ol-pua (Maa)

Habitat: forests, dense bush usually not far from water **Height:** 61–100 cm **Length:** 105–150 cm **Horns:** 25–57 cm (♂) **Weight:** 30–80 kg (♂); 24–60 kg (♀) **Status:** not endangered

Small, rufous-brown, white-spotted antelope with 6–7 vertical stripes across its back and a distinctive, white band at the base of its neck. Has a dark bushy tail, white below, best seen when animal is alarmed and running, when it also erects a dorsal crest. Male becomes darker, almost black, with age; has short spiral horns. Solitary, except when a female has young. Grazer and browser.

BEST VIEWING: Kenya: night-viewing lodges, Aberdare, Mount Kenya NPs; **Tanzania:** Arusha NP, Ngorongoro CA; **Uganda:** Murchison Falls, Queen Elizabeth NPs

BONGO
Tragelaphus euryceros   bongo, ndongoro (Swa)

Habitat: montane forests **Height:** 110–130 cm **Length:** 170–250 cm **Horns:** 75–99 cm **Weight:** 240–450 kg (♂); 210–253 kg (♀) **Status:** threatened

A strong-looking, bright chestnut antelope with a series of vertical white stripes running from the shoulders to the hindquarters. These join a short dark crest, which runs along the spine. Male larger and becomes darker, almost black, with age. Both sexes have flat-sided, spiral horns but the male's are longer and thicker. Mostly nocturnal. Shy, generally solitary, but groups of females form nursery herds. Feeds on shrubs, herbs and, for part of the year, bamboo.

BEST VIEWING: Kenya: Aberdare NP, but difficult to see

SITATUNGA
Tragelaphus spekei   nzohe (Swa)

Habitat: swamps and dense reed beds   **Height:** 88–125 cm (♂);
75–90 cm (♀)   **Length:** 150–170 cm (♂); 115–155 cm (♀)
Horns: 45–92 cm (♂)   **Weight:** 80–130 kg (♂); 40–85 kg (♀)
Status: rare and endangered

Long-legged, semi-aquatic antelope. Shaggy coat of long fine hair,
covered in oily, water-repellent secretion. Male greyish, larger, with
long, spiralled horns; female redder, lacks horns. There are 6–8
vertical pale stripes on the body, white spots on the cheeks, a white
throat patch and a distinctive, white chevron between the eyes.
Browses and grazes, mostly deep in swamps.

BEST VIEWING: Kenya: Saiwa Swamp NP, Lewa Wildlife Conservancy;
Uganda: Queen Elizabeth NP

LESSER KUDU
Tragelaphus imberbis   tandala ndogo (Swa)

Habitat: *Acacia* bush, semi-arid bush country   **Height:** 90–110 cm
Length: 110–175 cm   **Horns:** 50–92 cm (♂)   **Weight:** 92–108 kg (♂);
56–70 kg (♀)   **Status:** near threatened

A medium-sized antelope. Male blue-grey, darkening with age,
female and young rufous-coloured. Both sexes have up to 15 white,
lateral stripes and two distinctive white patches on upper and lower
throat. Tail is bushy, pale below; raised and fanned and conspicuous
when the animal is running. Horns present in male only, with two
or three spirals. Females live in groups of two or three, accompanied
by their young. Male solitary. A browser, feeding on leaves, shoots
and twigs, can go without water for long periods.

BEST VIEWING: Kenya: Tsavo East, Tsavo West NPs; **Tanzania:** Ruaha NP

GREATER KUDU
Tragelaphus strepsiceros   tandala mkubwa (Swa); ol-maalo (Maa)

Habitat: forest, woodlands, stony hilly country and thickets
Height: 122–150 cm (♂); 100–140 cm (♀)   **Length:** 195–245 cm (♂);
185–235 cm (♀)   **Horns:** average 120 cm (♂)   **Weight:** 190–315 kg (♂);
120–215 kg (♀)   **Status:** not endangered

A tall, majestic antelope; body grey-fawn with 6–10 narrow, white,
vertical stripes and a distinctive white chevron between the eyes.
Large rounded ears and a heavy fringe of hair along the throat and
chest. Male has horns, a wide-spreading, open spiral, up to 181 cm
long. Herds consist of females and young. Males solitary but often
near female herds. A browser, feeding on herbs and flowers of vines.

BEST VIEWING: Kenya: Lake Bogoria NR, Lewa Wildlife Conservancy;
Tanzania: Ruaha, Selous NPs; **Uganda:** Kidepo Valley NP

ELAND
Taurotragus oryx   pofu (Swa); o-sirua (Maa)

Habitat: open plains, highland forests and montane grasslands
Height: 137–178 cm (♂); 125–160 cm (♀)   **Length:** 240–345 cm (♂);
200–280 cm (♀)   **Horns:** 43–65 cm (♂); 51–68 cm (♀)
Weight: 400–942 kg (♂); 300–600 kg (♀)   **Status:** not endangered

Africa's largest antelope, fawn-tawny, with faint, narrow white
stripes and a long, tasselled tail. Male is larger than female and has
a large dewlap and a large mat of dark brown hair on the forehead.
Both sexes have short, spiralled, straight horns, but female's are
thinner and often longer. Lives in herds whose numbers constantly
change. Old bulls often solitary. Browser and grazer.

BEST VIEWING: Kenya: Nairobi NP, Masai Mara NR; **Tanzania:** Serengeti
NP; **Uganda:** Lake Mburo NP

COMMON (BUSH) DUIKER
Sylvicapra grimmia   nsya (Swa)

Habitat: scrub country, bush savanna **Height:** 45–70 cm
Length: 70–105 cm (♂); 90–115 cm (♀) **Horns:** 18 cm (♂)
Weight: 11–21 kg (♂); 12–25.5 kg (♀) **Status:** widespread and common

A medium-sized antelope, body colour variable but generally
grizzled-fawn, turning greyish on the hindquarters. Has a dark tuft
of hair between large ears and a distinctive, dark stripe from the
forehead to the nose. Only male has horns, which are short and
straight. Female is slightly larger than male. Lives in pairs, feeding
on leaves, fruits, seeds and flowers; does not need water.

BEST VIEWING: Kenya: Aberdare, Lake Nakuru NPs; **Tanzania:** Arusha,
Lake Manyara NPs, Ngorongoro CA; **Uganda:** Murchison Falls, Queen
Elizabeth NPs

SUNI
Neotragus moschatus   paa mwekundu (Swa)

Habitat: coastal and highland forests **Height:** 30–41 cm
Length: 57–62 cm **Horns:** 13 cm (♂) **Weight:** 4–6 kg
Status: not endangered

Tiny and graceful, the region's smallest antelope. Grey-brown,
with white underparts. Only the male has horns, which are
straight and ringed. Large, distinctive glands below the eyes and
no tuft of hair between the horns. Mostly solitary or in pairs, and
most active in the early morning and late afternoon. Mainly a
browser, feeding on leaves, herbs and fruits.

BEST VIEWING: Kenya: Aberdare, Mount Kenya, Nairobi NPs;
Tanzania: Arusha NP

Chris & Mathilde Stuart

STEENBOK
Raphicerus campestris   isha dondor (Swa)

Habitat: *Acacia* savanna and grasslands with bush
Height: 45–60 cm **Length:** 70–95 cm **Horns:** 9–19 cm (♂)
Weight: 7–16 kg **Status:** widespread and localised

A bright, reddish-fawn, long-legged antelope with large, white
ears, which have conspicuous black markings on the inside. A
distinctive, triangular mark on the nose and black-rimmed dark
eyes. Only the male has horns. Easily confused with an Oribi. Lives
in pairs and mostly browses, feeding on new shoots of shrubs and
trees, but also roots and tubers, which it digs up with its sharp
hooves. Not dependent on water.

BEST VIEWING: Kenya: Aberdare, Nairobi NPs, Masai Mara NR;
Tanzania: Serengeti NP

ORIBI
Ourebia ourebi   taya (Swa); en-jusie (Maa)

Habitat: grasslands **Height:** 50–67 cm **Length:** 92–140 cm
Horns: 8–19 cm (♂) **Weight:** 12–22 kg **Status:** not endangered
but very localised

A graceful antelope with a longish neck. Body sandy-fawn, with
white underparts; tail short and black, conspicuous against rump.
Large ears but not as distinctly marked as a Steenbok's. No markings
on face; the dark eyes are not black rimmed. Has distinctive black
gland patches below the ears and blackish knee tufts. Male has thin,
upstanding horns. Grazes but will browse in the dry season. Usually
seen solitarily. When fleeing, has a characteristic rocking-horse gait.

BEST VIEWING: Kenya: Meru NP, Masai Mara, Ruma NRs;
Tanzania: Serengeti NP; **Uganda:** Lake Mburo, Murchison Falls NPs

KLIPSPRINGER
Oreotragus oreotragus   **mbuzi mawe (Swa); en-kine oo soito (Maa)**

Habitat: steep rocky terrain **Height:** 43–60 cm **Length:** 75–155 cm
Horns: 9–16 cm **Weight:** 8–18 kg **Status:** locally common

A small antelope with large ears and large orbital glands below
the eyes. Yellowish-brown coat is long, rough and dense. Has
short legs and is unique in walking on the tips of its hooves. In
Kenya, both sexes have short upright horns but in Tanzania and
Uganda only males have horns. Occurs singly or in small family
groups on rocky hills and outcrops. Individuals usually seen
standing on the top of a rock on the lookout for predators.
Feeds on shrubs, herbs and grass.

BEST VIEWING: Kenya: Tsavo West NP, Shaba NR; **Tanzania:** Lake
Manyara, Serengeti NPs; **Uganda:** Lake Mburo NP

KIRK'S DIK-DIK
Madoqua kirkii   **digidigi, suguya (Swa); e-rongo (Maa)**

Habitat: dry bush, thickets and coastal bush **Height:** 35–45 cm
Length: 55–72 cm **Horns:** 8–11 cm (♂) **Weight:** 3.8–7.2 kg **Status:** not
endangered but under pressure outside of protected areas

A small, delicate-looking antelope with an elongated, almost trunk-
like nose. Coat grizzled grey-brown, paler tan on flanks and legs.
Has large ears, large white-rimmed eyes and distinct preorbital
glands. A tuft of hair on the crown is raised in alarm. Male has short
horns that slant backwards. Lives in monogamous pairs and marks
its territories with middens. Mostly active during late afternoons.
Browser, feeding on leaves, shoots and fruits.

BEST VIEWING: Kenya: Samburu, Buffalo Springs NRs; **Tanzania:** Arusha,
Serengeti NPs

GUENTHER'S DIK-DIK
Madoqua guentheri   **digidigi ya pua murefu (Swa)**

Habitat: arid bush country **Height:** 34–38 cm **Length:** 55–65 cm
Horns: 5–6 cm (♂) **Weight:** 3.7–5.5 kg **Status:** widespread, not
endangered

Very similar to Kirk's Dik-Dik, but slightly smaller, coat colour
greyer and has a more elongated rufous-coloured nose. Prominent,
preorbital glands but white ring around the eyes often indistinct.
Like Kirk's Dik-Dik, has a tuft of hair on crown, which is raised
when alarmed. Males have short horns that slant rearwards, often
hidden if head crest is raised. Habits similar to Kirk's, but this species
is found in hotter, drier areas. The large nose is an adaptation for
living in hot climates; it acts as a cooling passage for its blood.

BEST VIEWING: Kenya: Samburu NR; **Uganda:** Kidepo Valley NP

CHANLER'S MOUNTAIN REEDBUCK
Redunca fulvorufula chanleri   **tohe ya milima (Swa)**

Habitat: open grasslands on hills and mountains **Height:** 60–80 cm
Length: 110–136 cm **Horns:** 14–17 cm (♂) **Weight:** 22–38 kg (♂);
19–35 kg (♀) **Status:** vulnerable

A small to medium-sized, stocky antelope. Its coat is soft and grey-
tan, with white underparts. Its ears are long and narrow, with a
distinct bare, blackish patch beneath. Only male has horns, which
are distinctly curved upwards and forwards. Sociable, living in
small groups of 2–6 females, their young and a territorial male.
Mostly a grazer, but also browses in dry season.

BEST VIEWING: Kenya: Lake Nakuru NP, Masai Mara NR (Siria
Escarpment); **Tanzania:** Serengeti NP (Banagi Hill); **Uganda:** Kidepo
Valley NP

BOHOR REEDBUCK
Redunca redunca tohe, forhi (Swa); en-kijpuruk (Maa)

Habitat: grasslands, marshy areas with long grass, never far from water **Height:** 65–89 cm **Length:** 100–135 cm **Horns:** 20–41 cm **Weight:** 43–65 kg (♂); 35–45 kg (♀) **Status:** common, not endangered

A medium-sized, yellowish-sandy antelope with a white belly. A pale patch of bare skin below the ear. Under the tail is white, which is very conspicuous when tail held erect. Male has very distinctive, sharply hooked horns, which curve backwards then sharply forwards. Female similar, but smaller and slimmer. Occurs singly or in small family groups, spending the day lying hidden in thick vegetation. A grazer, feeding mostly at night but, during the dry season, often forced to graze during the day due to lack of food.
BEST VIEWING: most wildlife areas in the region

UGANDA KOB
Kobus kob thomasi mraye (Swa)

Habitat: grassland and savanna, never far from water **Height:** 90–100 cm (♂); 82–92 cm (♀) **Length:** 160–180 cm **Horns:** 45–92 cm (♂) **Weight:** 85–121 kg (♂); 60–77 kg (♀) **Status:** not endangered

A stocky, medium-sized antelope. Body rich, dark rufous with white markings around the eyes, on the face, ears and undersides. The legs have distinctive black markings on the front and white rings above the hooves. Male has thick, lyrate horns. Lives in large herds of 20–40, which can change in size and composition every day. Dominant males hold territories, while other males live in bachelor herds.
BEST VIEWING: Uganda: Queen Elizabeth, Murchison Falls NPs

DEFASSA WATERBUCK
Kobus ellipsiprymnus defassa kuru (Swa); ol-kibulekeny (Maa)

Habitat: riverine grassland and woodlands where there is permanent water **Height:** 120–136 cm **Length:** 177–235 cm **Horns:** 50–99 cm (♂) **Weight:** 200–300 kg (♂); 160–200 kg (♀) **Status:** not endangered

A stocky, thickset antelope with a shaggy, brownish coat, which darkens with age, and a white rump, bib, muzzle and eyebrows. Male has large, heavily ringed horns, which diverge widely at the base and curve upwards and backwards. Gregarious, living in groups composed of females, their young and a dominant male. Other males live in bachelor herds. Grazes mostly but browses during dry seasons.
BEST VIEWING: Kenya: Lake Nakuru NP, Masai Mara NR; **Tanzania:** Ngorongoro CA; **Uganda:** Queen Elizabeth, Murchison Falls NPs

COMMON WATERBUCK
Kobus ellipsiprymnus kuru ndogo (Swa)

Habitat: riverine grassland and woodlands with permanent water **Height:** 120–136 cm **Length:** 177–235 cm **Horns:** 55–99 cm (♂) **Weight:** 200–300 kg (♂); 160–200 kg (♀) **Status:** widespread

Similar to Defassa Waterbuck, but with a shaggy, grey-brown coat, which darkens with age, and a distinctive, white ring on rump. Has a white bib, muzzle and eyebrows. Male has large, heavily ringed horns, which diverge at the base and curve upwards and backwards. Gregarious, living in groups composed of females, their young and a dominant male. Other males live in bachelor herds.
BEST VIEWING: Kenya: Aberdare, Amboseli, Meru, Tsavo East, Tsavo West NPs, Samburu, Buffalo Springs NRs; **Tanzania:** Lake Manyara, Mikumi, Ruaha, Tarangire NPs, Selous GR

Paolo Torchio

THOMSON'S GAZELLE
Eudorcas thomsonii   swala tomi (Swa); enk-oilii (Maa)

Habitat: grasslands and open plains **Height:** 55–82 cm
Length: 80–120 cm **Horns:** 70–102 cm **Weight:** 20–35 kg (♂);
15–25 kg (♀) **Status:** not endangered

'Tommy', the common small gazelle of East African plains, is mainly fawn-rufous, with white underparts, separated by a broad black band. Rump white up to root of tail, bordered by black. Gregarious, in constantly changing herds with a single adult male. Breeding males mark territories with dung and tar-like deposits from a gland on the face. Non-breeding males usually solitary. Male is larger, with short ridged horns. A grazer, but browses in the dry season.
BEST VIEWING: Kenya: Amboseli NP, Masai Mara NR;
Tanzania: Serengeti NP

GRANT'S GAZELLE
Nanger granti   swala granti (Swa); ol-oibor sjadi (Maa)

Habitat: arid open plains and semi-desert country
Height: 85–91 cm (♂); 78–83 cm (♀) **Length:** 140–166 cm
Horns: 50–80 cm **Weight:** 60–81 kg (♂); 38–67 kg (♀)
Status: widespread and common; not endangered

Large, pale fawn coloured, with long legs and a distinctive, white rump, which extends above white tail. Most females have a faint dark stripe along their flanks. Both sexes have horns, male's are larger and graceful, extending upwards and outwards. Gregarious, living in small herds consisting of females, their latest offspring and a territorial male. Other males live in bachelor groups.
BEST VIEWING: common in most wildlife areas, except in the highlands;
Kenya: Masai Mara NR; **Tanzania:** Serengeti NP; **Uganda:** Kidepo Valley NP

GERENUK
Litocranius walleri   swala twiga, njonga (Swa); rigoo (Sam)

Habitat: dry thornbush country **Height:** 80–105 cm
Length: 140–160 cm **Horns:** 32–44 cm (♂) **Weight:** 31–52 kg (♂);
28–45 kg (♀) **Status:** not endangered

A distinctive, tall, long-necked antelope, with a relatively small head and large ears. Body colour fawn, back chestnut and underparts white. Male larger, with thick, heavily ringed horns. Can stand erect on its hindlegs and, with its long neck extended, browse on tall bushes. At times, uses its front legs to pull down higher branches. Does not require water and rarely drinks. Lives in small groups of females and their young, passing through various male territories.
BEST VIEWING: Kenya: Samburu, Buffalo Springs NRs;
Tanzania: Tarangire NP

IMPALA
Aepyceros melampus   swala pala (Swa); ol-olubo (Maa)

Habitat: *Acacia* savanna and light woodlands **Height:** 75–95 cm
Length: 120–160 cm **Horns:** 45–92 cm (♂) **Weight:** 45–80 kg (♂);
40–60 kg (♀) **Status:** not endangered

A common, medium-sized, graceful, rufous-fawn antelope. The rump is white, with a black line either side. Sexes similar but male has widespread S-shaped horns. Females live in herds of 10–100, usually accompanied by a territorial male. Males spend a considerable time chasing off other males; seldom able to hold their territories longer than a few months. Both a grazer and browser.
BEST VIEWING: Kenya and Tanzania: common in most wildlife areas, except mountain parks; **Uganda:** Lake Mburo NP

HIROLA/HUNTER'S ANTELOPE
Beatragus hunteri   hirola (Swa)

Habitat: open grassy plains **Height:** 100–125 cm **Length:** 120–200 cm
Horns: 60–72 cm **Weight:** 80–118 kg **Status:** critically endangered by
increase of livestock, but a number introduced into Tsavo East NP in
the 1960s and in 1996 are sustaining their number

An unusual-looking, sandy-coloured antelope with long legs,
a long body and a short stocky neck. The face is long, with
distinctive white-ringed eyes, a chevron between the eyes. Has
black-tipped white ears and a white tail. Male and female similar,
but female smaller. Both sexes have horns, which resemble Impala
horns. Herds usually made up of 5–30 females, their young and a
territorial male. Other males form bachelor herds. A grazer.
BEST VIEWING: Kenya: Tsavo East NP

Bruce Patterson

TOPI
Damaliscus lunatus   nyamera, topi (Swa); ol-konde (Maa)

Habitat: savanna and seasonally flooded grasslands
Height: 104–126 cm **Length:** 150–230 cm **Horns:** 150–180 cm
Weight: 120–160 kg (♂); 75–150 kg (♀) **Status:** not endangered

A distinctive, large antelope; colour rich, deep, glossy rufous, with
dark, purplish patches on legs and face. Legs yellowish. Horns
ridged, curving backwards and upwards, and often covered in mud.
Female similar to male, but smaller. Lives in small herds of females
and young, usually within a male's territory. Males have small
territories, with each taking up a prominent position, such as on a
termite mound. The fastest antelope, built for speed and endurance.
BEST VIEWING: Kenya: Masai Mara NR; **Tanzania:** Serengeti NP;
Uganda: Queen Elizabeth NP

COKE'S HARTEBEEST
Alcelaphus buselaphus cokii   kongoni (Swa); ol-korikor (Maa)

Habitat: open grassy plains and savanna woodland
Height: 107–150 cm **Length:** 160–245 cm **Horns:** 45–83 cm
Weight: 125–218 kg (♂); 116–185 kg (♀) **Status:** not endangered

A large, long-faced, uniformly fawn-coloured antelope with a pale
rump. Has high, humped shoulders and long, slim legs. Both sexes
have horns, which are short and thick, diverging almost horizontally
at the base, before turning upwards and backwards. Gregarious,
usually in herds of 5–10 females and their young. Territorial males
remain separate from the herds except when herding or breeding.
BEST VIEWING: Kenya: Amboseli, Nairobi, Tsavo East, Tsavo West
NPs, Masai Mara NR; **Tanzania:** Lake Manyara, Serengeti, Tarangire NPs;
Uganda: Murchison Falls NP

MOUNT KENYA (JACKSON'S) HARTEBEEST
Alcelaphus buselaphus jacksoni   kongoni (Swa)

Habitat: arid bush and grasslands **Height:** 124 cm
Length: 160–215 cm **Horns:** 45–70 cm **Weight:** 129–228 kg
Status: locally common

Typical hartebeest but colour much darker than previous species,
being uniformly tawny-red; horns more upright and V-shaped.
Female smaller than male and horns shorter. Lives in small herds
consisting of females, their young and a dominant male.
BEST VIEWING: Kenya: Ruma NP, Lewa Wildlife Conservancy;
Uganda: Murchison Falls, Kidepo Valley NPs

Ariadne van Zandbergen

LICHTENSTEIN'S HARTEBEEST
Alcelaphus buselaphus lichtensteinii   kongoni, konzi (Swa)

Habitat: dry bush and wooded country **Height:** 124 cm
Length: 160–200 cm **Horns:** 50–60 cm **Weight:** 118–145 kg
Status: not threatened

Similar to Mount Kenya Hartebeest but colour slightly lighter
and the legs have black markings on the front. Horns shorter
than Mount Kenya Hartebeest's, curving upwards, inwards and
backwards and, when viewed from the front, appear circular.
Female similar to male but horns smaller. Lives in small herds
consisting of a dominant male and 8–10 females and their
young. The herd is led by a female.
BEST VIEWING: Tanzania: Selous GR

EASTERN WHITE-BEARDED WILDEBEEST
Connochaetes taurinus albojubatus   nyumbu (Swa); o-enkat (Maa)

Habitat: grasslands **Height:** 115–154 cm **Length:** 170–240 cm
Horns: 76–81 cm **Weight:** 165–290 kg ($\male$); 140–260 kg ($\female$) **Status:** not
endangered, but increase of livestock a threat in the future

An unusual-looking antelope: the front of the body is heavily built,
the hindquarters are slender and it has thin, spindly legs. Light buff-
grey with a black mane, a conspicuous whitish beard and a long,
black tail. Both sexes have horns, the male's being larger and wider.
Lives in aggregations of small female herds and male bachelor herds;
mostly sedentary, only dispersing seasonally when conditions force
them to. All mating takes place during a three-week period; mature
males take up territories, which are marked by dung piles.
BEST VIEWING: Kenya: Amboseli, Nairobi NPs; **Tanzania:** Tarangire NP

WESTERN WHITE-BEARDED WILDEBEEST
Connochaetes taurinus mearnsi   nyumbu (Swa); o-enkat (Maa)

Habitat: grasslands **Height:** 117–123 cm **Length:** 170–240 cm **Horns:**
45–76 cm **Weight:** 200 kg ($\male$); 163 kg ($\female$) **Status:** not endangered

Similar to Eastern White-bearded Wildebeest, but much darker and
greyer, with smaller horns. Lives in large herds, consisting of female
groups and male groups. As wildebeest are highly migratory, males
are able to take up temporary territories only during the three-week
rutting season. The migratory population is about 1.4 million, with
smaller, more sedentary populations in the Ngorongoro Crater, the
Western Corridor, Serengeti NP. Occurs west of the Rift Valley, while
the previous species is found in, and east of, the Rift Valley.
BEST VIEWING: Kenya: Masai Mara NR; **Tanzania:** Serengeti NP,
Ngorongoro CA

Jenny Hartree

BLUE WILDEBEEST
Connochaetes taurinus taurinus   nyumbu (Swa)

Habitat: wooded grasslands **Height:** 106–114 cm **Length:** 300 cm
Horns: 66–76 cm **Weight:** 250 kg ($\male$); 204 kg ($\female$)
Status: not endangered

Very similar to Western White-bearded Wildebeest but darker,
with a black beard, an upstanding mane and brown lower legs.
This population is mostly sedentary, only dispersing seasonally for
better grazing conditions.
BEST VIEWING: Tanzania: Selous GR

ROAN ANTELOPE
Hippotragus equinus   **korongo (Swa); ol-oiborkutuk (Maa)**

Habitat: open wooded country and park-like savanna
Height: 126–145 cm **Length:** 190–240 cm **Horns:** 55–99 cm
Weight: 242–300 kg (♂); 223–280 kg (♀) **Status:** uncommon

A large, rufous-grey antelope with distinctive, black-and-white facial markings, and a short, black-tipped mane. Horns are thick, heavily ridged, scimitar-shaped; ears are long and tufted at tips. Sexes similar but female is smaller and has slimmer, shorter horns. Occurs in small herds of up to 20, each led by a dominant male. Other males live in small bachelor herds. Herds congregate during the dry season. Mainly a grazer but will occasionally browse and also eat seedpods.

BEST VIEWING: Kenya: Ruma, Shimba Hills NPs; **Tanzania:** Ruaha, Serengeti (rare in the Mbalageti Valley) NPs; **Uganda:** Kidepo Valley NP

SABLE ANTELOPE
Hippotragus niger   **pala hala, mbarapi (Swa)**

Habitat: light woodland and miombo woodland **Height:** 117–143 cm
Length: 190–255 cm **Horns:** 100–160 cm **Weight:** 200–270 kg (♂);
190–230 kg (♀) **Status:** probably endangered

An impressive-looking antelope. Male black or reddish-black, depending on age, with contrasting white underparts and black-and-white facial markings and long pointed ears. Very long, often exceeding 1 m, heavily ridged, scimitar-shaped horns. Female's horns similar to male's but smaller, paler, shorter and less curved. Female very similar to Roan Antelope but differs in the strongly demarcated white underparts, lack of ear tufts and facial patterns.

BEST VIEWING: Kenya: Shimba Hills NP; **Tanzania:** Ruaha NP, Selous GR

BEISA ORYX
Oryx beisa beisa   **choroa, bara bara (Swa); ikupoporog (Sam)**

Habitat: arid, semi-desert bush country **Height:** 110–120 cm
Length: 153–170 cm **Horns:** 60–110 cm **Weight:** 167–209 kg (♂);
116–188 kg (♀) **Status:** near threatened

A large, striking-looking antelope with long rapier-like horns. Pale grey with distinctive, black-and-white facial markings and long, pointed ears. Has a narrow, black spinal stripe and a black stripe separating lower flanks from white underparts. Forelegs are white, with a black ring above the knee and a black patch below. Sexes are similar, but female smaller with longer, more slender horns. Lives in mixed herds up to 60-strong, usually with more females than males.

BEST VIEWING: Kenya: Meru NP, Samburu, Buffalo Springs NRs;
Uganda: Kidepo Valley NP

FRINGE-EARED ORYX
Oryx beisa callotis   **choroa (Swa); ol-kimosorogi (Maa)**

Habitat: arid bush country **Height:** 110–120 cm
Length: 153–170 cm **Horns:** 60–110 cm **Weight:** 167–209 kg (♂);
116–188 kg (♀) **Status:** vulnerable

Similar in habits and appearance to Beisa Oryx, but rich brown and the long ears have a conspicuous fringe of black hairs at the tips. Oryx have adapted to living in hot, harsh conditions by feeding on grasses and herbs during late evening and early morning, when dew often forms. Will drink regularly if water available, but can go without it for weeks if necessary.

BEST VIEWING: Kenya: Amboseli, Tsavo East, Tsavo West NPs;
Tanzania: Tarangire NP; **Uganda:** Kidepo Valley NP

BIRDS

East Africa's birdlife is remarkable, and few visitors or residents can fail to be impressed by the large variety of colourful birds they see and by their relative tameness. Although many birds can be seen at close range in the region's parks and reserves, binoculars are essential for bird-watching.

Some 1 400 or more species have been recorded in East Africa, which represents approximately 15 per cent of the world's total. This figure is changing each year as new bird species are discovered, particularly in Tanzania. Discoveries in the first decade of the 21st century include a sunbird, a weaver, a cisticola and, perhaps the most exciting, a forest partridge whose closest relative is the Hill Partridge of Asia.

Even though the number of recorded species is slowly increasing, we cannot afford to be complacent: the destruction of habitats, due largely to an ever-increasing human population, has placed a number of species in danger. The forests of Kakamega, Nandi, Sokoke, Uluguru, Usambara, and many others, are vulnerable. A number of birds are threatened, including the Crowned Crane, Uganda's national bird, which is at risk because of the draining of its swamp habitat and the wild exotic bird trade. The latest threat to vultures and scavenging birds of prey is the use of a cheap and readily available poison, Furadan. It is being used widely to kill mammals such as Lion, Leopard and Hyaena, mainly on private land but also in protected areas. When these animals die they are fed upon by vultures, birds of prey and other scavengers, which are then also poisoned. Lake Natron, the only site where Lesser Flamingo breed in East Africa, is now under threat by a project to mine the soda ash in the lake. Despite concerns expressed by international authorities that the factory and infrastructure will severely disturb the flamingos, the project could still go ahead.

This chapter illustrates and describes 260 species of bird and a further 104 species are mentioned. Selecting birds for inclusion was a particularly difficult task, and preference was given to those species that can be easily seen and those that occur in areas visited by tourists.

In most cases, only the male is illustrated in this book, but the female and immature are described in the text. Also described in the text are subspecies, if they differ. For instance, in the west of the region, the White-eyed Slaty Flycatcher does not have white eyes and is plain grey. The text also gives brief descriptions of similar species. Measurements given for length include the tail.

Nomenclature and taxonomy is based on E.C. Dickinson's *The Howard & Moore Complete Checklist of the Birds of the World* (A&C Black/Croom Helm, London, 2003) for non-passerines; passerines follow Sangster *et al.* in *Ibis* 152: 181–186.

The common names are those in current use in the region, rather than those used by authors from outside of the region, but some alternatives are also given. Where known, the Kiswahili (Swa) and Maasai (Maa) names are included.

OSTRICH
Struthio camelus  bbuni masai (Swa); e-sidai (Maa)

Habitat: open plains and lightly wooded grassland below 2 000 m
Length: 2–2.5 m **Status:** common resident

Unmistakable, the male has a black body with contrasting white wings and tail, which is often stained brown. Two distinct races occur: nominate *S. camelus* has grey-pink legs and neck, and brown eyes; Somali Ostrich (*S. molybdophanes*), has grey-blue eyes, distinctive, blue-grey neck and legs, and the bill and the front of the lower legs pink. Female and immature of both races are grey-brown. Chicks are buffy, with black stripes on the head and neck. Feeds on grasses, seeds, insects and lizards.
BEST VIEWING: (*S. camelus*) **Kenya:** Masai Mara NR; **Tanzania:** Serengeti NP; (*S. molybdophanes*) **Kenya:** Buffalo Springs, Samburu NRs

HELMETED GUINEAFOWL
Numida meleagris kanga (Swa); enkersure (Maa)

Habitat: savanna, thornbush and cultivated areas, sea level to 2 000 m
Length: 58–64 cm **Status:** common resident

A familiar bird with greyish-black body covered in small white spots. Distinctive bright blue face and neck, horn-coloured bony crest and red-tipped blue wattles. Sexes similar; immature is drabber than adult, with smaller and duller wattles. Usually in flocks, except when breeding; most active at dawn and dusk. Feeds mostly on seeds but also on berries and insects, especially flying termites. Highly vocal at times, particularly if a predator is spotted. Spends most of the time on the ground, but roosts in trees and flies into trees if threatened.
BEST VIEWING: almost all national parks and reserves

VULTURINE GUINEAFOWL
Acryllium vulturinum kicheleko, koiolo-tumbusi (Swa)

Habitat: dry desert and thornbush country, sea level to 1 900 m
Length: 61–71 cm **Status:** locally common resident

A large, distinctive-looking guineafowl with long legs and long, pointed tail feathers. The small, bare, grey head, with a tuft of velvety, brown feathers on the nape, is distinctive. Neck and chest feathers are long and pointed, with white stripes and cobalt-blue edges. The breast and sides of the chest are bright cobalt-blue. The back, belly and wings are black, with small white spots. Sexes alike, the female slightly smaller than the male. Immature is duller than adult. Highly gregarious, occurring in large flocks, usually seen at dawn and dusk, often when approaching water.
BEST VIEWING: Kenya: Buffalo Springs, Samburu NRs

CRESTED FRANCOLIN
Francolinus sephaena kwale kishungi (Swa); en-kurle (Maa)

Habitat: dry bush country, often near watercourses, sea level to 2 100 m **Length:** 24–30 cm **Status:** locally common resident

A brown francolin with a distinctive white eye stripe, white streaking on the upperparts and buffy underparts, with darker triangular spots on the side of the neck. The dark crest on the head is seen only when the bird is excited. The legs are red and the tail is typically cocked at a 45° angle. In flight, the black tail is conspicuous. Sexes similar; immature resembles adult but is duller. Its harsh, rattling call, usually at dawn, is a characteristic sound of the bush where it occurs. Usually found in pairs or small family parties.
BEST VIEWING: widespread in suitable habitats

RED-NECKED SPURFOWL (FRANCOLIN)
Francolinus afer   kwale, shingo-nyekundu (Swa)

Habitat: light woodland and savanna country with thickets, sea level to 1 500 m **Length:** 35–41 cm **Status:** common resident

Varies in colour from grey to brown, with underparts streaked chestnut or black-and-white. The red throat, bill and legs are distinctive. Sexes alike, but female smaller than male. Immature is similar to adults but duller. Occurs in pairs or small family parties. Grey-breasted Spurfowl (*F. rufopictus*) is similar but has a bright orange throat and is restricted to the Serengeti NP, Tanzania.

BEST VIEWING: widespread in suitable habitats

YELLOW-NECKED SPURFOWL (FRANCOLIN)
Francolinus leucoscepus   kwali shingo-njano (Swa)

Habitat: dry bush country and savanna, sea level to 2 400 m **Length:** 34–43 cm **Status:** common resident

A distinctive-looking spurfowl with a bright yellow throat and bare, red skin around the eyes. Back greyish-brown, streaked whitish; underparts paler, with buffy streaks. In flight, shows conspicuous pale wing patches. Sexes alike; immature similar to adults. Often seen perched on a low branch or on top of a bush or termite mound. A common bird, usually found in pairs or small family parties.

BEST VIEWING: Kenya: Samburu NR, Meru, Tsavo East, Tsavo West NPs; **Tanzania:** Tarangire NP; **Uganda:** Kidepo Valley NP

WHITE-FACED WHISTLING DUCK
Dendrocygna viduata   bata miti uso mweupe (Swa)

Habitat: swamps, lakes, floodplains and dams **Length:** 43–48 cm **Status:** at times very common, resident

A distinctive duck with a white face, forehead and throat, often stained from feeding in muddy water. The body is rich brown, with barring on the flanks, and the belly is black. The bill is black, with a blue bar at its tip, and the legs and feet are blue. Sexes alike; immature similar to adult but the face, forehead and throat are greyish. A gregarious duck, often occurring in large numbers when feeding conditions are suitable. Its clear, whistling, three-note call is a feature of this bird.

BEST VIEWING: most national parks and reserves

EGYPTIAN GOOSE
Alopochen aegyptiaca   bata bukini, mmisri bata bakini (Swa)

Habitat: almost anywhere there is water, sea level to 3 000 m **Length:** 63–73 cm **Status:** common resident

A large, brown water bird with pink legs and a pink bill. The conspicuous rufous-coloured patch around the eyes and the dark patch in the centre of the belly are diagnostic. A white patch on the wing is particularly noticeable in flight. Sexes similar; immature resembles adult but is duller, lacks the rufous eye patch and the dark chestnut chest patch. Usually found in pairs, at times can be very noisy, especially when breeding. Often takes over Hamerkop nests or large holes in trees. At times builds a nest high on cliffs. When moulting, gathers in large numbers.

BEST VIEWING: any water habitat

CAPE TEAL
Anas capensis   **bata kusi (Swa)**

Habitat: alkaline lakes **Length:** 44–48 cm **Status:** locally common resident

A small, pale, speckled duck with a bright pink, slightly upturned bill. The male's eyes are yellow-brown, the female's orange-brown. The wings are darker and, in flight, show a distinctive white patch with a green-blue speculum. Sexes alike; immature is similar to adult but less spotted. A characteristic duck of the alkaline lakes, usually found in pairs, although occasionally large flocks do occur in the Rift Valley lakes. Feeds mostly by sieving the top surface of the water for aquatic food items, much like the Lesser Flamingo.

BEST VIEWING: Rift Valley alkaline lakes

YELLOW-BILLED DUCK
Anas undulata   **bata domonjano (Swa)**

Habitat: fresh-water lakes, swamps and dams, especially in the highlands above 1 600 m **Length:** 51–58 cm **Status:** locally common resident

A medium-sized, distinctive duck with a bright yellow bill, which has a black patch on the upper mandible and a black tip. The head is grey, finely streaked, and the body is grey-brown, with pale-edged feathers. In flight, a green-blue speculum is visible. Sexes similar; immature is similar to adult but duller. A characteristic duck, usually found in pairs or small groups, of fresh-water lakes, swamps and dams, especially in the highlands, where it is the most common resident duck.

BEST VIEWING: widespread in suitable habitats

RED-BILLED TEAL
Anas erythrorhyncha   **bata domojekundu (Swa); e-motoroki (Maa)**

Habitat: fresh-water lakes, dams and floodplains **Length:** 43–48 cm **Status:** locally common resident

A medium-sized, red-billed, buffy-coloured duck, mottled with brown spots. May be confused with the Cape Teal, both having red bills, but distinguished from that bird by its larger size and a distinctive dark cap, which contrasts with its pale cheeks. The wing is dark and, in flight, shows pale secondaries with a pink speculum. Sexes alike; immature similar but generally duller-looking. Occurs in small groups on lakes, dams and floodplains.

BEST VIEWING: widespread in suitable habitats

BLUE-BILLED TEAL
Anas hottentota   **bata hotento (Swa)**

Habitat: shallow water, swamps, marshes, dams and ponds, sea level to 3 000 m **Length:** 30–35 cm **Status:** common resident

Africa's smallest duck, with a blue bill and a distinctive dark cap. The body is brown, the wings darker and, in flight, secondaries show a green speculum with a distinctive white trailing edge. Sexes similar; immature duller with a brown-blue bill. Distinguished from Red-billed Teal by its smaller size and blue bill. Usually found in pairs or small groups.

BEST VIEWING: widespread in suitable habitats

SOUTHERN POCHARD
Netta erythrophthalma   bata jichojekundu (Swa)

Habitat: deep, mainly fresh-water lakes, to 3 000 m **Length:** 48–51 cm
Status: resident, not as common as it was

A medium-sized brown duck with a blue-grey bill. Male has distinctive red eyes and the head is darker than the body. Female is duller, with a white throat, dark eyes and a distinctive, pale whitish, crescent-shaped mark on the side of its head. In flight, both sexes show a distinctive white bar on the wing. Immature resembles female but paler. Usually found in pairs or in small groups. Male Maccoa Duck (*Oxyura maccoa*) is distinguished from male Southern Pochard by its chestnut body, bright blue bill and stiff tail, which is held upright.
BEST VIEWING: widespread in suitable habitats

LITTLE GREBE (DABCHICK)
Tachybaptus ruficollis   kiwizi mdogo (Swa)

Habitat: fresh-water lakes, dams and ponds, sea level to 3 000 m
Length: 20–29 cm **Status:** common resident

A small, stout-looking, tailless water bird with a 'powder-puff' rear end. The back is grey-brown, underparts paler. The bill is short, with a distinctive pale spot at its base. When breeding, the neck and cheeks become bright rufous and the throat and face turn black. Sexes alike; immature is similar to non-breeding adult. Juvenile has distinct grey-and-brown markings on the face. It dives regularly and also runs on the surface of the water. The call is a distinctive, loud, slightly descending trill.
BEST VIEWING: widespread in suitable habitats

GREATER FLAMINGO
Phoenicopterus roseus   heroe mkubwa (Swa)

Habitat: alkaline lakes, coastal lagoons, occasionally fresh-water lakes
Length: 127–142 cm **Status:** less common than Lesser Flamingo

Much larger than Lesser Flamingo and paler in colour. The body is pinkish-white and the upper and lower wing coverts, best seen in flight, are bright coral-red. The bill is pink, with a black tip. Distinctive red wings with black tips, best seen in flight. Sexes alike but male larger; immature greyish-white, with a pale bill. Feeds by filtering small invertebrates from the bottom mud in shallow waters. Displaying birds hold their necks fully extended, wag their necks from side to side, then flash open their wings for a few seconds. Occurs in much smaller numbers than Lesser Flamingo.
BEST VIEWING: Rift Valley lakes and the East African coast

LESSER FLAMINGO
Phoeniconaias minor   heroe mdogo (Swa); en-gusar (Maa)

Habitat: almost exclusively on alkaline lakes **Length:** 81–90 cm
Status: locally abundant

Unmistakable, but distinguished from Greater Flamingo by its deeper pink plumage and smaller size. The dark red, black-tipped bill also distinguishes it and is diagnostic. Sexes alike, but male larger. Immature drab greyish-white, with grey-brown bill and legs. Highly gregarious, occurring in large flocks. A surface feeder, filtering blue-green algae from the top few centimetres of the water. Displaying birds form distinctive, deep-pink, compact groups, the breast of one touching the back of the one in front, while holding their necks erect and bobbing their heads up and down, taking very small steps.
BEST VIEWING: Rift Valley alkaline lakes

YELLOW-BILLED STORK
Mycteria ibis korongo domonjano (Swa)

Habitat: prefers fresh-water lakes, swamps, but also alkaline lakes
Length: 95–105 cm **Status:** common resident

A medium-sized, mostly white stork, immediately distinguished from White Stork (*Ciconia ciconia*) by its slightly decurved yellow bill and its aquatic habits. Adult tinged with pink and has black wing tips, a black tail and bare, red skin on the forehead and face. When breeding, plumage is more diffused with pink and wing covert tips are crimson. Sexes alike; immature grey-brown with brown wing tips and tail, a pale yellow-brownish bill. In flight, its all-black tail distinguishes it from similar White Stork, which has an all-white tail. Feeds with bill partly open in shallow waters.

BEST VIEWING: any of the Rift Valley Lakes

AFRICAN OPEN-BILLED STORK/AFRICAN OPENBILL
Anastomus lamelligerus korongo domowazi (Swa)

Habitat: lakes, floodplains, rice paddies, up to 1 500 m
Length: 81–94 cm **Status:** inter-African migrant

A medium-sized, uniformly dark-plumaged stork with a long, heavy-looking bill, which, when closed, has a characteristic gap between the mandibles. Sexes alike; immature is duller than adult and, depending on age, has a noticeably shorter bill with almost no gap. Uses its uniquely shaped bill to extract its main food, water snails, from their shells. Flocks suddenly appear when feeding conditions are good, before moving on. Highly gregarious – flocks often number in the thousands.

BEST VIEWING: widespread in suitable habitats, especially during the rainy season

ABDIM'S STORK
Ciconia abdimii korongo mayobwe (Swa)

Habitat: savanna grasslands and pastures **Length:** 76–81 cm
Status: inter-African migrant

A small black-and-white stork. The head, back and wings are black, with a purple-green gloss. The lower back, uppertail and underparts are white, which extends above the shoulder of the wing. The bare skin around the face is greenish, with a red spot in front of the eyes. The bill is greenish, with a red tip, and the legs are dull-greenish with red joints. Sexes alike; immature is browner and duller than adult. The similar Black Stork (*C. nigra*) can be distinguished by its red bill and legs and it shows no white above the shoulders.

BEST VIEWING: Kenya: Masai Mara NR; **Tanzania:** Serengeti NP; **Uganda:** Murchison Falls NP

SADDLE-BILLED STORK
Ephippiorhynchus senegalensis korongo domoganzi (Swa)

Habitat: fresh-water lakes, swamps and rivers, sea level to 1 500 m
Length: c. 145 cm **Status:** uncommon resident

This striking, unmistakable, large black-and-white stork has a massive, sharp-pointed bill with a black band around it and a distinctive, yellow saddle-shaped shield at its base. The black wings often have a purple-green sheen. The legs are black with dull-red 'knees' and toes. There is also a bright red spot of naked skin on the chest. Sexes similar but female has bright golden-yellow eyes, while male has dark brown eyes and two small, yellow wattles at the base of the bill. Immature is duller and greyer than adult, with a dull, red-and-black bill, which lacks the yellow shield.

BEST VIEWING: Kenya: Masai Mara NR

MARABOU STORK
Leptoptilos crumeniferus   **korongo mfuko shingo (Swa);
eno-Ikirau (Maa)**

Habitat: savanna and wetlands, but also towns **Length:** c. 152 cm
Status: common resident

A large, ungainly looking stork with a massive bill. The pinkish skin of the neck and chest is sparsely covered in down. An extendable pink air sac hangs down from the base of the neck. The wings and tail are glossy green-black and the underparts are white. When breeding, the bare skin intensifies in colour and there is a white border to the wing coverts. Sexes alike; immature is brownish, with extensive woolly down on the head. A scavenger, but also feeds on rodents and insects.

BEST VIEWING: almost everywhere, often nests in tall trees in towns/cities

SACRED IBIS
Threskiornis aethiopicus   **kwarara mweupe (Swa)**

Habitat: swamps, floodplains, pastures and along rivers and lake shores, sea level to 3 000 m **Length:** 64–82 cm
Status: common resident

Unmistakable, a mostly white ibis with a contrasting naked black head and a long, decurved, black bill. During breeding, a long plume of black feathers grows over the tail and the bare skin along the base of the underwings turns bright red (seen only when the wing is lifted). Sexes alike; immature similar to adults but has black-and-white mottled feathers on the head and neck. Very gregarious birds, typically fly in a V-formation.

BEST VIEWING: widespread in suitable habits

HADADA (HADEDA) IBIS
Bostrychia hagedash   **kwarara hijani (Swa); en-kaaka (Maa)**

Habitat: swamps, pastures and urban gardens, sea level to 3 000 m
Length: 76–89 cm **Status:** common resident

A very noisy, dull brown, short-legged ibis with a glossy, green-bronze sheen on the shoulders and back, and a purple sheen on the wings. The bill is long and curved, with the upper mandible mostly red, and there is a distinctive white line on the cheeks. Sexes alike; immature similar to but duller than adult. Its well-known 'haa-de-daa' call is heard mostly at dawn and dusk, as it flies to or from roosting sites, which are usually in tall trees. Occurs in pairs or small groups. Glossy Ibis (*Plegadis falcinellus*) is similar, but is much slimmer looking, with long legs and a slender bill and neck.

BEST VIEWING: widespread in suitable habits

AFRICAN SPOONBILL
Platalea alba   **domomwiko Afrika (Swa)**

Habitat: floodplains, shallow lakes, both fresh and alkaline, and coastal lagoons, sea level to 3 000 m **Length:** c. 91 cm
Status: sparse resident

An unmistakable, all-white bird with a distinctive, flattened, spoon-shaped bill. There is bare red skin on the forehead and face. The legs are red. The upper mandible is blue-grey edged with red (visible at close range) and the lower mandible is darker. Sexes alike; immature duller, with a horn-coloured bill and dark legs. Occurs singly or in flocks. Flies in V-formation with neck outstretched, when the silhouette of the bill is noticeable.

BEST VIEWING: Rift Valley lakes

BLACK-CROWNED NIGHT HERON
Nycticorax nycticorax korongo kiparacheusi (Swa)

Habitat: riverine trees and bushes, lakes and dams
Length: 56–61 cm **Status:** locally common resident in suitable habitats

A medium-sized, short-legged heron with distinctive, large, red eyes. Body is white, with grey wings and a contrasting black crown and back. Two distinct, long, white plumes extend from the nape. Sexes alike; immature is pale brown with buffy spots on the back and wings, and the underparts are paler, with darker streaking. Usually found in small groups, sitting in a characteristic hunched position, in dense foliage along lakes and rivers. Although nocturnal, it can often be seen in the late afternoon.
BEST VIEWING: widespread in suitable habitats

SQUACCO HERON
Ardeola ralloides korongo maji (Swa)

Habitat: swamps, lakes and rivers **Length:** 46 cm **Status:** widespread, sometimes common resident

A small, short-legged, heron. Breeding birds are deep cinnamon-buff on the back and buff below; they develop long, black-edged, white plumes, which reach as far as the tail. The bill is greenish-yellow, with a black tip, the legs are yellowish and the eyes yellow. For a few days during breeding, the bill turns blue and the legs turn red. Non-breeding and immature birds are pale grey-brown, strongly streaked and have brown eyes. In flight, the white of the wings can be seen, as can the rump and tail, which contrast strongly with the body. Mostly solitary.
BEST VIEWING: Kenya: Amboseli NP

CATTLE EGRET
Bubulcus ibis yangeyange (Swa)

Habitat: swamps, marshes, grasslands and pastures **Length:** 50–56 cm
Status: common resident

A small, short-legged, short-necked egret, entirely white, except during the breeding season, when the crown, chest and mantle turn a rich buff colour. A short, yellow bill, yellow eyes and yellow-green legs, all of which turn coral-red for a few days during breeding. Sexes alike; immature similar. Gregarious and tame, usually seen feeding on insects disturbed by cattle and large herbivores. Roosts and nests in large groups. They fly to and from roosts in early mornings and late evenings, in long lines or V-formations.
BEST VIEWING: widespread in suitable habitats

GREY HERON
Ardea cinerea kongoti kijivu (Swa)

Habitat: lakes, swamps, rivers and coastal lagoons **Length:** 90–100 cm
Status: a widespread resident

A large, slim, grey heron with a distinctive grey neck with a line of black streaks down the front. The white forehead and crown contrast strongly with a black line that runs from behind the eyes and ends in a wispy crest. The bill and legs are yellowish-brown; the eyes yellow. When breeding, eyes are red and the bill and legs are reddish. In flight, the head and neck is tightly tucked in, as in all herons, and the underwings are uniform grey. Sexes similar; immature paler and has a grey crown. Shy, usually solitary.
BEST VIEWING: widespread in suitable habitats

BLACK-HEADED HERON
Ardea melanocephala   koikoi majoka, kongoti majoka (Swa)

Habitat: grasslands and pastures, not necessarily near water
Length: 84–96 cm **Status:** common resident

Similar to Grey Heron, but with a black head and hindneck, which contrast strongly with a white throat. The upperparts are dark grey and the chest and belly are paler. Sexes similar; immature is brownish-grey with a darker grey head. The bill and legs of adults and immature are grey. In flight, the underwings appear white, contrasting with the black flight feathers, unlike the all-grey underwing of the Grey Heron. Mostly solitary, often feeding far from water, although numbers congregate when the food supply is good. Nests communally, often in towns.
BEST VIEWING: widespread

GOLIATH HERON
Ardea goliath   pondagundi mkubwa, kongoti jutu (Swa)

Habitat: lakes, swamps, rivers and coastal creeks **Length:** 140–152 cm
Status: sparse resident

The world's largest heron. Its size, bushy crest on the top of the crown and large, heavy bill are distinctive. The upperparts are slate-grey and the head, neck and underparts are rich chestnut. The chin and throat are white; the white foreneck has black streaking. Sexes alike; immature is generally paler. The call is a distinctive '*karrrk*'. Flies with slow wing beats, with legs hanging below the horizontal. Usually occurs and nests alone, deep in reed beds and just above water level. Occasionally may nest colonially in trees, such as at Lake Baringo.
BEST VIEWING: Kenya: Lake Baringo

PURPLE HERON
Ardea purpurea   kongoti pondagundi (Swa)

Habitat: swamps and dense reed beds in larger lakes
Length: 79–84 cm **Status:** widespread, sparse resident

A shy, usually solitary, heron, very similar in appearance to Goliath Heron, but about half the size. It is also much slimmer-looking, with a long, slender neck and a thin, pointed bill. Adult is grey and chestnut, with a rufous neck and a black (not chestnut) crown. The throat is white, and distinctive black lines run from the gape to the nape and from the gape down the neck. Immature is mottled brown and pale rufous, and the black stripes on the head and neck are less distinct. Shy and solitary.
BEST VIEWING: widespread where there is suitable habitat

GREAT WHITE EGRET
Ardea alba   yange mkuu (Swa)

Habitat: swamps, lakes and rivers **Length:** 89–92 cm
Status: widespread common resident

Largest of the white egrets and almost as large as Grey Heron. This egret is all-white, slender-bodied and long-necked. It has a long, strong yellow bill and a distinctive, thin, black line extending from the gape to behind the eyes. The legs are all-black. The similar Yellow-billed Egret is smaller and has a thin, black line extending from the gape to immediately below the eyes. During breeding, the bill turns black, the lores become green and long nuptial plumes grow down the back. Sexes alike; immature is similar but has a black-tipped yellow bill.
BEST VIEWING: almost any wetland habitat

YELLOW-BILLED (INTERMEDIATE) EGRET
Egretta intermedia   yangi domonjano (Swa)

Habitat: swamps, lakes and flooded areas **Length:** 61–69 cm
Status: widespread resident

Very similar to Great White Egret but considerably smaller, shorter necked with a stumpy, yellow bill. The legs and toes are black, the upper leg yellowish (often difficult to see). The eyes are yellow, and the black line extending from the gape ends immediately below the eyes. During breeding, the bill turns orange, the eyes red and the area around the eyes green, and short plumes grow from the shoulders. Sexes alike; immature similar to non-breeding adults. Usually solitary but often feeds alongside Great White Egret.

BEST VIEWING: Kenya: Amboseli NP

LITTLE EGRET
Egretta garzetta   yange dandala (Swa)

Habitat: fresh and alkaline lakes, coastal waters **Length:** 56–65 cm
Status: common resident

An all-white, medium-sized egret with a long neck, a long, black bill and black legs with distinctive, bright yellow toes. When breeding, has long plumes from the head and nuptial plumes down the back. Sexes alike; immature similar to non-breeding adults, but has dull, not bright yellow, toes. Grey-coloured Little Egrets occur occasionally, most commonly along the East African coast from Mombasa southwards. Usually solitary or in loose groups. The Western Reef Heron (*E. gularis*) has an all-white phase, which can cause confusion, but is larger and has a yellowish bill and pale legs.

BEST VIEWING: at almost any wetland habitat

HAMERKOP
Scopus umbretta   msingwe, fundi chuma (Swa); en-kutel (Maa)

Habitat: almost any shallow water **Length:** 48–56 cm
Status: common resident

An unmistakable, dull-brown, short-legged water bird. The hammer-shaped head, with its large, thick, backward-pointing crest and large, black bill, is distinctive. Sexes alike; immature similar to adults, but with a less-developed head crest. Usually solitary, sometimes feeds in groups. Well known for its habit of building huge, domed nests, usually in the fork of a tree, but occasionally on a large rock. The small entrance hole usually faces eastwards. The tops of the nests are often decorated with old bone and bits of skin.

BEST VIEWING: common in suitable habitats

GREAT (EASTERN) WHITE PELICAN
Pelecanus onocrotalus   mwari mweupe (Swa); en-celelok (Maa)

Habitat: mostly soda lakes, but occasionally fresh-water lakes
Length: 140–180 cm **Status:** common resident on Rift Valley lakes

Large, gregarious, all-white. Bill huge, blue-pink with a red nail at tip; pouch, feet and skin around eyes yellow. Feathers on the head meet in a sharp point above the bill. In flight, white wings with black flight feathers, are distinctive. Sexes similar. Breeding birds are tinged pink with swollen knobs above bill; in male this knob turns yellow, in female bright orange. Juvenile and immature are dark brown, bill, pouch and feet blackish, becoming paler with age. Roosts and nests on the ground and flies in V-formation.

BEST VIEWING: Rift Valley soda lakes

PINK-BACKED PELICAN
Pelecanus rufescens   mwari (Swa)

Habitat: fresh-water lakes **Length:** 135–152 cm
Status: widespread resident

Smaller than the previous species, this grey pelican occurs singly or in small groups. Sexes alike. The back and rump are tinged pink and the bill is grey-pink, with an orange nail at the tip. The pouch and bare skin around eye are flesh-coloured and the feet are yellow. The feathers on the head form an arc above the bill. In flight, the wing tips are black but secondaries are brownish, not black, as Great White Pelican. Breeding birds develop a crest, the pouch turns yellow and the feet orange-red. Roosts and nests in trees.

BEST VIEWING: likely to turn up on any fresh water; **Tanzania:** breeding colonies Lake Manyara NP, Mto wa Mbu

REED (LONG-TAILED) CORMORANT
Phalacrocorax africanus   mnandi mkiamrefu (Swa)

Habitat: fresh-water lakes, rivers, swamps, dams and mangrove creeks
Length: 51–56 cm **Status:** widespread resident

A small, long-tailed cormorant with a short neck and bill. Adults' bodies are glossy black, with paler wings, distinctive red eyes and a short, stiff crest on the forehead. Immature and non-breeding birds are brownish to dull black, often paler on the throat, with brown eyes. Usually occurs singly or in small groups, often seen perched on a branch overhanging water. Swims very low in the water, often with only the head showing.

BEST VIEWING: widespread in suitable habitats

GREAT CORMORANT
Phalacrocorax carbo   mnandi kifuacheupe (Swa)

Habitat: lakes, alkaline and fresh, dams and rivers **Length:** 80–100 cm
Status: common resident

Larger than Reed Cormorant, with a noticeably shorter tail and a hook-tipped bill. Breeding birds are glossy black, with white cheeks, throat and upper breast and often a distinctive white patch on the side of the rump. The eyes are emerald, the male's lores are orange and the female's scarlet. Immature brownish above, whitish below. Usually found in large numbers, commonly along the shoreline. Roosts and nests in large colonies in tall trees.

BEST VIEWING: widespread in suitable habitats

PYGMY FALCON
Polihierax semitorquatus   kozi kuya (Swa)

Habitat: semi-desert, thornbush country and savanna, up to 1 800 m
Length: 18–20 cm **Status:** fairly common resident

A tiny, stocky, shrike-sized falcon with conspicuous, coral-red legs and a red cere. The upperparts are grey, with a white collar, the face and underparts and uppertail coverts are white. Male and female similar but female has a chestnut-coloured mantle. In flight, the white rump, black tail and black flight feathers with white spots are very distinctive. Immature similar to adults but duller. Usually seen perched conspicuously on bushes and trees, often near White-headed Buffalo Weaver nests, in which it breeds.

BEST VIEWING: Kenya: Samburu, Buffalo Springs NRs;
Tanzania: Tarangire NP; **Uganda:** Kidepo Valley NP

LESSER KESTREL
Falco naumanni **kozi mdogo (Swa)**

Habitat: open grassland, savanna and open cultivated country
Length: 26–33 cm **Status:** locally common Palaearctic passage migrant

A small, gregarious and, at times, a very common falcon. Male differs from other kestrels in its smaller size, uniform chestnut-coloured back and generally pale appearance. Female and immature are mainly buffy-brown, with darker streaks and spots and a barred, brown tail. Usually in loose flocks, hovering while searching for prey. Generally in the region October–November, on its passage southwards, and in March–April, on its passage northwards.

BEST VIEWING: Kenya: Masai Mara NR; **Tanzania:** Serengeti NP; **Uganda:** Kidepo Valley NP

COMMON KESTREL
Falco tinnunculus **kozi kozi (Swa)**

Habitat: grasslands and near rocks and cliffs, up to 4 000 m
Length: 30–33 cm **Status:** migrant and an uncommon resident

At first sight, similar to Lesser Kestrel but male has distinctive black spotting on the back. Two races occur in East Africa, one a migrant from Eurasia. The local race, Rock Kestrel (*F. rupicolus*), is usually darker and the female has a grey-barred tail, while migrant females have a brown-barred tail. Local kestrels occur in pairs, usually near rocks and cliffs; migrants generally occur in small flocks in open country. Both races hunt by hovering, before dropping onto their prey.

BEST VIEWING: widespread in suitable habitats

GREATER (WHITE-EYED) KESTREL
Falco rupicoloides **kozi machomeupe (Swa)**

Habitat: grasslands, savanna and semi-desert with scattered trees, up to 1 800 m **Length:** c. 36 cm **Status:** local resident

Similar to a female Common Kestrel, but larger, more heavily barred and with a pale grey rump, a pale grey-black, barred tail and distinctive, pale, creamy-coloured eyes. The cere and feet are yellow. Sexes similar; immature resembles adult but has dark eyes. Occurs sparsely in open *Acacia* and semi-desert areas. Usually hunts from a perch, rarely hovering. Feeds mainly on small mammals and lizards. Breeds in abandoned Cape Rook nests, unlike other kestrels, which breed on rocks and cliffs.

BEST VIEWING: Tanzania: Serengeti NP

Nigel Dennis/IOA

SECRETARYBIRD
Sagittarius serpentarius **karani tamba (Swa); ol-mamura (Maa)**

Habitat: grassland and savanna, up to 3 000 m **Length:** 125–150 cm
Status: widespread resident, but not common

Unmistakable, a large, slim, grey bird with long legs and long, projecting central tail feathers; usually seen walking in the open plains. Flight feathers, belly and legs black, with two black bands on the tail. A conspicuous, long, loose crest of black feathers on the nape is often raised when bird is excited. Bare skin on face orange-red. In flight, both legs extend well beyond the tail. Sexes similar; immature brownish-grey, with a shorter tail and bare yellow skin on the face. Feeds mostly on snakes but also on reptiles and insects. When pursuing prey, spreads its wings and stamps on it.

BEST VIEWING: Kenya: Masai Mara NR; **Tanzania:** Serengeti NP

AFRICAN BLACK-SHOULDERED KITE
Elanus caeruleus   mwewe kipupwe, mwewe bawa jeusi (Swa)

Habitat: cultivated land and grasslands, sea level to 3 000 m
Length: 31–35 cm   **Status:** at times common resident

A small, pale raptor, usually seen hovering over open land or conspicuously perched on the top of a tree or telephone pole, often wagging its tail slowly up and down. The head, underparts and tail are white, the back is grey and there is a distinctive black patch on the shoulder. The feet and cere are bright yellow and the eyes are deep red. Sexes alike; immature darker than adults, with yellow eyes, white tips to the mantle and wing feathers. Most often seen hunting over grasslands, where it preys on rodents.

BEST VIEWING: widespread in suitable habitats

BLACK (YELLOW-BILLED) KITE
Milvus migrans   mwewe domo-njano (Swa); ol-wuapishoi (Maa)

Habitat: urban areas, sea level to 3 000 m   **Length:** 51–60 cm
Status: common resident

An all-brown raptor with a conspicuous yellow bill, brown eyes and a distinctive forked tail. Sexes alike; immature resembles adults but has streaking on the chest and belly, a black bill, pale eyes and a less distinctively forked tail. The European nominate race, which visits East Africa from September to April, differs in being slightly darker, with a paler head, fine streaking, a black bill, pale eyes and a less distinctively forked tail. Mainly a scavenger, often seen flying low over roads, looking for road kills just after sunrise.

BEST VIEWING: widespread in suitable habitats

AFRICAN FISH EAGLE
Haliaeetus vocifer   tai miasamaki (Swa)

Habitat: almost any type of water habitat   **Length:** 63 cm (♂); 73 cm (♀)
Status: common resident

A distinctive eagle, easily recognised by its white head, chest, back and tail, a contrasting chestnut belly and shoulders and black wings. Sexes alike but female larger; immature is heavily streaked. Its loud, evocative, yelping call, given by both sexes often in a duet, is one of Africa's most distinctive sounds. Feeds almost entirely on fish, but also on water birds such as Red-knobbed Coot, which it catches by swooping down and snatching them from the water. Hunts and eats flamingos at soda lakes, where fish do not occur.

BEST VIEWING: at almost any wetland habitat

WHITE-BACKED VULTURE
Gyps africanus   tumbusi mgongomweupe (Swa); ol-ng'iro (Maa)

Habitat: savanna, sea level to 3 000 m   **Length:** 89–98 cm
Status: locally common resident but endangered

A large, uniformly brown vulture with a long, almost-bare neck with a pale ruff at its base. The eyes are dark and the bill black. The white back and rump are seen only in flight or when perched on the ground with its wings held open. The white forewing, seen in flight, is distinctive. Sexes alike; immature darker with pale streaking and lacks the white back and rump. Immature distinguished from immature Rüppell's Vulture by its darker appearance, shorter neck and shorter bill. The most common vulture at a carcass. Roosts and nests in trees, often near water.

BEST VIEWING: any game-viewing area

RÜPPELL'S VULTURE/RÜPPELL'S GRIFFON VULTURE
Gyps rueppellii tumbusi-mbuga (Swa)

Habitat: savanna **Length:** 95–107 cm **Status:** locally common resident but endangered

A large, brown vulture, distinguished from White-backed Vulture by the creamy-white edging to the body and wing feathers, which gives it a scaly appearance. The head and almost-bare neck are grey, with sparse, whitish down. The cere and the face are blue-grey, the bill horn-coloured, tinged pink, and the eyes are bright orange-yellow. Blue-grey bare patches on either side of the crop are distinctive, as are the three narrow, whitish bars, seen on the underwing in flight. Sexes alike; immature is paler and has a dark bill. Habitually roosts and nests on cliff faces, but perches on trees in open country.

BEST VIEWING: any game-viewing area

LAPPET-FACED VULTURE
Torgos tracheliotus tumbusi ngusha (Swa)

Habitat: savanna, sea level to 3 000 m **Length:** 98–115 cm
Status: resident

The largest African vulture. The bare, crimson skin on the head and neck and the massive, ivory or greenish-brown bill are diagnostic. The feathers on the flanks are white and contrast with the dark body. Sexes alike; immature similar but has pale pink, bare skin on the head and neck and, dark, not white, flanks. When seen in flight from below, the white flanks and legs are distinctive. Usually seen in pairs and often dominant at carcasses. Roosts and nests in the tops of small balanites and *Acacia* trees, often using abandoned Secretarybird nests.

BEST VIEWING: any game-viewing area

BLACK-CHESTED SNAKE EAGLE
Circaetus pectoralis tai kifuacheusi (Swa)

Habitat: savanna and light woodland, sea level to 3 400 m
Length: 63–68 cm **Status:** sparse resident

A distinctive eagle with an almost owl-like head, large, yellow eyes and bare, unfeathered, legs. Upperparts, head and breast blackish-brown, with a white belly. Sexes alike; immature pale blotchy-brown. In flight, the white belly and wings and barred tail are conspicuous. Usually seen perched high in a tree or soaring over the plains. Frequently hovers, the only eagle to do this regularly. Can be confused with a Martial Eagle but that eagle has a black-spotted belly and feathered legs and is much larger.

BEST VIEWING: Kenya: Masai Mara NR; **Tanzania:** Serengeti NP;
Uganda: Queen Elizabeth, Murchison Falls NPs

BROWN SNAKE EAGLE
Circaetus cinereus tai kijivu (Swa)

Habitat: savanna, woodland and cultivated country, sea level to
2 000 m **Length:** 66–71 cm **Status:** locally common resident

An all-brown eagle; like the previous species, has an owl-like head, large, yellow eyes and bare, unfeathered legs. Sexes alike; immature paler with a scaly appearance. In flight, the dark brown body and underwings contrast with the paler flight feathers and three dark bands in the tail. Usually seen perched high in a tree. In flight, its thin, narrow tail, not fanned, is distinctive. Preys mostly on snakes, but also on mongooses, lizards and small birds.

BEST VIEWING: Kenya: Tsavo East, Tsavo West NPs; **Tanzania:** Tarangire NP; **Uganda:** Queen Elizabeth, Murchison Falls NPs

BATELEUR
Terathopius ecaudatus pungu (Swa)

Habitat: open savanna, below 3 000 m **Length:** 55–70 cm
Status: locally common resident

A very distinctive, mainly black eagle with a chestnut back, red
face and legs and a short tail. Unmistakable in flight when the
black body contrasts with the long, white wings and the red legs
protrude beyond the tail. Sexes similar but, in flight, male shows
broad, black trailing edge to the wing, compared with the thin,
black trailing edge of the female's wing. Immature is all-brown,
with a short tail (although longer than the adult's), a distinctive,
large head and greenish-blue cere, which distinguishes it from
other brown eagles.

BEST VIEWING: any national park in savanna

AFRICAN HARRIER HAWK/GYMNOGENE
Polyboroides typus kipanga marungi (Swa)

Habitat: forests and woodland, and savanna with large trees,
sea level to 3 000 m **Length:** 60–66 cm **Status:** locally
common resident

A distinctive, long-legged, long-tailed, grey hawk. The head is small
and has bare yellow skin on the face, which turns bright red when
the bird is breeding or excited. The feathers on the back of the
head are long and sometimes raised to form a broad crest. The legs
are yellow. Sexes similar but female larger than male; immature is
brown with the characteristic small head. In flight, the broad, grey
wings, with contrasting black primaries and secondaries, and the
long, black tail, with its white band, are distinctive.

BEST VIEWING: widespread in suitable habitats

DARK CHANTING GOSHAWK
Melierax metabates kipanga domonjekundu (Swa);
ekoiepo (Maa)

Habitat: open country and light woodland west of Rift Valley,
up to 3 000 m **Length:** 43–51 cm **Status:** common resident

An all-dark grey hawk with a finely barred grey-and-white rump,
red-brown eyes, red legs and a red cere. Sexes similar; immature is
brown above and streaked below, with yellow eyes, a grey cere and
greenish-yellow legs. Usually seen sitting upright on a low tree or
bush. Overlaps with Eastern Pale Chanting Goshawk near Baringo
and Kedong Valley (Kenya) and in southern Serengeti (Tanzania).

BEST VIEWING: Kenya: Masai Mara NR; **Tanzania:** Serengeti NP;
Uganda: Queen Elizabeth, Murchison Falls NPs

EASTERN PALE CHANTING GOSHAWK
Melierax poliopterus kipanga-mkuu domonjano (Swa)

Habitat: arid country, east of the Rift Valley, sea level to 2 000 m
Length: 46–54 cm **Status:** locally common resident

Paler than Dark Chanting Goshawk and larger than similar-looking
Gabar Goshawk. The upperparts, head and neck are pale grey, with
a distinctive white rump, the breast and belly are finely barred grey,
the eyes are red, the cere is yellow and the legs are orange-red. Sexes
similar; immature is pale brown with a white rump, whitish eyes,
a grey cere and pale yellow legs. Similar habits to Dark Chanting
Goshawk but occurs east of the Rift Valley.

BEST VIEWING: Kenya: Samburu District; **Tanzania:** eastern Serengeti NP,
Mkomazi GR; **Uganda:** Kidepo Valley, Murchison Falls NPs

GABAR GOSHAWK
Micronisus gabar   kipanga-gabari (Swa)

Habitat: woodland and thornbush country, sea level to 2 000 m
Length: 28–36 cm **Status:** widespread, common resident

Occurs in two distinct colour phases: a grey form, the more common, and a melanistic form. Grey form has a grey head, back, throat and breast, a white rump, finely barred underparts and a dark-barred tail. The eyes, cere and legs are red. Female larger and more heavily barred than male. Melanistic form is all-black (lacks white rump), with a dark-barred tail, the cere, eyes and legs are distinctively dark red. Immature is boldly blotched brown, with a white rump and yellow eyes, and the cere and legs are pale orange.

BEST VIEWING: widespread in suitable habitats

AFRICAN GOSHAWK
Accipiter tachiro   kipanga misitu (Swa)

Habitat: forests, particularly highland forests, woodlands and gardens, sea level to 3 000 m **Length:** 36–47 cm
Status: common resident

The most common goshawk. Upperparts are dark grey, with a barred uppertail. The underparts are barred brown-rufous and the cere, eyes and legs are yellow. The female is larger and browner than the male. Melanistic birds do occur, which have grey bands on the tail and pale, contrasting flight feathers in the underwing. Immature is dark brown above and pale below, with heavy, dark blotches. Often seen and heard flying over the forests, with a characteristic fast wing beat, followed by a short glide, uttering a '*krik krik*' call.

BEST VIEWING: widespread in suitable habitats

AUGUR BUZZARD
Buteo augur   shakivale mweupe (Swa)

Habitat: common in the highlands, but also low country with isolated hills, 400–4 600 m **Length:** 55–60 cm **Status:** appears to be declining

The head, sides of neck and back are black, with contrasting white underparts and a distinctive, rufous-coloured tail. The eyes are dark and the cere and gape are yellow. Melanistic birds, all-black apart from grey-black wing feathers and a rufous tail, are not uncommon. Sexes similar; immature brownish, with white-streaked underparts and a pale rufous tail.

BEST VIEWING: widespread in suitable- habitats

TAWNY EAGLE
Aquila rapax   tai-kahawia (Swa)

Habitat: open country **Length:** 65–73 cm **Status:** fairly common resident

A mostly uniformly brown eagle, although plumage can vary considerably, from dark brown to almost white. Distinguished from similar Steppe Eagle only at close range. This species' bill is smaller and the yellow gape extends only as far as the centre of the pale brown eye, not beyond it. Sexes similar; immature paler and shows pale bars on the wing. Distinguished from Brown Snake Eagle by its smaller head, darker eyes and feathered legs. Occurs singly or in pairs, usually perched in a tree or soaring over open country.

BEST VIEWING: widespread in wildlife areas

STEPPE EAGLE
Aquila nipalensis   tai-nepali (Swa)

Habitat: open country, grasslands and farmland **Length:** 70–84 cm
Status: a passage migrant and visitor

A large, stout-looking eagle, usually uniformly dark brown, but some individuals have a pale patch on the crown or nape. The bill is large, the nostrils oval and the yellow gape extends to behind the centre of the dark eye. The legs are heavy and feathered. Immature paler with two pale bars on the wing. In flight, the wings show a distinctive, white, trailing edge. Habitually perches on the ground or on low rocks. Occurs in small groups and occasionally in flocks, particularly in March and April.

BEST VIEWING: widespread in wildlife areas

AFRICAN HAWK EAGLE
Aquila spilogaster   tai-kipanga (Swa); ol-kupelua (Maa)

Habitat: savanna, open woodland and thornbush, sea level to 1 500 m **Length:** 60–65 cm **Status:** common, widespread resident

A small eagle, black above, white below, with black streaks on the throat and breast. The cere, eyes and feet are yellow. In flight, the dark forewing and black band at the end of the tail contrast with the white underparts. Sexes similar, but female larger and more heavily streaked below. Immature is brown above, with buffy underparts. Often confused with Augur Buzzard but its larger size, streaked front and feathered legs distinguish it. Augur Buzzard has a distinctive, rufous tail.

BEST VIEWING: widespread in suitable habitats, mostly in wildlife areas

LONG-CRESTED EAGLE
Lophaetus occipitalis   tai ushungi, tai-kisungi (Swa)

Habitat: well-wooded country in higher-rainfall areas, up to 2 000 m
Length: 52–58 cm **Status:** common resident

This small eagle with a distinctive, long, loose crest is unmistakable. The body is dark brownish-black, which contrasts with the distinctive, white-feathered legs. The eyes are yellow. Sexes similar but the female is larger and the head crest is shorter; immature similar to adults but has a shorter crest and greyish eyes. In flight, the white patches on the wing, the white legs and the black-and-white-barred tail readily distinguish this eagle. Commonly seen perched on telephone and power poles along highways.

BEST VIEWING: Kenya: Masai Mara NR; **Tanzania:** Serengeti NP;
Uganda: Queen Elizabeth NP

MARTIAL EAGLE
Polemaetus bellicosus   tai-tumbojeupe (Swa)

Habitat: *Acacia* savanna and thornbush, sea level to 3 500 m
Length: 78–83 cm **Status:** a widespread local resident

Africa's largest eagle, a powerful bird of prey. The back, throat and upper breast are dark grey-brown. The underparts are white, with small, dark spots. The eyes are yellow; there is a small crest on the nape. Female is larger and more heavily spotted. Immature has pale brown upperparts, face and throat and white underparts. Differs from Black-chested Snake Eagle in its larger size, spotted underparts, feathered legs and dark, not pale, underwings (seen in flight).

BEST VIEWING: Kenya: Masai Mara NR; **Tanzania:** Serengeti NP;
Uganda: Queen Elizabeth NP

KORI BUSTARD
Ardeotis kori   tandawala mkubwa (Swa)

Habitat: grasslands and open semi-desert country, 700–2 000 m
Length: 76–101 cm **Status:** locally common resident

Africa's largest bustard with a distinctive, dark head crest and a finely barred grey neck. Upperparts brown; underparts whitish. Has a distinctive, checked, black-and-white pattern near the bend of the wing. Female is similar but smaller than male; immature resembles adults but has duller plumage. Male performs a distinctive courtship display with crest raised, throat puffed out, wings drooped and tail cocked to meet head, revealing white undertail coverts.
BEST VIEWING: Kenya: Masai Mara NR; **Tanzania:** Serengeti NP; **Uganda:** Kidepo Valley NP

WHITE-BELLIED BUSTARD
Eupodotis senegalensis   tandawala tumbojeupe (Swa)

Habitat: grassland and savanna, below 2 000 m **Length:** 61 cm
Status: common resident

Often the most common bustard seen on safari. The male is distinctive, with a blue-grey neck, whitish belly, white face with distinct black markings, a bright red bill and a blackish-brown crown. The upperparts are brown with fine, dark brown vermiculations. The female and immature are duller, with a brown crown and hindneck and a brownish-grey foreneck. Occurs in pairs or in small family groups. The call is a strange, rhythmical croaking, uttered repeatedly at dawn and dusk.
BEST VIEWING: Kenya: Masai Mara NR; **Tanzania:** Serengeti NP; **Uganda:** Kidepo Valley NP

BUFF-CRESTED BUSTARD
Lophotis gindiana   tandawala kishungichekundu (Swa)

Habitat: dry thornbush country, below 1 800 m **Length:** 53 cm
Status: common resident

A small, stocky, short-legged bustard with a black belly and a thin, black, white-edged line from the throat, merging with the belly. Upperparts sandy-coloured, wings edged with white and the top of the head grey, with a pinkish-buffy face and crest. Crest seen only when raised. Female paler, with the top of the head grey, speckled with white, a white throat, a white-speckled foreneck and a black belly. Immature is similar to female but lacks white speckles down the neck. Occurs singly in dry thornbush country. Often confused with Black-bellied Bustard.
BEST VIEWING: Kenya: Samburu area; **Tanzania:** Tarangire NP

BLACK-BELLIED BUSTARD
Lissotis melanogaster   tandawla tumbojeusi (Swa)

Habitat: grasslands, up to 2 500 m **Length:** 61 cm
Status: common resident

A long-necked, long-legged, slender bustard. The upperparts are brown, with blackish vermiculations; the rump is brown, tail also brown, with indistinct bars. There is a distinctive, thin, black line behind each eye and a black line extending from the grey throat down the neck, to merge with the black belly. Female is paler, with a white belly, and does not have the black line down the neck. Hartlaub's Bustard (*L. hartlaubii*) is very similar but differs in being stockier, greyer, with a black rump and tail.
BEST VIEWING: Kenya: Masai Mara NR; **Tanzania:** Serengeti NP; **Uganda:** Kidepo Valley NP

BLACK CRAKE
Amaurornis flavirostra   **kiluwiri mweusi (Swa)**

Habitat: fresh-water lakes and swamps with fringing vegetation, sea level to 3 000 m **Length:** 20 cm **Status:** common resident

A small, all-black bird with a distinctive, bright chrome-yellow bill, deep red eyes and bright red legs, especially noticeable when breeding. Sexes alike; immature is greyish-brown, with a green-brown bill and brown legs. Usually seen in pairs or in small, loose groups, feeding along the water's edge or on water lilies, often on the backs of hippos. Occurs in almost any fresh-water habitat, as long as there is dense vegetation in which to take cover. Its call is a duet of repeated harsh, deep, growling churrs; it also makes small chucking sounds while walking about.

BEST VIEWING: widespread in suitable habitats

RED-KNOBBED COOT
Fulica cristata   **kiluwiri domokifundo (Swa)**

Habitat: fresh-water lakes **Length:** 41 cm **Status:** common resident

A dark grey water bird with a distinct white forehead and a white bill. The eyes are deep red and there are two red knobs above the forehead, which are often visible during breeding. The legs and feet are green. Sexes identical. Immature is ashy-brown overall and best distinguished from immature Common Moorhen (*Gallinula chloropus*) by its lack of white undertail coverts. Found in large open waters, singly or in large numbers, when not breeding. Dives for food but also feeds along the shoreline. Can be very aggressive, particularly at breeding time.

BEST VIEWING: widespread in suitable habitats

GREY CROWNED CRANE
Balearica regulorum   **mana taji (Swa); e-ng'ool (Maa)**

Habitat: swamps, lakes and grasslands, sea level to 3 000 m **Length:** 102 cm **Status:** common but threatened by habitat loss

A distinctive, well-known, long-legged bird (national bird of Uganda) with a conspicuous, large, golden-yellow crown, a bright, white patch on the cheeks, a black forehead and small red wattles. Upperparts are slate-grey, underparts paler and the wing is blackish, with a distinctive, white-tinged chestnut patch. Sexes are alike; immature is brownish, with a much smaller crown. Usually found in pairs but occasionally in large flocks outside the breeding season.

BEST VIEWING: widespread in suitable habitats

WATER THICK-KNEE
Burhinus vermiculatus   **chekeamwezi (Swa)**

Habitat: river banks, lake shores, beaches and mangrove swamps **Length:** 43 cm **Status:** common resident

A brown, plover-like bird with a large head and distinctive, large, yellow eyes. Plumage streaked grey-brown, with a conspicuous, black-edged, pale grey bar across the wing. Feeds in the early evening, at night and in the early morning, singly or in small groups. Spends the day sitting in any available waterside shade. When disturbed, is often reluctant to fly, usually running away with its head held low before finally, taking to flight. The Spotted Thick-knee (*B. capensis*) is larger, with mottled upperparts; its habits are similar to this species, but it occurs in dry rocky scrub country.

BEST VIEWING: widespread in suitable habitats

BLACK-WINGED STILT
Himantopus himantopus **msese milonjo, msese bawanyeusi (Swa)**

Habitat: fresh-water and soda lakes **Length:** 38 cm
Status: common resident

A distinctive, black-and-white wading bird with long, red legs, a very long, slender bill and bright red eyes. Sexes similar but the female has a blackish-brown back and wings and, outside the breeding season, the head and nape are washed grey. Immature has brown wings and back. Found in pairs or in small groups, mostly inland, on both soda and fresh-water lakes and pools. Feeds by wading through deep water, sweeping its bill over the surface to obtain food, typically insects and molluscs.
BEST VIEWING: widespread in suitable habitats

BLACKSMITH PLOVER (LAPWING)
Vanellus armatus **kiluwiluwi fundichuma, ndoero-mweusi (Swa)**

Habitat: exposed land alongside rivers and swamps **Length:** 30 cm
Status: common resident

A large, conspicuous, mainly black-and-white plover with deep-red eyes (difficult to see), a black bill and black legs. Sexes similar; immature resembles adults but is browner and has a buff-coloured forehead. Occurs singly or in pairs. May occur in large flocks outside the breeding season. Gives a very distinctive, metallic '*tink tink*' call when alarmed. Breeding birds are very aggressive towards intruders, dive-bombing anyone that threatens the nest. Long-toed Plover (*V. crassirostris*) has a white crown, neck and throat and occurs in aquatic habitats.
BEST VIEWING: widespread in suitable habitats

SPUR-WINGED PLOVER (LAPWING)
Vanellus spinosus **ndoero kizibaocheusi (Swa); ol-kok (Maa)**

Habitat: short grass alongside rivers, marshes, and soda and fresh-water lakes **Length:** 27 cm **Status:** common resident

A mainly black, brown and white plover. Differs from Blacksmith Plover in its slightly crested black crown and black throat, which contrasts with its white cheeks and neck. The back and wings are pale brown, the bill is black, as are the legs and feet, and it has dull red eyes. Sexes alike; immature resembles adults but duller looking. Hybrids of this species and the Blacksmith Plover occur from time to time, causing identification problems. Usually occurs in pairs.
BEST VIEWING: widespread in suitable habitat; appears to be increasing its range

CROWNED PLOVER (LAPWING)
Vanellus coronatus **ndoero kibandiko (Swa); ol-kerrai le papa (Maa)**

Habitat: short, grassy plains and semi-desert country, sea level to 3 000 m **Length:** 28 cm **Status:** common resident

A common, largely uniform, plover with a distinctive black cap ringed with white, and a black forehead, extending to behind the eyes. The throat and chest are brown, edged on the lower breast with a thin, black line; the belly is white. The black-tipped, red bill, bright red legs and bright yellow eyes are also distinctive. Sexes similar; immature resembles adults, but is duller. Occurs in pairs; can often be seen picking insects out of animal dung. A gregarious bird, often in flocks of 20 to 30 birds when not breeding. When breeding, can be very aggressive and noisy.
BEST VIEWING: widespread in suitable habitats

AFRICAN WATTLED PLOVER (LAPWING)
Vanellus senegallus   ndoero kiluwingozi (Swa)

Habitat: damp areas near lakes, streams, marshes and pools, 250–2 200 m **Length:** 33 cm **Status:** common resident

A large, grey-brown plover with distinctive yellow wattles hanging from in front of eyes and small, red wattles above the yellow ones. Forehead is white, the centre of the chin black and the face and neck are streaked black. The bill is yellow, with a black tip, and the legs and feet are yellow. Sexes are alike; immature is similar to adults, but duller. Occurs in pairs. White-crowned Plover (*V. albiceps*) also has yellow wattles, but a grey head with a white stripe on the crown.

BEST VIEWING: Kenya: Masai Mara NR; **Tanzania:** Serengeti NP; **Uganda:** Murchison Falls NP

THREE-BANDED PLOVER
Charadrius tricollaris   ndoero mikufumitatu (Swa)

Habitat: along muddy edges of streams, rivers, lakes and swamps, sea level to 3 000 m **Length:** 18 cm **Status:** common resident

A small plover with two distinctive black bands, separated by a white band, across the chest. The forehead is white, the throat grey and a white line extends from the forehead to behind the nape. The large, red ring around each eye and the black-tipped, red bill are conspicuous. Sexes alike; immature is mainly brownish, with brown, often incomplete, chest bands. Occurs most often in pairs, along muddy edges of small streams, rivers, lakes and swamps. Often seen running with jerky movements and has a distinctive habit of bobbing its head and tail.

BEST VIEWING: widespread in suitable habitats

AFRICAN JACANA
Actophilornis africanus   sile-maua, kibilinzi (Swa)

Habitat: fresh-water lakes and ponds with floating vegetation, sea level to 3 000 m **Length:** 23–28 cm **Status:** common resident

A well-known, chestnut-coloured bird with long legs and long toes. The head is distinctive, with a black crown and hindneck, a white face and a white foreneck with a golden-yellow band at the base. The bill and frontal shield are blue. Sexes similar, but the female is larger than the male. Immature is browner than adults and the bill and frontal shield are grey. Occurs in pairs or small family parties, on almost any fresh water with floating vegetation. Females are polyandrous (mate with several males) and only the males incubate the eggs and rear the young.

BEST VIEWING: widespread in suitable habitats

WHIMBREL
Numenius phaeopus   kitwitwi-kuoga (Swa)

Habitat: coastal creeks and lagoons, also small numbers on Rift Valley soda lakes **Length:** 41 cm **Status:** a passage migrant and visitor

A large, brown, long-legged wading bird with a distinctive, long, curved bill. At close range, two dark and one pale stripe can be seen on the head. In flight, it gives a distinctive trill and the white rump and back are conspicuous. Sexes alike but the female is slightly larger. A visitor to East Africa from Eurasia, it occurs singly or in small groups, along the coast, especially in creeks and lagoons. Small groups also occur regularly inland, mainly at or on the Rift Valley soda lakes.

BEST VIEWING: Kenya: Mida Creek

COMMON GREENSHANK
Tringa nebularia   **kitwitwi-mguukijani (Swa)**

Habitat: coastal and inland waters **Length:** 32 cm
Status: a common passage migrant and visitor

A common, pale grey, long-legged wader with a long, pointed,
slightly upturned bill. The underparts are white and the legs are
grey-green. In flight, the white rump and back are conspicuous.
Utters a very distinctive *'chew chew'* call and, when feeding, has
a habit of dashing about in shallow water. Sexes alike; immature
resembles adults. A common visitor from Eurasia, it occurs mostly
singly or in loose parties. Easily confused with the smaller (25 cm)
Marsh Sandpiper (*T. stagnatilis*), which is slimmer, has a fine,
straight bill and proportionally longer legs.

BEST VIEWING: widespread in suitable habitats

WOOD SANDPIPER
Tringa glareola   **kitwiwi-miti (Swa)**

Habitat: inland waters **Length:** 20 cm **Status:** common
Eurasian migrant

The most common wader in the region, with a characteristic
spotted appearance and a distinctive, pale eyebrow. The upperparts
are dark brown and the underparts paler, although not as white as
a Common Sandpiper, with green legs. In flight, it shows a white
rump and a barred tail, and the legs protrude well beyond the tail.
Sexes alike. When taking flight, it gives a very distinctive *'twee twee
twee'* call and, on landing, bobs its body.

BEST VIEWING: widespread in suitable habitats

COMMON SANDPIPER
Actitis hypoleucos   **kitwitwi kipwita (Swa)**

Habitat: rivers, streams and lake shores, both fresh and soda
Length: 20 cm **Status:** common Eurasian migrant

A small wader with a short, sharp bill and short, greenish legs. The
dark grey-brown upperparts contrast with the white underparts,
and the white on the breast curves over the shoulder. Has a
characteristic horizontal stance and often bobs its head and tail.
When disturbed, flies low over the water with flickering wings, and
makes a distinctive, piercing *'twee tee tee tee'* call. Shows a distinct,
white wing bar in flight. Usually solitary. Often confused with the
Green Sandpiper (*Tringa ochropus*), which is much darker on the
back, contrasting strongly with its white underparts.

BEST VIEWING: widespread in suitable habitats

LITTLE STINT
Calidris minuta   **kitwitwi mdogo (Swa)**

Habitat: both coastal and inland waters **Length:** 13 cm
Status: a very common Eurasian migrant.

A very common, small, compact-looking wader with a short,
straight, black bill. The upperparts are brown, with a mottled
appearance (feathers have dark centres) and the underparts are
pale. During April, the underparts are often a rich brown. Sexes
alike. Always busy, feeding or running along the shoreline of
coastal and inland waters. A visitor from Eurasia, occurring singly
or in small groups but sometimes in large flocks when migrating.
The similar Temminck's Stint (*C. temminckii*) is plainer above and
has shorter, yellow-green legs.

BEST VIEWING: Rift Valley soda lakes

RUFF
Philomachus pugnax   kitwitwi mgongomabaka (Swa)

Habitat: flooded grasslands and coastal and inland waters
Length: 24–30 cm **Status:** a very common Eurasian migrant

A common, stocky wader with a short, straight, black bill and orange legs. The upperparts are mottled brown, the dark brown feathers have distinct pale edges, the underparts are paler. Sexes alike but the male is larger. Males with a white head occasionally occur. Usually occurs in loose groups. Often confused with the Common Redshank (*Tringa totanus*) but the Redshank is mainly grey, with a long, straight bill and bright red legs, and is usually solitary; the Redshank also shows a conspicuous white rump and a white hindwing in flight, which are lacking in the Ruff.

BEST VIEWING: widespread in suitable habitats

TWO-BANDED (DOUBLE-BANDED) COURSER
Rhinoptilus africanus   kitwitwi mgongomabaka (Swa)

Habitat: arid grassland and semi-desert country, below 1 800 m
Length: 20 cm **Status:** common resident

A small, brown, long-legged bird with very short toes, large eyes and a distinctive, upright stance. The underparts are paler, with two characteristic, black bands across the chest. Sexes similar; immature resembles adults, but is duller and mottled. When disturbed, it prefers to run rather than fly. In flight, the wings have a distinctive, rufous appearance and the white uppertail coverts are conspicuous. Occurs in small loose groups in arid, barren country, where it is easily overlooked.

BEST VIEWING: Kenya: Amboseli NP; **Tanzania:** Lake Manyara NP

COLLARED PRATINCOLE
Glareola pratincola   manja shingonjano (Swa)

Habitat: open areas around lakes, marshes and coastal waters
Length: 25 cm **Status:** local resident

A brown, short-legged bird with a white rump and a deeply forked tail. The bill is black, with a red base, and the throat is buffy, edged with a thin, black band. In flight, the long, pointed wings, with a chestnut patch, and the forked tail are conspicuous. Sexes alike; the immature is paler and heavily mottled above. Occurs in large flocks and often seen feeding acrobatically in the sky over water. Occasionally also feeds on the ground. The similar Black-winged Pratincole (*G. nordmanni*) is an uncommon Palaearctic visitor, which differs in having black undertail coverts.

BEST VIEWING: Rift Valley lakes

GREY-HEADED GULL
Chroicocephalus cirrocephalus   shakawe kichwa kijivu (Swa)

Habitat: inland waters, both fresh and alkaline **Length:** 40 cm
Status: common resident

A distinctive gull with a pale grey head, a bright red bill and red legs. The rest of the body is white, with grey-black-tipped wings; eyes pale yellow. Non-breeding birds lack the grey head and there is a grey spot behind the eyes. Sexes similar; immature has a whitish head with a sooty mark behind each eye, a black bill and black feet, and the wings are greyish-brown. Non-breeding birds and immature may be confused with the much smaller Black-headed Gull (*C. ridibundus*) but the former have paler eyes, darker underwings and more black on the wing tips.

BEST VIEWING: Rift Valley lakes

GULL-BILLED TERN
Gelochelidon nilotica   **buabua domokuu (Swa)**

Habitat: inland waters both fresh and alkaline   **Length:** 38 cm
Status: common Eurasian migrant July–April

A stocky tern with a distinctive, stout, black gull-like bill, a short, forked tail, pale grey upperparts and white underparts. The head has a black cap. Non-breeding and immature lack the cap, and have a dark smudge behind the eye. Sexes alike. A common visitor to East Africa on inland waters, it also occurs in large flocks over the Serengeti NP, where it feeds on emerging dung beetles and flying insects that have been disturbed by the migrating herds.

BEST VIEWING: widespread in suitable water habitats July–April;
Kenya: Lake Nakuru NP; **Tanzania:** Serengeti NP; **Uganda:** Queen Elizabeth NP

WHITE-WINGED BLACK TERN
Chlidonias leucopterus   **buabua bawaieupe (Swa)**

Habitat: fresh and alkaline inland waters   **Length:** 24 cm
Status: common Eurasian migrant August–May

A common migrant, usually seen in non-breeding plumage. Except for the white forehead, the head is grey-black, with a dark spot in front of the eyes. The wings and back are grey and the rest of the body, including the rump, is white. The bill is black and the legs red. Some birds may be in breeding plumage, with a black cap, body and underwing coverts, which contrast strongly with the rest of the body. Immature is browner than adult, with a broad, white collar. Best separated from similar Whiskered Tern (*C. hybridus*) in flight by its white rump and contrasting grey upperparts.

BEST VIEWING: Rift Valley lakes

CHESTNUT-BELLIED SANDGROUSE
Pterocles exustus   **firigogo tumbojekundu (Swa)**

Habitat: semi-desert and arid plains below 1 700 m   **Length:** 30 cm
Status: common resident

A yellowish-brown sandgrouse with distinctive, pointed, central tail feathers, which are easily visible in flight. Male has a thin, black line across the chest and a dark belly. Female is darker, with barred and streaked upperparts and a broad, pale, buffy breast band. Immature resembles the female. Most often seen flying to water in the mornings or late afternoons. Usually circles a water hole before landing a short distance away, then walking to the water. When disturbed, has a habit of slowly creeping away before taking flight.

BEST VIEWING: Kenya: Buffalo Springs, Samburu NRs;
Tanzania: Tarangire NP

BLACK-FACED SANDGROUSE
Pterocles decoratus   **firigogo usomweusi (Swa)**

Habitat: bush and semi-desert country, sea level to 1 600 m
Length: 28 cm   **Status:** common resident

A small sandgrouse with a distinctive black pattern on the face. Upperparts are brown with black barring, the neck and chest are brown and a narrow, black line separates the chest from a white chest band. Remaining underparts are black. Female and immature are similar, but lack male's black face pattern, and have a buff, not white, breast band. Occurs in pairs or small flocks. Similar Lichtenstein's Sandgrouse (*P. lichtensteinii*) male lacks the black throat and white breast band and has a more spotted appearance.

BEST VIEWING: Kenya: Buffalo Springs, Samburu NRs;
Tanzania: Tarangire NP

SPECKLED PIGEON
Columba guinea njiwa madoa (Swa); en-turkulu (Maa)

Habitat: towns and villages, and rocky habitats, 500–3 000 m
Length: 41 cm **Status:** common resident

A large, blue-grey and maroon-brown pigeon with white-spots on the wings. A large, red patch of bare skin around the eyes and the dark red legs are distinct. Sexes similar; immature resembles adults, but is grey where adult is maroon-brown and has bare, greyish skin around the eyes. Commonly found in towns and villages and in open and rocky country. The similar-sized African Olive Pigeon (*C. arquatrix*) is darker, has a yellow bill and yellow legs, and is found in highland forests.

BEST VIEWING: widespread in suitable habitats

AFRICAN MOURNING DOVE
Streptopelia decipiens kuyu jichonjano (Swa)

Habitat: arid bush and *Acacia* woodland, up to 1 500 m **Length:** 28 cm
Status: common resident

A pale grey dove with a black collar on the hindneck. The underparts have a pinkish wash, which distinguishes this dove from the Ring-necked Dove, as does the bare, red skin around the yellow, not dark, eyes. The black collar is edged with white and the tips of the tail show white in flight. Sexes alike; immature browner than adults. Utters a very distinctive '*garoow*' call. Found in *Acacia* woodland, often near water.

BEST VIEWING: widespread in suitable habitats

RED-EYED DOVE
Streptopelia semitorquata tete jichojekundu (Swa)

Habitat: woodlands, forest edges and gardens, up to 3 000 m
Length: 30 cm **Status:** widespread common resident

The largest of the grey doves, this dove has a conspicuous pale grey forehead, a pinkish neck and underparts. The eyes are red, surrounded by a dull maroon eye-ring and there is no white in the tail. Sexes alike; immature similar but duller in appearance. Occurs at higher altitudes than and in different habitats from the similar African Mourning Dove, and also the very similar Vinaceous Dove (*S. vinacea*), which occurs in Western Uganda and differs in having a pink forehead. A common garden bird in Nairobi. Most often solitary or in pairs.

BEST VIEWING: widespread in suitable habitats

RING-NECKED DOVE
Streptopelia capicola tetere mdogo (Swa)

Habitat: dry thornbush and savanna, up to 2 000 m, occasionally higher **Length:** 25 cm **Status:** widespread common resident

An all-grey dove with prominent dark eyes and a black collar on the hindneck. The underparts are grey, graduating to almost white on the belly. In flight, white tips and white sides of the tail are conspicuous. Sexes similar; immature is grey-tinged buff. Smaller than both the African Mourning Dove and the Red-eyed Dove. Widespread and common in dry thornbush savannas. Its call, often translated as '*tell father tell father*' is one of the best-known sounds of Africa.

BEST VIEWING: widespread in suitable habitats

LAUGHING DOVE
Streptopelia senegalensis **fumvu-songoro-kanturi (Swa)**

Habitat: thornbush and *Acacia* woodland, up to 2 000 m, occasionally higher **Length:** 24 cm **Status:** widespread common resident

A small pinkish-grey dove with no black hindneck collar. The wings are bluish and brown, and there are distinctive black specks on the breast. The eyes are black, encircled by a thin, pink eye-ring. In flight, the white tips on the tail are very conspicuous. Sexes similar; immature much duller and lacks the black breast marks. Occurs singly or in pairs, in thornbush and *Acacia* woodland, and often around towns and villages. Utters a distinctive '*co co co*' call.

BEST VIEWING: widespread in suitable habitats

EMERALD-SPOTTED WOOD DOVE
Turtur chalcospilos **pugi kituku (Swa)**

Habitat: savanna woodland, thickets and coastal shrub, up to 2 100 m **Length:** 20 cm **Status:** common resident

A small, inconspicuous, ground-living dove with a grey head and neck, a paler belly and a red bill with a black base. The upperparts are brown and there are two metallic green spots on the wing. When flushed, typically flies a short distance before settling. In flight, rufous wing patches and two bands across the rump are conspicuous. Sexes alike; immature browner. The call is a distinctive, descending, slow, low, '*du du du du du du*', which speeds up towards the end. Occurs singly or in pairs in savanna woodlands, thickets and coastal scrub.

BEST VIEWING: widespread in suitable habitats

NAMAQUA DOVE
Oena capensis **pugi kombamwiko (Swa)**

Habitat: arid and semi-desert country, up to 2 000 m **Length:** 25 cm **Status:** common resident

Africa's smallest dove with a long, graduated tail. Male is brownish-grey above and white below, and has a distinct black face, throat and chest. The bill is orange-yellow, with a red base. The female lacks the black on the face, throat and chest and has a dark grey bill. Immature resembles the female but is browner and more spotted. In flight, the rufous colour of the wings and the long tail make this dove unmistakable. Usually solitary or in pairs, although numbers often gather at water holes.

BEST VIEWING: widespread in suitable habitats

YELLOW-COLLARED LOVEBIRD
Agapornis personatus **kwaru shingonjano (Swa)**

Habitat: grassland and open woodland, 1 100–1 800 m **Length:** 15 cm **Status:** locally common

A mainly bright green bird with a dark brown head, a red bill and a noticeable white eye-ring. A yellow chest band continues around the neck to form a distinctive collar. Sexes alike; immature resembles adults but is duller coloured. A very noisy bird, usually occurring in flocks in grassland and open woodland, especially near Baobab trees. Occurs naturally in Tanzania but introduced into Kenya as a caged bird. Escapees now well established and, unfortunately, it hybridises with Fischer's Lovebird.

BEST VIEWING: Kenya: Lake Naivasha; **Kenya and Tanzania:** coastal strip

FISCHER'S LOVEBIRD
Agapornis fischeri kwaru manjano (Swa)

Habitat: wooded grassland, 1 100–2 000 m **Length:** 14 cm
Status: common

A mainly bright green bird with a red forehead, a red bill and a distinct white eye-ring. The cheeks and throat are orange, merging to brownish-yellow on the crown. The uppertail coverts are blue. Sexes alike; immature resembles adults but is duller. Occurs in noisy flocks in dry *Acacia* country. Introduced into Kenya as a cage bird. Escapees now well established in Nairobi, Mombasa and Naivasha, where it hybridises with Yellow-collared Lovebird. Occurs naturally in northwestern Tanzania.

BEST VIEWING: Tanzania: Serengeti NP; **Kenya and Tanzania:** coastal strip

BROWN (MEYER'S) PARROT
Poicephalus meyeri kasuku meya (Swa)

Habitat: savanna woodland and scrub, up to 2 200 m **Length:** 25 cm
Status: common resident

A mainly brown parrot with a conspicuous yellow crown and yellow shoulders. The back and rump are blue-green, the underparts green and the eyes are dull red. Sexes alike; immature is similar to adults but lacks any yellow colouring. Occurs in pairs or small family parties, in savanna woodland and scrub. The Brown-headed Parrot (*P. cryptoxanthus*) has a brown head and green wings, with bright yellow underwing and is confined to the coastal strip.

BEST VIEWING: widespread in suitable habitats

AFRICAN ORANGE-BELLIED PARROT
Poicephalus rufiventris kasuku tumbonjano (Swa)

Habitat: dry thornbush country, below 1 200 m **Length:** 25 cm
Status: locally common resident

The orange breast and belly of the male are distinctive. The upperparts are ashy-brown, with a green-blue rump and green undertail coverts. The female is less distinctive, lacking the orange of the male, with a green breast and belly. The eyes are orange-red. Immature resembles the female. This is the characteristic parrot of dry, thornbush country and is particularly partial to Baobab trees. It occurs in pairs or small family parties but, apparently, never flocks.

BEST VIEWING: widespread in suitable habitats

GREAT BLUE TURACO
Corythaeola cristata shorobo-mkuu (Swa)

Habitat: forests and well-treed farmland, 700–2 500 m
Length: 71–76 cm **Status:** local resident

Unmistakable, the largest turaco in East Africa. The blue head, with its distinctive blackish-blue crest and the red-tipped, bright yellow bill are conspicuous. Upperparts are blue, the breast green, merging into yellow, and the belly is chestnut. There is a black band at the end of a very long, greenish-yellow tail. Sexes are alike; immature resembles adult but is duller coloured. Gregarious, occurring in forests, where its distinctive, rapid '*gonk gonk gonk*' call, habit of flopping from tree to tree and large size make it very conspicuous.

BEST VIEWING: Kenya: Kakamega Forest; **Uganda:** Entebbe Botanical Garden; **Rwanda:** Nyungwe NP

Amedeo Buonajuti

HARTLAUB'S TURACO
Tauraco hartlaubi shorobo buluu (Swa); en-giwua (Maa)

Habitat: highland forest, 1 600–3 000 m **Length:** 41 cm
Status: locally common resident

A mostly green turaco with a noticeable, rounded, blue-black crest and a distinctive, white patch above and in front of the eyes. There is a white line below the eyes, which are encircled by a coral-red ring and the bill is red. Wings and tail are dark violet-blue, wings have crimson-red wing tips. In flight, the crimson-red colouring on the wings is eye-catching. Sexes alike; immature resembles adults but is much duller coloured. Common in highland forests, where it draws attention to itself by its loud, distinct, croaking '*karh karh*' call.

BEST VIEWING: Kenya: Aberdare, Mount Kenya NPs;
Tanzania: Kilimanjaro, Ngorongoro Crater rim; **Uganda:** Mount Elgon NP

ROSS'S TURACO
Musophaga rossae shorobo-uzuri (Swa)

Habitat: riverine forest and woodland, 700–2 300 m **Length:** 21 cm
Status: widespread locally common resident

A striking-looking turaco with a large, bright yellow bill, yellow around the eyes and a bright red crest. The body is dark purple-blue. Immature similar but duller, with a blackish bill. In flight, the crimson-red colouring on the wings is eye-catching. Usually shy, occurs singly or in pairs, in riverine forests and woodland.

BEST VIEWING: widespread in suitable habitat; **Kenya:** Kakamega Forest, Masai Mara NR; **Uganda:** Murchison Falls NP

WHITE-BELLIED GO-AWAY-BIRD
Corythaixoides leucogaster shorobo tumbojeupe (Swa)

Habitat: arid woodland and dry thornbush, up to 2 200 m
Length: 51 cm **Status:** locally common resident

A distinctive, slim-looking, mainly grey turaco with a white belly, a pronounced crest and a long tail. The wings are grey, with black bars and black tips, and the bill is brownish, turning green when breeding. Sexes alike; immature similar to adults but browner. Occurs in pairs or small flocks. Typically announces itself by its well-known, drawn-out '*wah wah wah*' call. Bare-faced Go-away-bird (*C. personatus*) has a distinctive black face, which contrasts strongly with its white neck and breast; it occurs in wetter areas.

BEST VIEWING: widespread in suitable habitat; **Kenya:** Buffalo Springs, Samburu NRs; **Tanzania:** Tarangire NP; **Uganda:** Kidepo Valley NP

EASTERN GREY PLANTAIN-EATER
Crinifer zonurus shorobo tumbomichirizi (Swa)

Habitat: savanna woodland, riverine forests, up to 1 800 m
Length: 51 cm **Status:** locally common resident

A mainly greyish-brown turaco with white-tipped feathers on the nape and hindneck forming a shaggy crest. The bill is yellow-green. In flight, a white bar is very noticeable on the wings, as is the black, grey and white pattern in the tail. Sexes alike; immature resembles adult but lacks the crest. A very noisy bird with a strange, chuckling call. Occurs in pairs or small parties in savanna woodland, cultivated areas and riverine vegetation. Extremely common around Lake Victoria. Should not be confused with the Bare-faced Go-away-bird (*C. personatus*), which has a distinctive black face and a white neck.

BEST VIEWING: widespread in suitable habitats

RED-CHESTED CUCKOO
Cuculus solitarius   **kekeo kifuachekundu (Swa)**

Habitat: woodlands, forests and gardens, up to 3 000 m **Length:** 31 cm
Status: common resident

A common cuckoo, but heard more than it is seen. The upperparts are dark blue-grey, the underparts are buffy-white, finely barred black, and with a rufous throat and upper breast. Sexes similar; immature darker than adults, with a blackish throat and a barred white belly. A treetop bird, occurring in a variety of habitats, from woodland to gardens, where its well-known, persistent call, rendered as '*it-will-rain*', is a feature just before and during the rainy season. This cuckoo mostly parasitises the Cape Robin-Chat.

BEST VIEWING: widespread in suitable habitats

DIEDERIK CUCKOO
Chrysococcyx caprius   **kekeo-mdiria (Swa)**

Habitat: thornbush and wooded grassland, up to 2 200 m
Length: 19 cm **Status:** common resident

Common and often conspicuous, with a well-known '*dee-dee-dee-deedric*' call. The upperparts are metallic green, with a coppery-coloured wash, and there are white blotches on the wing. The underparts are white, with coppery-green bars on the flanks. The white eye stripe, red eyes and black bill are distinctive. Female is more coppery on the back and wings, with coppery flank bars. Immature similar but has a red bill. Similar Klaas's Cuckoo (*C. klaas*) lacks white spots on the wings, is greener above, whiter below and has dark eyes; female Klaas's Cuckoo is finely barred below.

BEST VIEWING: widespread in suitable habitat

WHITE-BROWED COUCAL
Centropus superciliosus   **dudumizi (Swa); elube (Maa)**

Habitat: coastal scrub, rank grass and bush, sea level to 2 300 m
Length: 41 cm **Status:** common resident

A large, clumsy-looking bird with a black cap, chestnut wings and a long, black tail. A white eye stripe, pale streaks on the nape and the deep red eyes are distinctive. The underparts are buffy-white and the flanks are finely streaked. Sexes alike; immature is similar to adult but has browner underparts and a brown eye stripe. Occurs in coastal scrub, rank grass and bush, where its well-known bubbly call – likened to water being poured out of a bottle and accounting for its popular name of the 'Water Bottle Bird' – is commonly heard. A skulking bird, often seen walking on the ground.

BEST VIEWING: widespread in suitable habitats

SPOTTED EAGLE OWL
Bubo africanus   **bundi machonjano (Swa)**

Habitat: rocky ravines, koppies in dry bush country, sea level
to 2 100 m **Length:** 51 cm **Status:** locally common resident

This owl occurs in two colour phases: a greyish form and a brown form. Both forms have finely barred upperparts and show dark spotting on the breast. The large ear tufts and bright yellow eyes are diagnostic. Sexes alike; immature is browner than adults, with less spotting. Usually found in pairs in rock ravines on koppies and sometimes on buildings (e.g. safari lodges) in dry bush country. The similar Greyish Eagle Owl (*B. cinerascens*), which occurs in northern Kenya, has dark eyes.

BEST VIEWING: widespread in suitable habitat; **Kenya:** Lake Baringo Lodge; **Tanzania:** Serengeti NP (on koppies); **Uganda:** Murchison Falls NP

VERREAUX'S (GIANT) EAGLE OWL
Bubo lacteus   kokoko (Swa); toosho to Itukus (Maa)

Habitat: *Acacia* woodland and savanna country, sea level to 3 000 m
Length: 61–66 cm **Status:** common resident

Africa's largest owl, generally grey in colour, finely vermiculated brown, the face is distinctively paler and is edged with black. The eyes are dark, with conspicuous pink eyelids, and the bill is white. The ear tufts are small and not always visible. Sexes alike but the female is larger. Immature resembles adults but generally browner. Occurs singly. Prefers large trees where it typically roosts on a large branch in deep shade. The bird's call, a deep low '*hu hu-hu hoo*', is often heard – during the day and night.

BEST VIEWING: widespread in suitable habitats

PEARL-SPOTTED OWLET
Glaucidium perlatum   kitaumande madoa (Swa)

Habitat: dry, arid *Acacia* bush, mainly below 2 200 m **Length:** 20 cm
Status: locally common resident

A very small owl with a longish, white-spotted tail. The upperparts are rich brown, spotted with white, and the underparts are white, with dark rufous-brown streaks. The bill and eyes are yellow. Has distinctive dark marks surrounded with white, which look like eyes, on the back of the head. Sexes alike; immature resembles adults. Often seen during the day, at times being mobbed by other birds. Occurs in dry *Acacia* bush country. Its call is characteristic: a series of '*pwee pwee pwee*' notes, rising in volume.

BEST VIEWING: widespread in suitable habitats

MONTANE NIGHTJAR
Caprimulgus poliocephalus   mbarawiji-mlima (Swa); e-supaker (Maa)

Habitat: woodlands and along forest edges in the highlands,
1 500–3 000 m **Length:** 24 cm **Status:** locally common resident

Dusky-brown, best identified by its highland habitat and its distinctive, plaintive '*pee-ee pee-ee*' call. It has a diagnostic rufous collar on the hindneck. In flight, two white spots on the wings and the two white outer tail feathers are distinctive. The latter serves to distinguish it from most other nightjars in the region. Sexes similar, but the female has buffy, not white, wing spots. Occurs in the highlands in woodlands, wooded gardens and along forest edges.

BEST VIEWING: widespread in suitable highland habitats

AFRICAN PALM SWIFT
Cypsiurus parvus   teleka-tui (Swa)

Habitat: associated with palm trees, up to 2 000 m **Length:** 18 cm
Status: common resident

This small, slim-bodied, brown swift has slender wings and a deeply forked tail. It has a distinctive, flickering flight and the tail is more often closed, forming a sharp point. Sexes alike; immature resembles adult but has a shorter tail. A widespread resident, it is always associated with tall palm trees, where it nests – using its saliva to glue both nest material and its eggs to the inside of vertical, hanging palm leaves. The similar Scarce Swift (*Schoutedenapus myoptilus*) is larger, with a greyish-brown throat; it is a highland bird, preferring rocky crags for nesting.

BEST VIEWING: widespread where suitable palm trees exist

Albert Froneman/IOA

LITTLE SWIFT
Apus affinis　　　　　　　　　　　teleka mdogo (Swa)

Habitat: cliffs and tall buildings in cities and towns, up to 3 000 m
Length: 14 cm **Status:** common resident

A small, black swift with a white rump, white chin and square-ended tail. Sexes alike. A colonial bird occurring in noisy flocks, it breeds on cliffs and also on buildings and under bridges in cities and towns. Its flight is fluttery, interspersed with short glides. The very similar White-rumped Swift (*A. caffer*) has less white on the rump and has a distinctive, forked tail. Horus Swift (*A. horus*) also has a white rump, but is larger, more thickset and the white on its throat extends to the chest and forehead.

BEST VIEWING: widespread except in arid areas, but common in many cities and towns

SPECKLED MOUSEBIRD
Colius striatus　　　　　pasa-mchirizi (Swa); olkasero (Maa)

Habitat: woodland, cultivated areas and gardens, up to 2 600 m
Length: 33 cm **Status:** common resident

A generally brown bird with a very long tail and a distinctive head crest. The body feathers are edged with white, imparting a speckled appearance. The face is black, with white cheek patches, the bill is black above and pinkish below and the legs are red. Sexes alike; immature is similar but has a shorter head crest, a shorter tail and a pale bill. A gregarious bird, often seen dust-bathing on the ground. The White-headed Mousebird (*C. leucocephalus*) is similar, but greyer, and has a distinctive white head and barred underparts; it occurs in dry bush country.

BEST VIEWING: widespread

BLUE-NAPED MOUSEBIRD
Urocolius macrourus　　　　　pasa kisogobuluu (Swa)

Habitat: dry bush country, below 1 900 m **Length:** 36 cm
Status: common resident

A long, slim, ash-grey mousebird with a crest, a distinctive, turquoise-blue patch on the nape and a long, slender, pointed tail. The face and the base of the bill are bright red and the feet are dull red. Sexes alike; immature is paler, with a pale bill, a greenish face and less distinct nape patch. Flies fast in small parties, uttering its very distinctive '*peee-peee*' call.

BEST VIEWING: widespread in suitable habitats

LILAC-BREASTED ROLLER
Coracias caudatus　　　　　chole (Swa); ol-anga (Maa)

Habitat: thornbush, savanna and open woodland, up to 2 000 m
Length: 41 cm **Status:** common resident

A striking, common bird with a bright lilac throat and breast, deep-blue underparts and distinctive, elongated outer tail feathers. The back is olive-chestnut and the wings have dark blue coverts. Perches on open branches, large termite mounds and even on power and telephone wires, from where it swoops down onto its insect prey, clearly displaying its brilliant blue wings. Sexes alike; immature duller and lacks the long outer tail feathers. Often seen along roadsides. The lilac on birds occurring in the northeast of Kenya is confined to the throat and they have a greenish-blue breast.

BEST VIEWING: widespread in suitable habitats

EURASIAN ROLLER
Coracias garrulus   chole-ulaya (Swa)

Habitat: savanna and open woodland, up to 1 500 m **Length:** 31 cm
Status: locally common Palaearctic passage migrant

The adult bird unmistakable, with its bright blue head, throat,
belly and wings, a brown back and a short tail. Sexes alike;
immature paler. A passage migrant from eastern Europe and Asia,
visiting the region in October–April, particularly conspicuous
on its return migration in March–April. The similar Abyssinian
Roller (*C. abyssinica*) is slimmer and has long, elongated outer tail
feathers; immature very similar to immature Eurasian Roller.

BEST VIEWING: Kenya: Tsavo East NP; **Tanzania:** widespread;
Uganda: Queen Elizabeth NP

GREY-HEADED KINGFISHER
Halcyon leucocephala   kurea tumbo-jekundu (Swa)

Habitat: savanna and wooded country, often near watercourses, up
to 2 200 m **Length:** 20 cm **Status:** locally common resident

An insect-eating kingfisher with a distinctive, rich chestnut belly,
cobalt-blue wings and a cobalt-blue tail. The head is grey or grey-
brown and the bill and feet are bright red. Sexes alike; immature
resembles adults but is duller looking. Immature and some adults
may be confused with the Brown-hooded Kingfisher (*H. albiventris*)
but that species lacks the chestnut belly. Grey-headed occurs singly
or in pairs, often along watercourses, where it feeds on a variety of
insects and small lizards but rarely, if ever, on fish.

BEST VIEWING: Kenya: Buffalo Springs, Samburu NRs; **Tanzania:** Selous
GR; **Uganda:** Murchison Falls NP

STRIPED KINGFISHER
Halcyon chelicuti   kichi michirizi (Swa)

Habitat: savanna and woodland **Length:** 17 cm **Status:** locally
common resident

A small insect-eating kingfisher with a dark streaky head, a black
eye stripe, a distinctive, buffy-white collar and a red-and-black
bill. The rump and tail are bright azure-blue, clearly seen only in
flight. Sexes alike; immature resembles adults but is duller coloured.
This kingfisher's loud, trilling call is a feature of its savanna and
woodland habitat. Feeds on insects, grasshoppers and lizards. The
Brown-hooded Kingfisher (*H. albiventris*) is similar and larger, and
has an all-red bill and a paler head.

BEST VIEWING: Kenya: Masai Mara NR; **Tanzania:** Serengeti NP;
Uganda: Lake Mburu NP

WOODLAND KINGFISHER
Halcyon senegalensis   kichi buluu (Swa)

Habitat: savanna and woodlands, sea level to 1 600 m **Length:** 20 cm
Status: resident and intra-African migrant

Distinctive, mainly bright blue kingfisher with a large, striking red-
and-black bill. The area around the dark eyes is black; in southern
race this extends behind the eyes. Upperparts are blue-grey,
underparts are whitish and the feet are black. The wings, back and
tail are blue, the shoulders are black. Sexes alike; immature similar
but duller coloured. Feeds on a variety of insects, frogs and, at times,
fish. Its call is a loud distinctive trill. Similar Mangrove Kingfisher
(*H. senegaloides*) is confined to coastal creeks and has an all-red bill.

BEST VIEWING: widespread in suitable habitat; **Kenya:** Masai
Mara NR (common)

MALACHITE KINGFISHER
Alcedo cristata **kichi kishungibuluu (Swa)**

Habitat: near permanent fresh water with fringing vegetation, sea level to 3 000 m **Length:** 14 cm **Status:** common resident

Tiny, brilliantly coloured, with a large, red bill, a green-blue crest that extends to the eye, and red feet. Upperparts ultramarine; underparts rufous. There is a white patch on either side of the neck and the throat is white. Sexes alike; immature duller, with a black bill. Feeds on small fish, frogs, tadpoles and small insects. Immature, with its black bill, sometimes mistaken for larger Half-collared Kingfisher (*A. semitorquata*). Similar African Pygmy Kingfisher (*Ispidina picta*) has small, dark blue crown and violet-coloured cheeks; occurs in woodland habitats.

BEST VIEWING: widespread in suitable habitats

PIED KINGFISHER

Ceryle rudis **kichi mtilili (Swa)**

Habitat: inland and coastal waters, sea level, up to 2 300 m
Length: 25 cm **Status:** common resident

Africa's best-known kingfisher. A highly social, black-and-white kingfisher with a crested head and a long, black bill. The male has two black bands across the white chest, while the female has one incomplete band. Commonly hunts for fish by hovering, before diving, beak-first into water. Will readily use perches, even telephone lines or boats, to hunt from. Occurs at most inland waters and also at the coast. Usually found singly or in pairs but at times very gregarious; can be very noisy.

BEST VIEWING: Rift Valley lakes in the region

LITTLE BEE-EATER
Merops pusillus **kinega mdogo (Swa); en-coshoroi (Maa)**

Habitat: open grasslands and along the shores of lakes and swamps, sea level to 2 200 m **Length:** 17 cm **Status:** common resident

A common bee-eater, mainly green with a bright yellow throat and a black gorget, which has a thin blue line along its upper edge. A distinctive, bright blue line above the eyes borders a broad black eye band. The upper chest is chestnut, becoming paler below. Sexes alike, the immature is duller, lacks the black gorget and has a greenish, not chestnut, chest. Usually occurs in pairs. Habitually perches on low bushes or rocks, from where it hawks for insects. The similar Blue-breasted Bee-eater (*M. variegatus*) differs in having noticeable white patches on the sides of its neck.

BEST VIEWING: widespread in suitable habitats

CINNAMON-CHESTED BEE-EATER
Merops oreobates **kinega kifuamarungi (Swa)**

Habitat: highland forests and forest edges, 1 800–2 300 m
Length: 22 cm **Status:** common local resident

A common highland resident with deep green upperparts, a yellow throat, a conspicuous white cheek spot and a black gorget. There is a distinctive black band through the eyes. Sexes alike; immature is greenish and lacks the black gorget. Occurs in pairs or small groups, especially when breeding, along forest edges and clearings. Often common in Nairobi suburban gardens. May be confused with Little Bee-eater, but that species is much smaller, has a distinctive blue line above the eye and occurs in different habitats.

BEST VIEWING: Kenya: Aberdare NP; **Tanzania:** Ngorongoro Crater rim; **Uganda:** Bwindi Impenetrable NP

WHITE-FRONTED BEE-EATER
Merops bullockoides **kinega usomweupe (Swa)**

Habitat: watercourses in wooded country, up to 2 000 m
Length: 23 cm **Status:** a decreasingly common resident

A distinctive bee-eater with a bright red throat contrasting with a white forehead, and a white chin and a broad black band through eye. The underparts are cinnamon, the upperparts are mainly green and the head and neck are golden-brown. The deep blue undertail coverts are best seen in flight. Sexes alike; immature similar to adults but duller. Common in the Rift Valley, breeding in colonies in sandy banks and cliffs. Very noisy, especially around its nesting colony, where its loud, characteristic *'waark waark'* call is a common feature. Has become much less common of late.

BEST VIEWING: Kenya: Lake Nakuru NP; **Tanzania:** Arusha NP

WHITE-THROATED BEE-EATER
Merops albicollis **kinega koojeupe (Swa)**

Habitat: grassland and arid bush country, sea level to 2 000 m
Length: 28 cm **Status:** locally common inter-African migrant

A distinctive, slim bee-eater with a long, thin tail. It has a black crown, eye stripe and chest band, all of which contrast strongly with a white throat and forehead. The rest of the plumage is pale green, becoming paler on the belly. In flight or when displaying, it shows conspicuous cinnamon colouring on the wings. Sexes similar, but the female has a shorter tail. Immature is duller coloured than adults and has a short tail. Gregarious, especially in the breeding season. Often excavates nest holes in flat, bare ground.

BEST VIEWING: Kenya: Buffalo Springs, Samburu NRs; **Tanzania:** Selous GR; **Uganda:** Queen Elizabeth NP

EURASIAN BEE-EATER
Merops apiaster **kinega-ulaya (Swa)**

Habitat: open country, up to 3 000 m **Length:** 28 cm **Status:** common mainly passage Palaearctic migrant

A distinctive, mainly blue-and-green bee-eater. The head and upper back are rich chestnut in colour, the lower back is gold and the throat is bright yellow. Sexes alike; immature is duller coloured and has a green-brown back. Mainly a passage migrant to East Africa, passing through September–November and March–April, although some do winter in the area, mostly in Tanzania. Usually seen in small groups, gracefully hawking insects in the sky, when their distinctive, rufous-coloured wings can be seen, uttering their characteristic liquid call.

BEST VIEWING: widespread

NORTHERN CARMINE BEE-EATER
Merops nubicus **kinega mwekundu (Swa)**

Habitat: wooded grassland, up to 1 200 m **Length:** 38 cm
Status: locally common inter-African migrant

An unmistakable, large, bright carmine-red bee-eater with a long, pointed tail. The head and throat are dark blue-green and the rump is light blue. Sexes alike; immature is similar to adults but duller coloured and has a shorter tail. Gregarious, especially at roosts. Also often seen perched on roadside telephone wires or flowering Sisal plants. Breeds in colonies in Kenya's Lake Turkana area. Has a distinctive *'tuk tuk'* call. The similar Southern Carmine Bee-eater (*M. nubicoides*) differs in having a red throat.

BEST VIEWING: East African coast; Kenya: Lake Turkana; **Uganda:** Western Rift Valley

HOOPOE
Upupa epops hudihudi wa Africa (Swa); ol-masi (Maa)

Habitat: grasslands and open woodlands, sea level to 2 200 m
Length: 28 cm **Status:** a common resident and a Palaearctic migrant

An unmistakable, fairly common bird, generally cinnamon-rufous in colour, with contrasting black-and-white wings and tail. Feeds on the ground, probing with a long, decurved black bill. Raises its distinctive, black-tipped, fan-shaped crest when alarmed. Its undulating flight is distinctive, during which the black-and-white wings are conspicuous. Sexes similar; immature is duller coloured and has a shorter crest. European migrants differ in having a noticeable white band across the primaries and are generally paler in colour. Has a distinctive, soft, low 'hoo-poo-poo' call.
BEST VIEWING: widespread in suitable habitats

GREEN WOOD HOOPOE
Phoeniculus purpureus gegemela domojekundu (Swa)

Habitat: woodlands and forests, sea level to 2 800 m **Length:** 38–41 cm
Status: common widespread resident

A slim, blackish bird with a green-blue gloss and a long, graduated tail. It has a conspicuous, long, curved, red bill and red legs. In flight, the white wing bar and white-tipped tail feathers are noticeable. Sexes similar, but the female is smaller and has a shorter bill. Immature is duller coloured and has short, curved black bill. May be confused with the Scimitarbill (*Rhinopomastus cyanomelas*) but the latter has a slender, curved black bill. Common in woodlands, where it occurs in noisy parties, climbing about on tree trunks and in branches, searching for insects.
BEST VIEWING: widespread in suitable habitats

CROWNED HORNBILL
Tockus alboterminatus kwembe (Swa)

Habitat: woodland and forest edges, sea level to 3 000 m
Length: 48–51 cm **Status:** locally common resident

Slender, mainly blackish-brown, with a dusky-red bill and casque. The lower chest and belly and the outer tips of the tail feathers are white. A small head crest is sometimes visible. Sides of head and the nape are streaked white and there is a pale, sometimes indistinct, yellowish band at base of bill. Sexes similar, but the female is smaller and lacks a casque. Immature is duller than adults and has an orange-yellow bill. Found mostly in pairs; distinctive its piping call and buoyant flight. Hemprich's Hornbill (*T. hemprichii*) is a similar but uncommon species, confined to dry, rocky country.
BEST VIEWING: widespread in suitable habitats

RED-BILLED HORNBILL
Tockus erythrorhynchus hondohondo domojekundu (Swa)

Habitat: semi-arid savanna and thornbush country, up to 2 000 m
Length: 43–46 cm **Status:** locally common resident

The slender, all-red bill and white-spotted, black wings render this hornbill unmistakable. Female similar but smaller and has a smaller bill. Immature resembles adults but has a much shorter, brownish bill. A common hornbill, usually in seen in pairs, feeding on the ground on insects, seeds and scorpions. Ruaha Hornbill (*T. ruahae*, discovered in 2001) differs in having a black patch around the eye extending to the base of the bill and bare patches of pink skin on either side of the throat.
BEST VIEWING: Kenya: Buffalo Springs, Samburu NRs;
Tanzania: Tarangire, Ruaha NPs; **Uganda:** Kidepo Valley NP

EASTERN YELLOW-BILLED HORNBILL
Tockus flavirostris   hondohondo domonjano (Swa)

Habitat: dry thornbush country, up to 1 400 m **Length:** 46–53 cm
Status: locally common resident

Similar to the Red-billed Hornbill but larger, with a distinctive, large, yellow bill. There are two bare, pink skin patches on the throat and the eyes are yellow. Sexes similar but female is smaller and has black, not pink, bare skin throat patches. Immature is similar to adults but with shorter, pale yellow bill. Frequents dry, thornbush country. Typically feeds on the ground, where it has a special relationship with the Dwarf Mongoose, feeding on flying insects escaping from the mongoose and, in turn, warning it of any threats.
BEST VIEWING: Kenya: Samburu NR; **Tanzania:** Ruaha NP;
Uganda: Kidepo Valley NP

VON DER DECKEN'S HORNBILL
Tockus deckeni   hondohondo mweupe (Swa)

Habitat: semi-arid savanna country, up to 1 700 m **Length:** 43–51 cm
Status: widespread common resident

A distinctive, black-and-white hornbill with an ivory-tipped, red bill. Face and underparts white, contrasting with black wings and conspicuous pink throat patches. Sexes are similar, but the female is smaller with an all-black bill. Immature similar, with a shorter, blackish bill. Usually found in pairs, often feeding on the ground. The similar Jackson's Hornbill (*T. jacksoni*) differs in having white-spotted wing coverts. Hornbills nest in tree cavities; after laying eggs the female seals herself inside with mud and excrement, leaving a small hole for the male to feed her.
BEST VIEWING: widespread in suitable habitat

BLACK-AND-WHITE CASQUED HORNBILL
Bycanistes subcylindricus   hondohondo rangimbili (Swa)

Habitat: tall trees in woodland and riverine forests, 700–2 600 m
Length: 69–76 cm **Status:** locally common resident

Large, mainly black hornbill, distinguished from Silvery-cheeked Hornbill by the large white patch on the wings, and large black-and-white casque. Sexes similar, but female has a much reduced, almost absent, casque. Immature similar to adult female. Found in pairs or small groups in western areas of East Africa. Loud '*hawack hawack*' call is spectacular. Smaller (up to 66 cm) Trumpeter Hornbill (*B. bucinator*) differs from the last two species in having white lower chest and belly; occurs in riverine forests and scrub in coastal areas.
BEST VIEWING: Kenya: Masai Mara NR; **Uganda:** Bwindi Impenetrable, Kibale NPs

SILVERY-CHEEKED HORNBILL
Bycanistes brevis   hondohondo kijivu (Swa)

Habitat: highland forests, up to 2 600 m **Length:** 66–74 cm
Status: locally common resident

A very large, mainly black hornbill with the lower back, rump, belly and tips of tail feathers white. Male has a distinctive, large, horn-coloured casque, a faint pale line at the base of a brown bill, bare blue skin around eyes, red eyes and silvery-tipped facial feathers. Female is smaller and lacks the large casque. Immature has smaller bill, lacks a casque and facial feathers are edged brown. A forest hornbill, found in pairs or small parties east of the Kenya/Tanzania Rift Valley. Particularly common when fig trees are fruiting, when it often enters towns and cities, e.g. Nairobi.
BEST VIEWING: Kenya: Aberdare NP; **Tanzania:** Lake Manyara NP

SOUTHERN GROUND HORNBILL
Bucorvus leadbeateri   mumbi (Swa); ol-muntut (Maa)

Habitat: wooded grasslands, up to 3 000 m **Length:** 107 cm
Status: locally common resident

An unmistakable, black, turkey-sized hornbill with a large, black
bill, distinctive, bare red skin on face and throat and bright red eyes.
Sexes similar but the female has an additional small, blue patch of
bare skin below the bill. Immature is brown-black with a shorter bill.
Usually found in pairs or small family parties, walking through open
country, looking for snakes, lizards and large insects. The male's call,
usually at dawn or dusk, is a deep, booming '*ho ho ho*', followed by
the female's slightly higher '*hu hu hu*'.
BEST VIEWING: Kenya: Masai Mara NR; **Tanzania:** Serengeti NP;
Uganda: Lake Mburo NP

YELLOW-RUMPED TINKERBIRD
Pogoniulus bilineatus   tingitingi kiuonjano (Swa)

Habitat: forests, woodlands and gardens, sea level to 3 000 m
Length: 10 cm **Status:** locally common resident

A small, black-and-white bird with distinctive white stripes above
and below the eyes. When seen at close quarters, the yellow wash
on the belly, yellow edges to wing feathers and the bright orange-
yellow rump can be seen. Sexes similar; immature resembles adults
but is duller coloured. A common bird inhabiting forests and
gardens and usually heard but difficult to see. The call, '*tok tok tok
tok*', uttered in a long series of short bursts, is a characteristic sound
of its forest habitat. Coastal birds have a different call, which is
more rapid and almost a trill.
BEST VIEWING: widespread in suitable habitats

RED-AND-YELLOW BARBET
Trachyphonus erythrocephalus   zawakulu kichwachekundu (Swa)

Habitat: dry bush country with termite mounds, below 2 100 m
Length: 23 cm **Status:** locally common resident

A very distinctive, red-and-yellow bird with a large, red bill and a
black crown. The wings and tail are black, spotted with white and
yellow. The underparts are yellow, with an orange wash on the
chest; there is a spotted, black-and-white chest band and a black
streak down the throat. Female is similar to male but lacks black
throat streak and has a red crown tipped with black. Immature is
paler than adult. The call is a duet that sounds like '*red and yellow,
red and yellow*', is uttered repeatedly.
BEST VIEWING: Kenya: Lake Baringo; **Tanzania:** Tarangire NP;
Uganda: Kidepo Valley NP

D'ARNAUD'S BARBET
Trachyphonus darnaudii   zuwakulu usambro (Swa); ol-tilokeri (Maa)

Habitat: dry bush country and grasslands, up to 2 000 m
Length: 16–18 cm **Status:** locally common resident

A mainly yellowish-brown barbet with a yellowish head, marked
with black spots. The wings and back are brown, spotted with white
and it has a white-spotted black tail. There is a black patch in the
centre of the throat and the undertail coverts are bright red. Sexes
alike; immature is similar to adults. Has a distinctive courtship
display. A pair sit opposite each other, swinging their tails in an
almost mechanical way, and at the same time uttering their duet
call '*doo doo dee dok, do do dee dok*', over and over again.
BEST VIEWING: widespread in suitable habitats

GREATER HONEYGUIDE
Indicator indicator   kiongozi mkubwa (Swa); en-coshoroi (Maa)

Habitat: open country with a scattering of trees, sea level to 3 000 m
Length: 20 cm **Status:** common resident

A distinctive bird with a stout, bright pink bill, white cheek patches and a black throat. The upperparts are greyish-brown and the underparts are buffy. In flight, the white outer tail feathers are very conspicuous. Female duller than male, has a pale bill and lacks black throat and white cheek patches. Immature has a brown head and back and yellowish underparts. Common in various habitats, except for very arid areas. Its call, a characteristic '*weet purr, weet purr*', is given from high in a tree and attracts honey hunters, which it often leads to a beehive.

BEST VIEWING: widespread in suitable habitats

NUBIAN WOODPECKER
Campethera nubica   kigong'ota-mnubi (Swa); ol-tito (Maa)

Habitat: dry bush, *Acacia* woodland and savanna, sea level to 2 300 m
Length: 18 cm **Status:** locally common resident

The green-brown upperparts of this woodpecker are spotted and barred yellowish. The tail feathers are barred yellow and brown and have distinctive yellow shafts. The underparts are buffy-white with dark spots, which become streaks on the flanks. Male has a red crown, nape and moustachial stripe; the female's crown is black, spotted white with a small red patch on nape. The call is a loud, shrill '*week week*', often performed by a pair, which is characteristic of the species. Very similar Golden-tailed Woodpecker (*C. abingoni*) is greener and has streaks, not spots, on the underparts.

BEST VIEWING: widespread in suitable habitats

CARDINAL WOODPECKER
Dendropicos fuscescens   kigong'ota kiparachekundu (Swa)

Habitat: almost any wooded habitat, sea level to 3 000 m
Length: 14 cm **Status:** common resident

A small, green-backed woodpecker with streaked underparts and a spotted back. Male has a distinctive red cap, female has a blackish-brown cap. Both sexes have dark moustachial stripes and brown foreheads, and the tail has golden-yellow shafts. Immature is similar to adults but duller. This is the most common woodpecker, usually found singly or in pairs, foraging in trees, pecking at the bark in search of insects. The similar Brown-backed Woodpecker (*Picoides obsoletus*) has a large, brown patch, which is encircled with white, on the face and a brown tail with white spots.

BEST VIEWING: widespread in suitable habitats

AFRICAN GREY WOODPECKER
Dendropicos goertae   kigong'ota kijvu (Swa)

Habitat: forest edges and *Acacia* woodland, 700–3 000 m
Length: 18 cm **Status:** common resident

A distinctive-looking woodpecker with grey head and underparts, green wings and back and a brown tail with yellowish bars. The rump is red and the male has a red patch on rear of crown, which extends onto nape. Female lacks red on the head but has a little red patch on the lower belly. Immature resembles adults but is greener and the red colouring is more diffused. Olive Woodpecker (*D. griseocephalus*) is similar but can be distinguished by its olive, not grey, breast; it furthermore occurs in the interior of highland forests up to 3 700 m.

BEST VIEWING: widespread in suitable habitats

CHIN-SPOT BATIS
Batis molitor tatata kidoacheusi (Swa)

Habitat: forest edges, *Acacia* woodland and gardens, 500–3 000 m
Length: 10 cm **Status:** widespread common resident

A small, dumpy, short-tailed flycatcher. Male is grey above with black wings, a black tail and a black face. The underparts are white, with a broad black band across chest. Female is similar to male but has a rufous chest band and a small rufous spot on the throat. Both sexes have distinct, bright yellow eyes. Immature is similar to female but duller, streaked on upperparts and throat. Gives a distinctive, thin, flute-like song of three descending notes, which can be interpreted as *'three blind mice'*, uttered repeatedly. Usually found in pairs or small family parties.

BEST VIEWING: widespread in suitable habitats

GREY-HEADED BUSHSHRIKE
Malaconotus blanchoti mbweta nzgive (Swa); olkirapash (Maa)

Habitat: forest edge, woodland and *Acacia* country **Length:** 25 cm
Status: common

This brightly coloured bushshrike is surprisingly more often heard than seen. It is a bulky bird with a grey head, a large hooked black bill and bright yellow eyes. The upperparts are bright green with yellow spots on the wing. The underparts are bright yellow with a rufous-orange wash across the breast. Birds occurring in western Tanzania lack the orange wash. Immature is paler, with dark eyes. The call, usually uttered from high in a tree, is an unusual, loud, hollow-sounding, drawn-out *'whooooooooooo'*, also loud clicks and harsh scolds.

BEST VIEWING: *Acacia* country

ROSY-PATCHED BUSHSHRIKE
Rhodophoneus cruentus kuwekuwe mwekundu (Swa)

Habitat: arid bush country, 150–1 600 m **Length:** 23 cm
Status: locally common resident

This slim, long-tailed shrike has buffy-brown upperparts and a rosy-red rump, which is conspicuous in flight. The tail is darker, with white tips to the outer feathers. Two races of this bird occur. The male of the northern race has a rosy-red stripe on the throat and breast. The male of the southern race has a rosy-red stripe and a black band across the throat. The female is similar but has a white throat, surrounded by black gorget and a rosy patch down the centre of the belly. Immature resembles adults but is duller.

BEST VIEWING: widespread in suitable habitats; **Kenya:** Samburu, Buffalo Springs NRs

SLATE-COLOURED BOUBOU
Laniarius funebris tiva kijivucheusi (Swa); olkududu (Maa)

Habitat: mostly arid areas but in the west and south prefers moist woodlands, sea level to 2 200 m **Length:** 18 cm **Status:** common widespread resident

A dark slaty-black bird with red eyes. Sexes similar; immature is brownish with indistinct barring above. A skulking bird, which can be very difficult to see and is perhaps best known for its distinctive call, a bell-like *'bop bop'*, uttered by the male, closely answered by a higher *'boop'* by the female. Mountain Black Boubou (*L. poensis*) is almost identical but has a distinctive call (a loud, high-pitched whistle, sometimes a duet) and occurs in the highland forests of Burundi, Rwanda and Uganda.

BEST VIEWING: widespread in suitable habitats

TROPICAL BOUBOU
Laniarius aethiopicus   **tiva rangimbili (Swa)**

Habitat: forests, dense thickets, gardens and coastal scrub, up
to 1 800 m **Length:** 23 cm **Status:** common resident

A stout-looking, black-and-white bird with a white wing bar, a
pinkish wash on the belly and a strong, hook-tipped bill. Sexes
similar; immature is brownish. Common and widespread, it is
found singly or in pairs but, because of its skulking nature, it can be
difficult to see. Its well-known, bell-like call, *'bou bou bouu'*, closely
followed by a harsh *'kweee'*, is a duet between the male and female.
The similar looking Common Fiscal is more conspicuous, slimmer
and has a long tail. The Black-backed Puffback (*Dryoscopus cubla*) is
also similar but is a treetop bird, with a greyish-white rump.
BEST VIEWING: widespread in suitable habitats

NORTHERN WHITE-CROWNED SHRIKE
Eurocephalus rueppelli   **mlali kichwacheupe (Swa)**

Habitat: *Acacia* bush country, sea level to 2 300 m **Length:** 23 cm
Status: locally common resident

A stocky, short-tailed shrike with a distinctive white crown and
forehead. The back and tail are dark brown, the underparts white,
becoming buffy on lower flanks and belly. There is a thin black
line through the eye and a black patch behind the eye. Sexes
similar; immature is duller than adults and has a brown crown.
Has a characteristic fluttering and gliding flight, with the wings
held slightly upwards; at this time its white rump is conspicuous.
Occurs in pairs or small family parties in *Acacia* bush country.
BEST VIEWING: widespread in suitable habitats

GREY-BACKED FISCAL
Lanius excubitoroides   **mbwigu kijivu (Swa)**

Habitat: *Acacia* woodland often near water, 600–3 000 m
Length: 25 cm **Status:** locally common resident

A long-tailed shrike with a broad, black band across the forehead
and eyes. The crown is grey, which extends down the back. There
is a small, white patch on the black wings and two white
patches on the upper outer tail feathers. The underparts are white.
The female is similar to the male but has a small chestnut-coloured
patch on its flanks. Immature is grey-brown with dusky barring.
Mackinnon's Shrike (*L. mackinnoni*) is similar but has a distinct
white V across its back and no white patches on the wings or tail.
BEST VIEWING: widespread in suitable habitat; **Kenya:** Lake
Naivasha (common)

LONG-TAILED FISCAL
Lanius cabanisi   **mbwigu mkiamrefu (Swa)**

Habitat: open woodland, grasslands with scattered bushes and
coastal bush, sea level to 1 600 m **Length:** 30 cm **Status:** locally
common resident

The upperparts of this large shrike are black, with a grey rump
and lower back, and completely black tail. A small, white bar is
visible in the closed wing. The underparts are white. Sexes similar;
immature is brown with fine, darker barring. A conspicuous bird
occurring in small parties, which often perch in the same bush,
swinging their tails up, down and around. The even larger Magpie
Shrike (*Urolestes melanoleucus*) is all-black with a distinct white V
across its back, white wing patches and a grey rump.
BEST VIEWING: widespread in suitable habitats; **Kenya:** Nairobi NP

TAITA FISCAL
Lanius dorsalis mbwigu-taita (Swa)

Habitat: dry bush country, sea level to 1 600 m **Length:** 20 cm
Status: locally common resident

Very similar to the better-known Common Fiscal, but distinguished by its grey-blue mantle and shorter tail. The sexes are alike; immature is brown-grey above, with fine barring, whitish below. Usually conspicuous, it perches on the tops of *Acacia* bushes or trees in dry, bush country. The Somali Fiscal (*L. somalicus*) is similar, but differs in having the secondaries broadly tipped with white, very conspicuous in flight and it occurs only in the Lake Turkana area and Marsabit in Kenya.
BEST VIEWING: widespread in suitable habitats

COMMON FISCAL
Lanius collaris mbwigu barabara (Swa)

Habitat: open areas with scattered trees, power and telephone lines, 500–3 350 m **Length:** 23 cm **Status:** common resident

A well-known, black-and-white shrike with a long, white-tipped tail. Has a distinct white V on the back. Sexes similar, but female has a small patch of chestnut colour on the flanks. A widespread and common bird in open country, especially in the highlands. Conspicuous, perching in the open, often on telephone wires, it also frequents villages, towns and gardens. Has a habit of spiking its insect prey on a thorn or barbed wire, and often has a store of such prey; because of this, it is sometimes known as the 'butcher bird'.
BEST VIEWING: widespread

BLACK-HEADED ORIOLE
Oriolus larvatus naiwa kubwiro (Swa); ologos (Maa)

Habitat: forests and woodlands, sea level to 2 300 m **Length:** 23 cm
Status: common resident

This distinctive, bright yellow bird has a black head and throat and a bright coral-red bill. The wings are black, with a small, white patch, which is particularly visible in flight. The upper side of the central tail feathers is green-yellow and the eyes are red. Sexes alike; immature duller and has streaking on the throat. Often difficult to see, as it typically feeds in the tops of trees. Best located by its distinctive call: a short, loud, far-carrying clear whistle that falls in pitch. The similar Montane Oriole (*O. percivali*) has black central tail feathers and is a highland forest bird.
BEST VIEWING: widespread in suitable habitats

COMMON (FORK-TAILED) DRONGO
Dicrurus adsimilis miamba mkiapanda (Swa)

Habitat: open areas in woodland, forest edges and cultivated areas, up to 2 000 m **Length:** 25 cm **Status:** common resident

A glossy black bird with a distinctive forked tail, bright red eyes and a strong hook-tipped bill. In flight, the pale inner webs of the flight feathers are very noticeable. Sexes alike; immature is greyer, with brown speckles on the wing, is finely barred buffy-grey below and its tail is less forked. A conspicuous, often noisy and aggressive bird, it perches on open branches, from which it hawks its insect prey. The call is a harsh, sometimes grating song; also imitates other birds. The Square-tailed Drongo (*D. ludwigii*) is smaller, the tail is only slightly forked, and it occurs in the interior of forests.
BEST VIEWING: widespread in suitable habitats

AFRICAN PARADISE FLYCATCHER
Terpsiphone viridis   chechele mwekundu (Swa)

Habitat: along forest edges, in woodlands and gardens, up to 2 500 m
Length: 30–36 cm (♂); 20 cm (♀) **Status:** locally common resident

A distinctive, unmistakable, eye-catching bird. The male has a
blackish-blue, slightly crested head, with a bright blue bill and eye-
ring. The back and long tail are chestnut, and the underparts are
grey. Female is similar but has a short tail and a duller blue eye-ring
and bill. Immature resembles the female but is duller. There is a
white colour phase: some males, particularly in dryer eastern areas,
have a white back and tail; female as above. Easily overlooked but
often draws attention to itself by its '*pi pi pi pi, pi pi pi pi*' call or as
it swoops for insects in flight.

BEST VIEWING: widespread in suitable habitat especially during the rains.

HOUSE CROW
Corvus splendens   kunguru barahindi (Swa)

Habitat: coastal strip **Length:** 42 cm **Status:** a very common resident

An increasingly common, slender-looking crow. The body is dark
grey, the head, wings and tail are black. Sexes alike; immature
resembles adults but is duller. Introduced from India, it is now very
common along the East African coast, particularly in Mombasa,
Zanzibar and Dar-es-Salaam. In Mombasa and Dar-es-Salaam, it
has become a very serious pest and is responsible for the decline
in numbers of several indigenous birds. It is very aggressive and
regularly raids the colonies of breeding weaver birds. There have
been a number of attempts to reduce its numbers.

BEST VIEWING: Kenya: Mombasa; **Tanzania:** Dar-es-Salaam,
Zanzibar Island

CAPE ROOK (CROW)
Corvus capensis   kunguru mweusi (Swa)

Habitat: open plains, light woodland and cultivated areas below
2 500 m **Length:** 43 cm **Status:** locally common

An all-black crow with a distinctive, slender bill. Sexes alike;
immature resembles adults. It occurs mainly in upland areas in
open plains, light woodland and cultivated areas, where it typically
builds a large untidy nest in a tree. Particularly common in the
Lake Turkana area and on Rift Valley highlands and may be
expanding its range southwards. The all-black Fan-tailed Raven
(*C. rhipidurus*) is similar in size but has a much heavier-looking
bill and a short tail; it is also an inhabitant of rocky and craggy
hillsides and cliffs in arid and semi-desert country.

BEST VIEWING: widespread in suitable habitats

PIED CROW
Corvus albus   kunguru mweupe (Swa)

Habitat: all areas apart from very arid country, up to 3 000 m
Length: 46 cm **Status:** very common resident

A predominantly black crow with a distinctive white collar, which
extends from the neck onto the breast. In flight, the white chest
and belly are very conspicuous. Sexes alike; immature resembles
adults. Common and gregarious, feeding and roosting in towns
and villages. The White-necked Raven (*C. albicollis*) is larger and
the areas of white on the body are restricted to the nape; it is a bird
of mountains and rocky areas but does wander extensively.

BEST VIEWING: widespread, particularly in towns and cities

BLACK SAW-WING
Psalidoprocne pristoptera   kizele mweusi (Swa); esarrampala (Maa)

Habitat: woodlands, forest clearings and along forest edges, sea level to 3 500 m **Length:** 18 cm **Status:** locally common resident

A slender, all-black swallow with a deeply forked tail. Sexes similar; immature resembles adults, with a shorter tail. The flight is distinctive, slow and fluttering. Usually found singly or in small, loose flocks. In flight, when its tail is fanned, distinct white spots can be seen near the end of the tail. The male White-headed Saw-wing (*P. albiceps*) is easily distinguished by its white head; the females are similar but White has a whitish throat patch. The Rock Martin (*Ptyonoprogne fuligula*) is all-brown with a rufous throat.
BEST VIEWING: widespread in suitable habitats

BARN SWALLOW
Hirundo rustica   mbayuwayu ulaya (Swa); esarrampala (Maa)

Habitat: throughout, sea level to 3 000 m **Length:** 18 cm
Status: common Palaearctic migrant

A common, well-known migrant, often occurring in large flocks, September–April. Upperparts are blue-black, the face and throat are red. The underparts are white or buffy and there is a dark band below the throat. Sexes similar, both have long tail streamers. Immature is much paler than adults and lacks the long outer tail feathers. The Angola Swallow (*H. angolensis*) is similar but smaller and has grey underparts and shorter outer tail feathers. Immatures of the two species may be confused, but Barn Swallow's underparts are always paler.
BEST VIEWING: widespread

WIRE-TAILED SWALLOW
Hirundo smithii   mbayuwayu mkiasindano (Swa);
esarrampala (Maa)

Habitat: widespread often near water, sea level to 2 400 m
Length: 15 cm **Status:** common resident

The distinctive, long, thin, outer tail feathers of this fast-flying swallow are sometimes difficult to see, particularly in flight. The back, wings and tail are glossy blue, the underparts are white and it has a bright chestnut-rufous crown. Sexes alike; immature resembles adults, but is duller and lacks the long tail feathers. Occurs in pairs and, although common, never numerous. The similar Ethiopian Swallow (*H. aethiopica*) is also white below but has a pale buffy throat and short outer tail feathers.
BEST VIEWING: widespread

LESSER STRIPED SWALLOW
Cecropis abyssinica   mbayuwayu-mchirizi (Swa);
esarrampala (Maa)

Habitat: variety of habitats apart from arid areas, sea level to 2 200 m
Length: 18 cm **Status:** common resident

A distinctive swallow with heavily streaked underparts, a bright chestnut head and rump, and deeply forked tail. The rest of the upperparts are dark glossy-blue. Sexes alike; immature is similar to adults but has a brownish-black head, a buffy-coloured breast and a shorter tail. Common, usually in pairs. Often nesting under eaves of homes and under bridges. The Greater Striped Swallow (*Hirundo cucullata*), a very rare swallow recorded only in southern Tanzania, is much paler and the streaks are indistinct.
BEST VIEWING: widespread

RED-RUMPED SWALLOW
Cecropis daurica   mbayuwayu kiunochekunau (Swa); esarrampala (Maa)

Habitat: occurs from 1 299–2 500 m **Length:** 18 cm **Status:** common
This swallow has a black cap that extends to the eye, down to the nape, and rufous ear coverts. The upperparts are blue-black with a contrasting black, deeply forked, tail. Underparts pale rufous, throat paler and undertail coverts blue-black. In flight, black undertail coverts, black forked tail and pale rufous wing coverts, contrasting with black flight feathers, help distinguish this swallow from the similar Rufous-chested (*Hirundo semirufa*) and Mosque (*Cecropis senegalensis*) swallows. Both of these swallows have rufous undertail coverts, and the latter has distinct white underwing coverts.
BEST VIEWING: widespread in suitable habitats

RUFOUS-NAPED LARK
Mirafra africana   kipozamataza kisogochekundu (Swa)

Habitat: open plains and bushed grassland, 1 000–3 000 m
Length: 18 cm **Status:** locally common resident
A common, large, short-tailed lark with a heavy bill, an obvious pale stripe above the eye, and a short shaggy crest. The upperparts are rich brown and the wings are brown, with rufous primaries, which are very conspicuous in flight. The rufous nape is often absent. The underparts are pale with black streaks on the chest and flanks. Sexes alike. This lark's call is characteristic, comprising 3–4 sweet musical notes, delivered from the top of a small bush, rock, fence post or termite mound. Very similar Red-winged Lark (*M. hypermetra*) is larger and has a noticeably longer tail.
BEST VIEWING: widespread in suitable habitats

RED-CAPPED LARK
Mirafra cinerea   kipozamataza kibenzichekundu (Swa)

Habitat: open plains and cultivated land, 1 000–3 000 m **Length:** 14 cm
Status: locally common resident
A small, rich brown lark with a distinctive chestnut cap and a distinct white line above the eye. The underparts are pale, with chestnut patches on each side of the chest. Sexes alike; immature resembles the adults but lacks the chestnut cap. In flight, the white outer tail feathers are visible and the dark tail contrasts with the rufous rump. Common, often in flocks in open plains and cultivated fields. The Fawn-coloured Lark (*M. africanoides*) is similar in size but lacks the chestnut cap and chest patches and occurs at lower altitudes (500–1 800 m).
BEST VIEWING: widespread in suitable habitats

HUNTER'S CISTICOLA
Cisticola hunteri   kidenenda-chamwindaji (Swa)

Habitat: forest edges and glades in the highlands, 1 500–4 400 m
Length: 14 cm **Status:** locally common resident
A plain-looking cisticola; the top of the head is rufous-brown, merging to brown on the mantle and back. The back is indistinctly streaked. Below grey, paler on the throat. Sexes similar; immature resembles adult but is duller. Common in the highlands. Its loud, far-carrying call, a rhythmic undulating trill, is given by two or more birds from the tops of bushes or grass stems. The similar Chubb's Cisticola (*C. chubbi*) also duets but occurs in thick bush and along forest edges in the west of the region.
BEST VIEWING: Kenya: Aberdares, Mount Kenya NPs;
Tanzania: Kilimanjaro NP; **Uganda:** Mount Elgon NP

RATTLING CISTICOLA
Cisticola chiniana **kidenenda-taratara (Swa)**

Habitat: dry *Acacia* thornbush, scrub and cultivated land, sea level to 2 100 m **Length:** 13 cm **Status:** locally common resident

This cisticola is often recognised by its distinctive rattling *'che che che cheee'* call. The crown is a dull rufous-brown, with indistinct streaking. The mantle is similar but is thickly streaked, the tail is brown with pale tips, and the underparts are paler. It has a short, strong-looking bill. Sexes similar, but the female is a little smaller. Immature is less streaked than adults and is yellowish below. Common, usually in pairs or small groups, in dry *Acacia* thornbush scrub and cultivated land. Typically calls from the tops of bushes.

BEST VIEWING: widespread in suitable habitats

STOUT CISTICOLA
Cisticola robustus **kidenenda-kinene (Swa)**

Habitat: grasslands and grasslands with scattered bushes, 1 200–2 700 m **Length:** 14 cm **Status:** common resident

A large distinctive cisticola with a bright rufous crown and nape; the crown is finely streaked with black. The brown back and wings are heavily blotched and the tail is black, with distinct white tips. Immature is very different, yellow below, with streaking on the head and nape. Occurs in pairs or noisy groups calling from the tops of grass clumps or bushes. Draws attention to itself by its loud, scolding *'chaaaa chaaaa'*.

BEST VIEWING: Kenya: Masai Mara NR; **Tanzania:** Serengeti NP; **Uganda:** Lake Mburo NP

TAWNY-FLANKED PRINIA
Prinia subflava **shoro bawakahawia (Swa)**

Habitat: rank grass, scrub and along forest edges, sea level to 2 300 m **Length:** 13 cm **Status:** common resident

This small, slim, long-tailed warbler is brown, with a conspicuous, pale eyebrow and a black line through the eye. The throat and breast are whitish and there is a tawny-buff wash on the flanks and belly. Sexes similar; immature resembles adults but is duller coloured and has a shorter tail. Usually occurs in pairs or family groups. Commonly attracts attention to itself by its persistent *'prezztt prezztt'* call, while at the same time frequently raising and lowering its tail. Pale Prinia (*P. somalica*) is similar but is greyer above and much paler below; occurs in dry bush country.

BEST VIEWING: widespread in suitable habitats

YELLOW-BREASTED APALIS
Apalis flavida **kolokolo kifuanjano (Swa)**

Habitat: woodland, forest edges and *Acacia* scrub, sea level to 2 200 m **Length:** 11 cm **Status:** common resident

A small, long-tailed bird with green upperparts, a grey forehead and face and red eyes. It is white below, with a distinctive, broad, yellow band across the chest. Many birds have a small, black mark in the centre of the chest. Sexes similar; immature duller than adults and with a shorter tail. Occurs in pairs in woodland, forest edges and *Acacia* scrub. Often carries its tail cocked, particularly when duetting. The call is a distinctive, rolling *'krek krek, kreek kreek'*, often likened to galloping hooves.

BEST VIEWING: widespread in suitable habitats

GREY-BACKED CAMAROPTERA
Camaroptera brachyura   **kibwirosagi (Swa)**

Habitat: woodland and thornbush country, sea level to 2 000 m
Length: 10 cm **Status:** common resident

This small warbler has a short tail, which it often holds up in the cocked position. The grey head, mantle, back, rump and underparts contrast with its bright green wings. Birds with green backs occur along the Tanzania coast and inland in southern Tanzania. The eyes are red. A widespread bird, it occurs singly or in pairs in the undergrowth of woodland and thornbush country. Although common, it is often difficult to see as it skulks low down in dense bushes. Often calls attention to itself by its bleating *'quee queee'* call. It also has a call that resembles two stones being knocked together.

BEST VIEWING: widespread in suitable habitats

COMMON BULBUL
Pycnonotus barbatus   **sholwe (Swa); e-motonyi ng'iro (Maa)**

Habitat: almost all habitats apart from forest interiors, sea level to 3 000 m **Length:** 18 cm **Status:** very common resident

A common and well-known bird. The head and throat are blackish-brown, the back is brown and the breast and belly are buffy-white. It has distinctive, yellow undertail coverts. Often raises feathers on the nape, which gives the head a crested appearance. Sexes alike; immature resembles adults but duller overall. A common and widespread bird, it occurs in pairs in almost any type of habitat; it is especially common in towns and gardens. The distinctive call, a rapid *'towee-too-tweeoo'*, is often translated as *'Come back to Calcutta'*.

BEST VIEWING: widespread

RED-FACED CROMBEC
Sylvietta whytii   **kibubutu usomwekunda (Swa)**

Habitat: woodland, *Acacia* bush and along forest edges, sea level to 2 000 m **Length:** 10 cm **Status:** common but shy resident

A plump, almost tailless warbler, grey above and rufous below, becoming paler on the lower belly. The sides of the face are rufous and the eyes are red. Sexes similar; immature is brownish-grey. Occurs in pairs in woodland, *Acacia* bush and along forest edges; usually seen climbing among branches of trees and bushes in search of small insects. Has a brief warbling song and also a *'tic tic'* call note. The similar Northern Crombec (*S. brachyura*) is smaller, has a pale eye stripe and prefers more arid habitats. Both species build a deep, pouch-shaped nest out of spider webs, grass heads and bark.

BEST VIEWING: widespread in suitable habitats

RUFOUS CHATTERER
Turdoides rubiginosa   **zogoyogo machomeupe (Swa)**

Habitat: scrub and coastal bush in arid areas, often near rivers, sea level to 2 000 m **Length:** 20 cm **Status:** locally common resident

A distinctive, cinnamon-and-rufous-coloured bird with noticeable pale eyes and a horn-coloured bill. Sexes alike; immature resembles adults but is duller. Gregarious but far less vocal than other members of this family. Occurs in small parties, foraging on the ground in thick scrub in arid areas and coastal bush. The Scaly Chatterer (*T. aylmeri*) is similar but is ashy-brown above and pale cinnamon-buff below, with a buff streaking that gives it a scaly appearance. It also has a small mask of bare, grey skin surrounding yellow eyes and a distinct long, decurved horn-coloured bill.

BEST VIEWING: Kenya: Samburu, Buffalo Springs NRs

ARROW-MARKED BABBLER
Turdoides jardineii   zogoyogo bawa-mishale (Swa)

Habitat: bush and wooded country, sea level to 2 000 m **Length:** 22 cm
Status: locally common resident

A loud, noisy, brown bird with bright orange-yellow eyes. Below paler, with small, white, arrow-shaped markings on the throat and chest. Gregarious, foraging on the ground and in the undergrowth, while constantly keeping in touch with each other. They fly one after the other from tree to tree. The similar Brown Babbler (*T. plebejus*) differs mainly in having bright yellow eyes, whitish face and chin, and less noticeable chest markings. The Black-lored Babbler (*T. sharpei*) has distinct white eyes and black lores.

BEST VIEWING: widespread in suitable habitats

AFRICAN YELLOW WHITE-EYE
Zosterops senegalensis   kinegenenge manjano (Swa)

Habitat: forest edges, woodlands and gardens, sea level to 3 400 m
Length: 10 cm **Status:** common resident, mostly west of the Rift Valley

A small, bright yellowish-green bird with a fine pointed bill, a narrow, distinct white eye-ring and a contrasting yellow forehead. Sexes similar; immature resembles adult but is duller. Occurs in pairs or small groups along forest edges, and in woodland, mostly west of the Rift Valley. The very similar Abyssinian White-eye (*Z. abyssinicus*) has an all-yellow head and a smaller eye-ring, is paler below and occurs mainly in and east of the Rift Valley. The Montane White-eye (*Z. poliogastrus*) is larger (11.5 cm) and greener, has a conspicuous broad white eye-ring and is found in the highlands.

BEST VIEWING: widespread in suitable habitats

WATTLED STARLING
Creatophora cinerea   kuzi kijivucheupe (Swa)

Habitat: savanna, *Acacia* woodland and pastures, sea level to 3 000 m
Length: 21 cm **Status:** locally common resident

A pale grey starling with black wings and tail and a white rump, which is conspicuous in flight. Male in breeding plumage is distinctive, with bare, black skin on the forehead, face and throat, long black wattles and a bright yellow patch behind the dark eyes. Female lacks the black wattles and yellow face patch; immature similar to female but duller. Highly gregarious at times, occurring in large flocks. Fischer's Starling (*Lamprotornis fischeri*) is also grey but has a white belly and white eyes.

BEST VIEWING: Kenya: Masai Mara NR; **Tanzania:** Serengeti NP;
Uganda: Queen Elizabeth NP

GREATER BLUE-EARED STARLING
Lamprotornis chalybaeus   kuzi machonjano (Swa)

Habitat: woodlands, open country and cultivated land, sea level to 3 000 m **Length:** 23 cm **Status:** common resident

The upperparts are glossy green-blue, with a row of black spots on the wing coverts. The underparts are bluer, darkening on the belly. The eyes are striking orange-yellow, contrasting with the dark, blackish ear coverts. Sexes alike; immature is blackish, not blue, below. The very similar Lesser Blue-eared Starling (*L. chloropterus*) (18 cm) is difficult to separate, but is smaller and slimmer and the immature is dark brown below. The Black-bellied Starling (*L. corruscus*) is similar but slimmer, has a longer tail and is a forest top species.

BEST VIEWING: widespread in suitable habitats

RÜPPELL'S (LONG-TAILED) STARLING
Lamprotornis purpuroptera   **kuzi bawazambarau (Swa)**

Habitat: woodland and savanna country, 1 000–2 200 m
Length: 33–36 cm   **Status:** locally common resident

A large, iridescent, dark blue-purple starling with a long, graduated tail and creamy-white eyes. The head and neck are darker, sometimes with a bronzy sheen. Sexes similar; immature is brownish with a shorter tail. Mostly found in pairs or small groups in *Acacia* woodland and savanna country, often feeding on the ground. The Bristle-crowned Starling (*Onychognathus salvadorii*) also has a long, graduated tail but has distinctive, chestnut-coloured primaries and a conspicuous tuft on the forehead. It is also found only in semi-desert country.
BEST VIEWING: widespread in suitable habitats

GOLDEN-BREASTED STARLING
Lamprotornis regius   **kuzi kifuanjano (Swa)**

Habitat: dry thornbush country, sea level to 1 200 m   **Length:** 30–36 cm
Status: locally common resident

The most beautiful of all the starlings, with a striking, golden-yellow breast and belly and a long, slim graduated tail. The upperparts are violet-blue and it has distinctive white eyes. Sexes similar; immature is paler than adults and has a short tail. A very shy starling, always on the move, occurring in pairs or loose flocks in dry, thornbush country. The all-grey Ashy Starling (*Cosmopsarus unicolor*) also has a long tail and similar habits, but occurs in wooded grasslands in Tanzania, where it is endemic.
BEST VIEWING: Kenya: Samburu, Buffalo Springs NRs, Tsavo East NP

SUPERB STARLING
Lamprotornis superbus   **kwezi maradadi (Swa); ol-kirapash (Maa)**

Habitat: a wide variety of habitats including towns, sea level to 3 000 m
Length: 18 cm   **Status:** common resident

East Africa's best-known starling, with iridescent, blue-green upperparts and black spots on the wing. The head is blackish and the eyes are pale yellow. The belly is rich orange-chestnut, separated from the throat by a narrow white line. The underwings (seen only in flight) and the vent are white. Sexes similar; immature is duller than adults and has dark eyes. Feeds on the ground, eating mainly insects such as grasshoppers, termites, moths and beetles but also occasionally fruit, *Acacia* flowers and seeds.
BEST VIEWING: Kenya: Masai Mara NR; **Tanzania:** Serengeti NP;
Uganda: Kidepo Valley NP

HILDEBRANDT'S STARLING
Lamprotornis hildebrandti   **kwezi-jangwa (Swa); o-le-kishu (Maa)**

Habitat: savanna woodland and *Acacia* country, 500–2 000 m
Length: 18 cm   **Status:** common resident

Endemic to East Africa, this bird differs from Superb Starling in its striking, red eyes and deep-rufous-coloured breast and belly; the vent and the underwings are also rufous. Sexes similar; immature resembles adults but is duller. Gregarious in small groups, feeding on the ground, in savanna woodland, *Acacia* country and cultivated land. Shelley's Starling (*L. shelleyi*) is similar, but darker, and richer coloured and has orange-red eyes; this is an uncommon starling occurring in dry bush country, from sea level to 1 300 m.
BEST VIEWING: widespread in suitable habitats

VIOLET-BACKED STARLING
Cinnyricinclus leucogaster   **kuzi mgongozambarau (Swa)**

Habitat: forests, woodlands and gardens, sea level to 3 000 m
Length: 16 cm   **Status:** locally common resident, also an inter-African migrant

A distinctive starling. The male's upperparts and throat are violet-blue, contrasting strongly with its white underparts. The eyes are bright yellow. The female conspicuously different from the male; the back is mottled brown-tawny and white below, with brown streaks. Immature is similar to the female. At times very common, particularly when fig trees are in fruit. The similar Sharpe's Starling (*C. sharpii*) is blue-black above and white below, with yellow eyes, and is an uncommon forest bird.

BEST VIEWING: widespread in suitable habitats

RED-BILLED OXPECKER
Buphagus erythrorhynchus   **shashi domojekundu (Swa)**

Habitat: widespread, sea level to 3 000 m   **Length:** 18 cm
Status: locally common resident

Has a bright red bill, and red eyes surrounded by a yellow eye-ring. The back, wings, rump and tail are uniformly ashy-brown, merging to buff on the belly. Sexes similar; immature duller, with dark-coloured eyes and a black bill. Oxpeckers are specially adapted to feed on ticks and insects found on mammals. Their claws are sharp and strong and their tail feathers are very stiff. This allows them to clamber all over their host, using the slender, flattened bill in a scissor-like motion.

BEST VIEWING: all national parks and reserves in the region

YELLOW-BILLED OXPECKER
Buphagus africanus   **shashi domo-njano (Swa)**

Habitat: widespread, sea level to 3 000 m   **Length:** 19 cm
Status: locally common resident

Differs from the previous species in having a distinctive, red-tipped, yellow bill and a pale, buffy rump. The pale rump contrasts with the ashy-brown back and is particularly noticeable in flight. The throat and upper chest are ashy-brown, merging to buff on the belly and the eyes are red. Sexes similar; immature is duller than adults, with a pale rump and dark eyes, and the bill is brown. The bill is stout and is used to pluck ticks and other parasites from the hide of its host (mostly buffalo and giraffe). Call a distinctive '*tseee, tseee*'.

BEST VIEWING: all national parks and reserves in the region

OLIVE THRUSH
Turdus olivaceus   **kiruwiji kijanikijivu (Swa)**

Habitat: forests, woodlands and cultivated areas with trees, above 1 600 m   **Length:** 23 cm   **Status:** common resident

A common thrush, with brown-olive upperparts, breast and throat paler, with dark streaking on the throat and an orange-rufous belly. The bill and feet are orange-yellow and there is a yellow ring around the eyes. Sexes alike; immature is duller than adults and has spotted underparts. Occurs in the highlands in pairs, especially common in gardens. The call is a monotonous '*chee-chee-chee-chee*', repeated over and over again. The very similar African Thrush (*T. pelios*) is paler, has a pale yellow-orange bill and the breast is pale grey-brown, with a buffy-orange wash on the flanks.

BEST VIEWING: widespread in suitable habitats

CAPE ROBIN-CHAT
Cossypha caffra **kurumbiza tumbojeupe (Swa)**

Habitat: forest edges, cultivated land and gardens in the highlands, 1 600–3 400 m **Length:** 17 cm **Status:** common resident

The orange-rufous throat and upper breast, contrasting with a grey belly, distinguish this robin-chat. The head, back and tail are dusky, rump and outer tail feathers are rufous. A distinctive white stripe above the eyes contrasts with the black face. Sexes alike; immature is brown with buffy spots above and mottling below and a duller, rufous tail. Has a distinctive habit of raising and lowering its tail. A shy bird, occurring in the highlands along forest edges and in scrub. Becomes tame and confiding in gardens. Often parasitised by the Red-chested Cuckoo.

BEST VIEWING: widespread in suitable habitats

RÜPPELL'S ROBIN-CHAT
Cossypha semirufa **kurumbiza-rupeli**

Habitat: highland forests and dense scrub, 1 400–3 300 m **Length:** 18 cm **Status:** locally common resident

This robin-chat is entirely bright orange-rufous below, which contrasts with its dark upperparts. The tail is rufous, with blackish central tail feathers. The crown and face are black, with a distinctive, long, white stripe above the eye, extending from the forehead to the nape. Sexes similar; immature is brownish and spotted buff. Its song is a loud, three-note whistle, repeated over and over again. It is a wonderful mimic, copying other birds, mammals, humans and many other sounds. Shy and skulking, it occurs in highland forests, dense scrub and gardens where it becomes tame and confiding.

BEST VIEWING: widespread in suitable habitats

WHITE-BROWED ROBIN-CHAT
Cossypha heuglini **kurumbiza mchirizimweupe (Swa)**

Habitat: woodland, thickets and coastal scrub, sea level to 2 200 m **Length:** 20 cm **Status:** common resident

Very similar to Rüppell's Robin-Chat, being orange-rufous below, with contrasting, dark upperparts. The tail differs in being rufous-orange with olive-brown, not blackish, central tail feathers, and the black head is separated from the greyish mantle by an orange collar. A distinctive white eye stripe extends from the forehead to the nape. Sexes similar; immature is brownish with buff spotting. A shy, skulking bird, which forages for insects on the ground. Well known for its melodious song, delivered in the early mornings and late afternoons.

BEST VIEWING: widespread in suitable habitats

SPOTTED MORNING (PALM) THRUSH
Cichladusa guttata **kurumbiza-miluzi (Swa)**

Habitat: coastal thickets and semi-arid bush, below 1 600 m **Length:** 16 cm **Status:** locally common resident

A shy, skulking bird with dull, rufous-brown upperparts, a thin white stripe above the eyes and a conspicuous, rufous tail. The underparts are buffy, with a line of black spots that runs from its bill to the sides of the throat, becoming larger black blobs on the breast. Sexes alike; immature resembles adult but is duller. Occurs in thickets in dry bush country, especially along dry river courses, also in coastal scrub. The call, a loud melodious song, is usually delivered from a prominent perch at dawn and dusk and, occasionally, at night. It also has a harsh alarm call and mimics other bird calls.

BEST VIEWING: widespread in suitable habitats

CAPPED WHEATEAR
Oenanthe pileata   mozo kiparacheusi (Swa)

Habitat: short grasslands, above 1 400 m **Length:** 18 cm
Status: locally common resident

A resident wheatear with a black cap and a characteristic white
rump. The cheeks and breast are black, with a distinct white stripe
above the eye. The forehead and throat are white, the belly is white,
with a pinkish wash on flanks. The upperparts are brown, with a
black tail. They have a distinctive upright stance and typically stand
on a rock or termite mound from where they fly to catch their prey;
they flutter straight upwards while singing. Sexes similar; immature
resembles adults but is duller, with a brownish colour replacing the
black areas of the adult.

BEST VIEWING: Tanzania: Serengeti NP (short grass plains)

ISABELLINE WHEATEAR
Oenanthe isabellina   mozo-isabela (Swa)

Habitat: arid and semi-arid areas and grasslands, usually below
2 000 m **Length:** 16 cm **Status:** common Eurasian migrant

A migrant from Europe and Asia, occurring in East Africa October–
March. It is overall pale sandy in colour, with a pale eye stripe and
a characteristic white rump. Found in arid and semi-arid areas,
often in stony places and on bare ground or short grasslands in
open country. Sexes similar; immature resembles adult. May be
confused with the female Northern Wheatear but it is larger and
longer-legged; its pale wings, with little or no contrast between the
wings and back, which are best seen in flight, distinguish it from
that species.

BEST VIEWING: widespread in suitable habitats

NORTHERN WHEATEAR
Oenanthe oenanthe   mozo mkiarangimbili (Swa)

Habitat: grasslands and open bush country **Length:** 15 cm
Status: common Eurasian migrant

A migrant from Europe and Asia, occurring in East Africa
September–March. Male in breeding plumage is distinctive, with a
grey crown and mantle, black cheeks, black wings and a pale stripe
above the eye. The underparts are white, with a buffy-pink wash on
the flanks. Non-breeding male is duller and the black on the cheeks
is much reduced. Female and immature are browner and lack any
black on the cheeks. Both sexes have a characteristic white rump
and the upper part of outer tail feathers is white, forming a T. In
flight, the pale back contrasts with darker wings.

BEST VIEWING: Kenya: Masai Mara NR; **Tanzania:** Serengeti NP

NORTHERN ANTEATER CHAT
Myrmecocichla aethiops   mozo kwapanyeupe (Swa)

Habitat: open grasslands, generally above 1 500 m **Length:** 20 cm
Status: locally common resident

A blackish-brown chat with conspicuous white wing patches,
which are visible only in flight. Sexes alike; immature is
brownish. Usually seen on the ground or perched on low bushes,
fence posts or termite mounds. Excavates a nest burrow in a
termite mound or Antbear hole or in a roadside cutting, which
is used as a year-round roost, as well as a nest site. The similar
Sooty Chat (*M. nigra*) is darker and has a conspicuous white patch
on the shoulder and shows no white on the wings in flight. The
female Sooty Chat is all-brown.

BEST VIEWING: widespread in suitable habitats

MOCKING (WHITE-SHOULDERED) CLIFF CHAT
Thamnolaea cinnamomeiventris   **mozo kichwacheusi (Swa)**

Habitat: cliffs, gorges and boulder-strewn slopes, 600–2 200 m
Length: 20 cm **Status:** locally common resident

The male is a distinctive, attractive bird with a glossy black head, breast, back, wings and tail. The belly, rump and both upper and lower tail coverts are rich rufous. There is a conspicuous white shoulder patch and a thin white line across the chest. The female is greyer, with rufous underparts, and lacks the white shoulder patch. Immature resembles the female. Occurs in pairs, on cliffs, gorges and boulder-strewn slopes. Has a sweet warbling song. A tame and confiding bird, especially in areas visited by tourists.

BEST VIEWING: Kenya: Lake Nakuru NP

WHITE-EYED SLATY FLYCATCHER
Melaenornis fischeri   **chechele machomeupe (Swa)**

Habitat: forest edges, scrub and gardens, 1 300–3 000 m
Length: 15 cm **Status:** locally common resident

A stocky flycatcher with a distinctive white ring around eyes. The upperparts are slate-grey, paler below. Sexes alike; immature is greyish-brown, with heavy white spots. Birds occurring in the west of the region lack the white eye-ring. This is a common garden bird in the highlands. Feeds mostly by picking up insects from the ground, but also occasionally hawks for them from a low bush or tree. In season, occasionally feeds on small, ripe berries. Very active at dawn and dusk, when it may be seen foraging on the ground along forest tracks.

BEST VIEWING: widespread in suitable habitats

NORTHERN BLACK FLYCATCHER
Melaenornis edolioides   **chechele mweusi (Swa)**

Habitat: woodland and cultivated areas, 400–800 m **Length:** 19 cm
Status: locally common resident

This dull, slate-black flycatcher has a long, slender, squared tail and dark brown eyes. Sexes alike, but immature is slate-black, with heavy, tawny spotting. Occurs singly or in pairs, in woodland and cultivated areas, west of the Rift Valley. Catches its insect prey on the ground. The Southern Black Flycatcher (*M. pammelaina*) is very similar, but has a glossy black plumage and occurs in more arid areas. Both species distinguished from adult Common Drongo by having a square, not forked, tail, dark, not red, eyes and a smaller, slender bill.

BEST VIEWING: widespread in suitable habitats

AFRICAN GREY FLYCATCHER
Bradornis microrhynchus   **chechele-kidomo (Swa)**

Habitat: dry bush and *Acacia* woodland, sea level to 2 000 m
Length: 14 cm **Status:** common resident

An all-grey flycatcher, paler below, with indistinct streaking on the crown, which is often difficult to see. Sexes similar; immature brownish. Juvenile is distinctly spotted. Found singly or in pairs, usually seen sitting on a low branch from where it catches insects on the ground. Very similar Pale Flycatcher (*B. pallidus*) is pale brown and longer tailed, has no streaks on crown and occurs in less arid habitats. Ashy Flycatcher (*Muscicapa caerulescens*) is pale blue-grey and has a thin, black stripe between the bill and the eye and a white line above it. Also has an incomplete white ring around the eye.

BEST VIEWING: widespread in suitable habitats

SILVERBIRD
Empidornis semipartitus   chechele tumbojekundu (Swa)

Habitat: dry bush and *Acacia* woodland, 500–2 300 m **Length:** 18 cm
Status: locally common resident

An unmistakable, distinctive flycatcher. The upperparts are silvery-grey and the underparts are rufous. Sexes alike; immature is buffy above, spotted below. Locally common, usually found in pairs, in dry bush and *Acacia* woodland, where it sits in the open, on the top of bushes or telephone wires. Hawks insects in the air but also captures its insect prey on the ground. The call is a sweet thrush-like song.

BEST VIEWING: widespread in suitable habitats

AFRICAN DUSKY FLYCATCHER
Muscicapa adjusta   chechele kijivucheusi (Swa)

Habitat: forest edges, woodlands and cultivated areas, 900–3 200 m
Length: 10 cm **Status:** locally common resident

A small, plump, short-tailed flycatcher, mainly brown-grey but paler on the throat and belly. Sexes alike; immature is spotted buff above and buffy with brown spots below. A tame bird, usually seen sitting on a bare branch, from which it makes short flights to capture its insect prey. More common in the highlands. The larger (14 cm) Spotted Flycatcher (*M. striata*) is also brownish, but has streaks on the crown and more indistinct streaks on the breast. Likewise, the Swamp Flycatcher (*M. aquatica*) is brown but larger (14 cm) and has a distinct white throat and belly.

BEST VIEWING: widespread in suitable habitats

EASTERN VIOLET-BACKED SUNBIRD
Anthreptes orientalis   chozi macheo (Swa)

Habitat: semi-arid bush country, sea level to 1 300 m **Length:** 12 cm
Status: locally common resident

The male has violet-blue upperparts and throat and is white below. The female is brown-grey above, white below and has a distinctive white stripe above the eyes; the uppertail coverts and tail are dark violet. Immature is similar to female. Locally common in semi-arid bush country, often near water. This sunbird is reputed to build its nest close to wasps' nests. The similar Western Violet-backed Sunbird (*A. longuemarei*) is larger (13 cm), the male is grey below and the female is yellowish below; it is much less common and is a woodland bird, occurring in the western parts of the region.

BEST VIEWING: widespread in suitable habitats

COLLARED SUNBIRD
Hedydipna collaris   chozi mkufu (Swa)

Habitat: widespread in gardens, forests and damp bush, sea level to 2 800 m **Length:** 10 cm **Status:** locally common resident

A small sunbird with a short tail. Male's upperparts, head, throat and breast iridescent green, lower breast and underparts yellow, separated from the breast by a narrow violet band, which is seen only in good light. Female similar, but all of the underparts, including the throat and breast, are yellow. The bill is short, which helps separate this species from the similar Variable Sunbird. Immature like female but duller. Usually seen in pairs foraging among flowers, feeding on the nectar. The quiet 'tsweeee tsweeee' contact call between male and female often draws attention.

BEST VIEWING: widespread in the region

AMETHYST SUNBIRD
Chalcomitra amethystina (*Nectarinia amethystina*)   **chozi mweusi (Swa)**

Habitat: a wide variety of habitats, sea level to 2 200 m **Length:** 14 cm
Status: common resident

A velvety-black sunbird with a long, decurved bill. Often appears
to be all-black but, in good light, the chin and throat are seen to
be rosy-purple and the top of the head metallic green. There is also
a small patch of purple on the shoulder. Female is brown, with a
narrow, pale eye stripe, and is paler below, with heavy streaking.
Immature is similar to female. Male has a pleasant warbling song.
The similar male Green-throated Sunbird (*C. rubescens*) is also
black but has an iridescent green cap and throat; the female and
immature are similar to Amethyst Sunbird.

BEST VIEWING: widespread, especially in gardens with flowers

SCARLET-CHESTED SUNBIRD
Chalcomitra senegalensis (*Nectarinia senegalensis*)   **chozi-gunda (Swa)**

Habitat: a variety of habitats, preferring medium- to high-rainfall areas,
sea level to 2 150 m **Length:** 15 cm **Status:** common resident

The male is velvety blackish-brown, with a metallic green cap
and moustachial streaks. Throat is also metallic green but is often
difficult to see. Its distinctive, vivid scarlet chest is spotted bright
metallic blue, also best seen in good light. Female is dark brown
above, buffy below with mottles and streaks. Immature is similar to
female but has blackish streaks on the throat. Usually occurs in pairs.
Male may be confused with Hunter's Sunbird, which is black, with
a scarlet chest but lacks the green throat. Male Red-chested Sunbird
also has a red chest but is green and has a long tail.

BEST VIEWING: sometimes large numbers occur at *Leonotis* flowers

HUNTER'S SUNBIRD
Chalcomitra hunteri (*Nectarinia hunteri*)   **neli mweusi (Swa)**

Habitat: bush and woodlands in semi-arid areas, 50–1 200 m
Length: 14 cm **Status:** locally common resident

Similar to, and often confused with, the Scarlet-chested
Sunbird. The male is all-black with a metallic green cap and
green moustache streaks. The throat is all-black, bordering onto
a bright scarlet chest. In good light, the violet-coloured rump
and violet patches on the wing can be seen. The female
is brown, mottled and streaked below. Immature similar to
female. Widespread in arid bush and woodlands.

BEST VIEWING: Kenya: Lake Baringo

BRONZE SUNBIRD
Nectarinia kilimensis   **neli kilima (Swa)**

Habitat: forest edges and woodlands, 1 200–2 800 m
Length: 14–23 cm **Status:** common resident

A blackish-looking, long-tailed sunbird with a metallic bronze-green
head, throat, shoulders and chest, which, in some lights, appear
green. Female is olive-grey, pale yellowish below, with darker
streaking and a short tail. Immature is similar to female. A highland
species. Sometimes confused with the Malachite Sunbird (*N. famosa*)
but male is an unmistakable bright emerald-green and the female is
unstreaked below. Can also be confused with the Tacazze Sunbird
(*N. tacazze*), which also has a green head but, in good light, the
body's purple, green and gold colours can be seen.

BEST VIEWING: common in gardens with nectar-bearing flowers

BEAUTIFUL SUNBIRD
Cinnyris pulchellus (Nectarinia pulchellus) chozi-uzuri (Swa)

Habitat: *Acacia* woodland and semi-arid bush, 400–1 900 m
Length: 12–15 cm **Status:** locally common resident
The male is a small and slender-looking sunbird with a long, thin tail. Bright metallic-green upperparts and a red chest, bordered with yellow patches. Belly colour varies according to region: east of the Rift Valley it is black, west of the Rift Valley it is green, apart from around Kisumu in western Kenya, where the male's belly is black. Female has a short tail, is grey with pale eye stripes, below yellow-grey with indistinct streaking. Immature is similar to female. Very similar Black-bellied Sunbird (*C. nectarinioides*) is smaller (9–12 cm) and male lacks the yellow chest patches; its belly is always black.
BEST VIEWING: widespread in suitable habitats

MARICO (MARIQUA) SUNBIRD
Cinnyris mariquensis (Nectarinia mariquensis) chozi-mariko (Swa)

Habitat: savanna and *Acacia* scrub and woodland, 800–2 000 m
Length: 13 cm **Status:** common resident
Male has a metallic, coppery sheen above and on the throat. A thin, blue line separates the throat from a broad maroon chest band, and the belly is black in the north, but southern birds have a more greyish-black belly. Female is grey-brown above, with a buffy eye stripe, and is paler below, with dusky streaks. Immature is similar to female but has a dark throat. The very similar Purple-banded Sunbird (*C. bifasciata*) is slightly smaller (10 cm) and has a shorter bill.
BEST VIEWING: widespread in suitable habitats

RED-CHESTED SUNBIRD
Cinnyris erythrocercus
(Nectarinia erythrocerca) chozi kifuachekundu (Swa)

Habitat: waterside vegetation near lakes, swamps and rivers, 600–1 800 m **Length:** 13–15 cm **Status:** common resident
Male is metallic, blue-green on the head, neck and mantle, with a deep-red chest band, a black belly and long, elongated central tail feathers. In good light, a metallic-violet band can be seen across the chest and on the rump and uppertail coverts. The female is dark brown above and buffy below, the central tail feathers are not elongated. Immature is similar to the female but has a darker throat. Sometimes confused with Scarlet-chested Sunbird, but the long tail, blue-green head and black belly and habitat should avoid confusion.
BEST VIEWING: Lake Victoria region

VARIABLE SUNBIRD
Cinnyris venustus (Nectarinia venusta) chozi tumbonjano (Swa)

Habitat: forest edges, woodlands and gardens, sea level to 3 000 m
Length: 9 cm **Status:** common resident
Male is metallic blue-green above with dark wings and a dark tail. The throat and the upper chest are bright, metallic purple-violet. The colour of the underparts varies from bright yellow to orange-yellow in the west and white in the north. Displaying male shows distinctive, yellow or orange-red pectoral tufts. Female is olive-grey above, with a blue-black tail and whitish below. Immature is similar to female. The male Collared Sunbird is similar but has a green head, neck and throat and yellow below.
BEST VIEWING: widespread in suitable habitats

WHITE-BROWED SPARROW WEAVER
Plocepasser mahali   **korobindo mchirizimweupe (Swa)**

Habitat: dry *Acacia* and savanna country, 400–2 000 m **Length:** 17 cm
Status: common resident

A mainly brown weaver with a conspicuous, broad, white stripe above the eyes. Below white, has white wing coverts and a white rump, which is noticeable in flight. Sexes similar; immature resembles adults but is duller. A very common bird, occurring in noisy flocks in dry *Acacia* and savanna country, where its untidy, round, dried-grass nest is a feature of the landscape. The nests have two entrances and are used year-round as roosting sites. When breeding, one entrance is closed by the female and the inside of the nest lined with fine grasses.

BEST VIEWING: widespread in suitable habitats

RUFOUS-TAILED WEAVER
Histurgops ruficauda   **korobindo mkiamwwekundu (Swa)**

Habitat: dry *Acacia* woodland and grasslands with scattered trees, 400–1 800 m **Length:** 22 cm **Status:** locally common resident

A very conspicuous and noisy weaver. The upperparts are brown, with pale edging to the feathers, giving it a distinctive, mottled effect. The underparts are paler, with brown mottling. In flight, the brown tail, with chestnut outer tail feathers and chestnut edges to the flight feathers, is conspicuous. The eyes are pale blue. Sexes similar; immature resembles adults but browner. Locally a very common bird, occurring in noisy flocks, feeding on the ground. Was endemic to Tanzania but now regularly recorded in Kenya.

BEST VIEWING: Kenya: Sand River, Masai Mara NR; **Tanzania:** Ngorongoro CA, Serengeti NP

GREY-CAPPED SOCIAL WEAVER
Pseudonigrita arnaudi   **korobindo kichwakijivu (Swa)**

Habitat: dry thorn and *Acacia* country, 500–1 800 m **Length:** 11 cm
Status: locally common resident

A small, short-tailed greyish-buff bird with a dove-grey cap. The eyes are deep red surrounded by a white eye-ring. Sexes similar; immature is buffy with the top of its head buffy-grey. In flight, a pale band can be seen at the end of the tail. Locally common in dry thorn and *Acacia* country where it is gregarious, breeding in small scattered colonies. A colony usually consists of a number of untidy grass nests hanging from the lower branches of an *Acacia* tree. The birds generally stay in the vicinity of these colonies, roosting year-round in the nests at night.

BEST VIEWING: widespread in suitable habitats

BLACK-CAPPED SOCIAL WEAVER
Pseudonigrita cabanisi   **korobindo kiparacheusi (Swa)**

Habitat: arid areas with large trees, 200–1 300 m **Length:** 13 cm
Status: locally common resident

A small, distinctive-looking weaver with a black cap, which contrasts with its brown back and tail. It is white below with black streaks in the flanks. The ivory-coloured bill has a greenish tinge and the eyes are bright red. Sexes similar, and immature has a brown cap and dark eyes. Gregarious, lives in colonies, building its grass nest towards the ends of branches, in tall, isolated *Acacia* trees. Feeds on the ground.

BEST VIEWING: widespread in suitable habitats

KENYA RUFOUS SPARROW

Passer rufocinctus   korobindo mwekundu (Swa)

Habitat: variety of habitats, including wooded grasslands, cultivated land and gardens, 1 000–3 000 m **Length:** 14 cm **Status:** Locally common resident

A typical sparrow, with a small black bib, a grey mantle and crown, a rich brown back with black streaking and a rufous rump. There is a distinctive rufous streak running from the pale eyes, around the grey cheeks and a thin, black streak through the eyes. Birds in the northwest of the region are paler, with pale cheeks and dark eyes. Female and immature are paler and have a grey bib. The male House Sparrow (*P. domesticus*) is similar but has a larger black bib, white cheeks and the rump is grey.

BEST VIEWING: widespread in suitable habitats

GREY-HEADED SPARROW

Passer griseus   korobindo-kaya (Swa)

Habitat: variety of habitats including towns and villages, sea level to 2 500 m **Length:** 15–18 cm **Status:** common widespread resident

A typical sparrow, with a grey head, neck and underparts, a rufous-brown back and a rufous rump and undertail coverts. A number of races of this sparrow (often treated as separate species) occur. The smallest has a buffy chin and throat and a small white mark on the shoulder; the largest has a distinctive, large, parrot-like bill. Sexes similar; immature resembles adults but is duller. Widespread and common in a variety of habitats, including towns and villages. Builds untidy nests, usually low in a tree or bush, occasionally in a tree hole or another bird's nest.

BEST VIEWING: widespread in suitable habitats

CHESTNUT SPARROW

Passer eminibey   korobindo mwekundu (Swa)

Habitat: dry *Acacia* bush often near water, sea level to 2 000 m **Length:** 11 cm **Status:** common resident

The breeding male is rich chestnut with a darker head and dark eyes. The wings and tail feathers are blackish, with white edging. The non-breeding male and female are similar, with ashy-brown heads and necks, a black-streaked mantle, a chocolate-brown eye stripe, rump and shoulders. The similar-looking Chestnut Weaver (*Ploceus rubiginosus*) is larger (17 cm); the breeding male is chestnut-brown, with a black head and red eyes; the non-breeding male and female are ashy-brown above, head and mantle streaked blackish, and are pale below, with an indistinct cinnamon chest band.

BEST VIEWING: widespread in suitable habitats

YELLOW-SPOTTED PETRONIA

Petronia pyrgita   korobindo doanjano (Swa)

Habitat: dry, open *Acacia* bush and savanna country, preferring rocky ground, sea level to 2 000 m **Length:** 15 cm **Status:** resident

A very plain-looking, sparrow-like bird with a pale bill, brownish-grey above, with a buffy eye stripe and a pale eye-ring. Below is greyish-white, with an often indistinct yellow mark at the base of the throat. The pale eye-ring and pale bill are the best way of identifying this bird. Found in dry, open *Acacia* bush and savanna country, prefers rocky ground. The Yellow-throated Petronia (*P. superciliaris*) is darker above, with a distinct buffy stripe above the eye, below pale buffy, with an indistinct, yellow mark on the throat, and occurs in woodland in central and southern Tanzania.

BEST VIEWING: widespread in suitable habitats

RED-BILLED BUFFALO WEAVER
Bubalornis niger   korobindo domojekundu (Swa)

Habitat: savanna and *Acacia* woodland, sea level to 1 500 m
Length: 23 cm **Status:** locally common resident

Male is large, stout, all-black, with a large, red bill, variable white
markings on the wings and small, white marks on the breast. Female
has a blackish bill and is grey-brown above, paler below, with streaks
above and below. Immature is similar to female but has white
edgings to feathers. Common and gregarious, usually seen feeding
on the ground, nesting colonially. The large, thorny stick nest, 1 m
or more across, with several entrances, is distinctive and most often
built in Baobabs.
BEST VIEWING: Kenya: Tsavo East, Tsavo West NPs, Lake Baringo;
Tanzania: Tarangire NP; **Uganda:** Kidepo Valley NP

WHITE-HEADED BUFFALO WEAVER
Dinemellia dinemelli   korobindo kichwacheupe (Swa)

Habitat: dry bush and *Acacia* woodland, sea level to 1 400 m
Length: 18 cm **Status:** locally common resident

An unmistakable, large, stocky weaver with a white head, chest
and belly, and a brown mantle, wings and tail. The rump is bright
orange and there are large white patches on the wing, which are
especially conspicuous in flight. Sexes similar; immature resembles
adults but is duller and browner. Widespread, occurring in pairs
or small groups, usually feeding on the ground. Breeds in loose
colonies, building a large, untidy, domed stick nest. Often an
unoccupied nest is taken over by a pair of Pygmy Falcons.
BEST VIEWING: Kenya: Samburu area; **Tanzania:** Tarangire NP;
Uganda: Kidepo Valley NP

GROSBEAK WEAVER
Amblyospiza albifrons   yombeyombe (Swa)

Habitat: forest edges and swamps, sea level to 3 000 m
Length: 17 cm **Status:** locally common resident

A large, thickset weaver with a distinctive, large, dark, heavy bill.
Male is slate-black or brownish-black, with a white patch on the
forehead and a small white patch on the wing, both conspicuous
in flight. Female and immature are brown above and paler below,
with dark streaks and a pale yellow bill. Builds a distinctive, neat,
domed nest of fine, shredded leaves or reeds. The similar Thick-
billed Seedeater (*Crithagra burtoni*), a shy highland forest bird, is
dark brown, with faint dark streaking and a small white patch
on the forehead; its wings and tail are edged green.
BEST VIEWING: widespread in suitable habitats

BAGLAFECHT WEAVER
Ploceus baglafecht   kwera usomweusi (Swa)

Habitat: forest edges, woodlands and gardens, 800–3 000 m
Length: 15 cm **Status:** common resident

This weaver occurs in a number of forms. The male in Kenya has
a black nape, back, tail and eye coverts, while that occurring in
the west of the region has a blackish crown. Female in Kenya is
distinctly different, having a black crown and face; female in the
west is similar to male. Immatures are similar to females but duller.
A non-colonial weaver, widespread and common. The similar Black-
necked Weaver (*P. nigricollis*) is more golden-yellow; the male has
a black chin and throat and a thin black line through the eyes; the
female has a black cap and neck and a black line through the eyes.
BEST VIEWING: widespread in suitable habitats

SPECTACLED WEAVER
Ploceus ocularis kwera koojeusi (Swa)

Habitat: forests, *Acacia* woodland, particularly along rivers and streams, sea level to 2 200 m **Length:** 14 cm **Status:** common resident

Bright yellow, with greenish wings and tail. The male has a black bib on chin and throat and a black patch through the eyes. The female is similar to the male but the bib on chin and throat is orange. Immature resembles female but is duller. The call is distinctive, a descending '*tee tee tee*'. A non-colonial weaver, locally common, but shy and more skulking than other weavers. Forages like a warbler for insects and fruit, often in damp places. Builds a round, conspicuous, compact nest of grass leaf strips, with a long entrance spout, usually on the ends of drooping branches of *Acacia* or palm trees.

BEST VIEWING: widespread in suitable habitats

HOLUB'S GOLDEN WEAVER
Ploceus xanthops kwera manjano mkubwa (Swa)

Habitat: variety of habitats, from dense vegetation to cultivated country, 900–2 300 m **Length:** 18 cm **Status:** locally common resident

A large, thickset, bright yellow weaver with a large, heavy, black bill and pale eyes. The male has an orange wash on throat and chest, the female usually paler overall and lacks the orange wash. Immature resembles female but is duller. Widespread and not gregarious, occurring singly or in pairs. The Orange Weaver (*P. aurantius*) has pale eyes and is smaller (13 cm), has a pale bill and the head is orange-yellow; occurs in lakeside vegetation around the shores of Lake Victoria. The African Golden Weaver (*P. subaureus*) is also smaller (14 cm), with pale red eyes.

BEST VIEWING: widespread in suitable habitats

SPEKE'S WEAVER
Ploceus spekei kwera kifuakahawia (Swa)

Habitat: *Acacia* country, woodlands and cultivated country, 1 200–2 200 m **Length:** 15 cm **Status:** locally common resident

Male has yellow forehead, crown and nape. The back is yellow, with distinctive black markings. Sides of face, chin, throat and bill are black and the eyes are pale. The underside is yellow. Female and immature are olive-brown above with darker mottling, and buffy-white below. Highly gregarious, breeding in dense colonies, often near human habitation. Lesser Masked Weaver (*P. intermedius*) is similar but has a black face mask, which extends over the forehead, and yellow eyes. Vitelline Masked Weaver (*P. vitellinus*) has a yellow-orange crown and red eyes.

BEST VIEWING: widespread in suitable habitats

VILLAGE (BLACK-HEADED) WEAVER
Ploceus cucullatus kwera nguya (Swa); ol-orogos (Maa)

Habitat: open country with scattered trees, woodlands and gardens, sea level to 2 500 m **Length:** 17 cm **Status:** common resident

A large-billed, bright yellow weaver with red eyes and a black mask, which tapers to a point on its chest. Wings are black, with distinct yellow markings. Two distinct races occur. The eastern race has a spotted mantle, while in the western race the mantle is blotched black. Female is olive-brown above, with dusky streaks, yellowish below, and has a yellow stripe above the red eyes. Non-breeding male and female have a greenish-yellow head, red eyes, greyish-olive streaked back, a yellow breast and a whitish belly. Highly gregarious, breeding in colonies, often near human habitation.

BEST VIEWING: widespread in suitable habitat during the rains

RED-HEADED WEAVER
Anaplectes melanotis (*A. rubriceps*)   **yombeyombe mwekundu (Swa)**

Habitat: woodland and *Acacia* bush country, sea level to 2 000 m
Length: 14 cm **Status:** local uncommon resident

A distinctive weaver. Male has a bright crimson-red crown, nape, throat and chest, contrasting with a black face and a red bill. The back, wings and tail are brown, belly white. There is a distinct red panel on the wings. Male in southeastern Tanzania has a red head, with yellow panels on the wing. Female is greyish, with conspicuous red edges to flight feathers (yellow in southeastern Tanzania), a pale pink bill and pale underparts. Builds a distinctive nest of loosely woven twigs, with a long entrance spout, with many projecting ends, suspended from a branch by a woven stem.

BEST VIEWING: widespread

RED-BILLED QUELEA
Quelea quelea   **kwelea domojekundu (Swa)**

Habitat: dry thornbush, grasslands and cultivated land, sea level to 3 000 m **Length:** 13 cm **Status:** locally common resident

Breeding male has a black face and bright red bill, the upperparts are brown and heavily streaked. There is a pinkish wash around the head, shoulders and chest, the underparts are buffy. Non-breeding male lacks the black face but retains the red bill. Female and immature similar to non-breeding male but have a pale eye stripe and red bill. At times highly gregarious. Breeding male Red-headed Quelea (*Q. erythrops*) has a red head, large, dark bill and streaked back. Cardinal Quelea (*Q. cardinalis*) breeding male has a red head but the red extends only to the nape.

BEST VIEWING: widespread

Albert Froneman/IOA

YELLOW BISHOP
Euplectes capensis   **kweche manjano (Swa)**

Habitat: along forest edges, grasslands and cultivated land, sea level to 2 300 m **Length:** 15 cm **Status:** common resident

Breeding male is black, with a conspicuous bright yellow rump, yellow shoulder patches and a short tail. Non-breeding male is brown, heavily streaked, with blackish wings, a blackish tail and the yellow rump and shoulders are much reduced. Female and immature similar to non-breeding male, not so heavily streaked, with brown wings and tail, a paler-yellow rump and without the yellow shoulders. Widespread and common, especially in the highlands. Very conspicuous when breeding, the male flutters from bush to bush with the yellow rump very noticeable.

BEST VIEWING: widespread in suitable habitat, best seen during the rains

Amedeo Buonajuti

RED-COLLARED WIDOWBIRD
Euplectes ardens   **kwelea kisogochekundu (Swa)**

Habitat: grasslands and open bush country, sea level to 3 000 m
Length: 26 cm (♂); 13 cm (♀) **Status:** common resident

Breeding male is all-black, with a red, crescent-shaped patch across the chest, a long tail and a black bill. The red on the chest of breeding male in the Kenya highlands extends onto the nape and crown. But breeding male in western Uganda, Rwanda and Burundi is all-black. Non-breeding males are dusky-brown above, with heavy streaking, wings blackish, below buffy. Female and immature resemble non-breeding male, but have less distinct streaking. Male is conspicuous during the breeding season, when it flutters slowly from bush to bush in display, with the long tail hanging down.

BEST VIEWING: widespread in suitable habitat during the rains

LONG-TAILED WIDOWBIRD
Euplectes progne   kweche mkia-mrefu (Swa)

Habitat: wet grassland and moorland, 1 800–2 800 m
Length: 61–76 cm (♂); 15 cm (♀) **Status:** locally common resident

Unmistakable, male in breeding plumage is all-black with an extremely long, floppy tail, red shoulder patches and a pale bill. Non-breeding male is tawny buff, heavily streaked above, retains red shoulder patches and has a short tail. Female and immature resemble non-breeding male but lack the red shoulder patches. The male displays by flying low over its area with very slow, heavy wing beats and with the tail conspicuously drooped. Male often seen sitting on the top of tall grass stems. Gregarious outside of breeding season. Builds a domed nest close to the ground.

BEST VIEWING: Kenya: Lake Nakuru NP (during the rains)

COMMON WAXBILL
Estrilda astrild   njiri (Swa)

Habitat: lush grasslands and overgrown cultivated land, sea level to 3 000 m **Length:** 10 cm **Status:** common resident

A small brown bird with a conspicuous red bill and a red streak through the eyes. The upperparts are dark brown, with very fine barring, below paler with dusky fine barring and a reddish patch in the centre of belly. Sexes similar; immature is duller than adult and has a brown bill. Occurs in flocks. The similar Crimson-rumped Waxbill (*E. rhodopyga*) also has a red streak through the eye but has a crimson rump and crimson on the wings, and is darker below. The male Black-rumped Waxbill (*E. troglodytes*) is also similar but has a black rump.

BEST VIEWING: widespread in suitable habitats

RED-CHEEKED CORDON-BLEU
Uraeginthus bengalus   njiri buluu shavujekundu (Swa)

Habitat: thornbush, *Acacia* grasslands, forest edges and in gardens, sea level to 2 300 m **Length:** 13 cm **Status:** common resident

A striking azure-blue-and-brown waxbill with a longish blue tail. Male has bright red patches on the cheeks and a dark red bill. Female similar but lacks the red cheek patches. Immature similar to female but a little duller. Widespread and common, found in pairs or family groups. Southern Cordon-bleu (*U. angolensis*) is similar but the male lacks red cheeks. Blue-capped Cordon-bleu (*U. cyanocephalus*) also lacks red cheeks and the male's head is entirely blue. Red-cheeked Cordon-bleu female is similar to the last two species. This species is found in more arid country than the other two.

BEST VIEWING: widespread

PURPLE GRENADIER
Granatina ianthinogaster   njiri mkiamrefu (Swa)

Habitat: semi-arid areas, thickets and bush, below 2 200 m
Length: 13 cm **Status:** common resident

A distinctive-looking, colourful waxbill. The male's head, neck and throat are cinnamon, merging to brown on the back and wings. The eyes are dark, with red eyelids surrounded by a blue patch. The bill is bright red, the rump and uppertail coverts are cobalt-blue and the underparts cobalt-blue with cinnamon splashes. Female has a much reduced blue eye patch and has paler red eyelids; the underparts are russet-brown, with small whitish bars on the flanks. Immature resembles female. Often parasitised by the Straw-tailed Whydah.

BEST VIEWING: widespread in suitable habitats

GREEN-WINGED PYTILIA
Pytilia melba njiri bawakijani (Swa)

Habitat: dry bush, *Acacia* bush and neglected cultivated land, sea level to 1 800 m **Length:** 14 cm **Status:** locally common resident

A distinctive bird, the male has a bright red face and bill, and a crimson rump and tail. The back of head is grey, the wings and back are green. The underparts are grey, with distinct dark barring. Female and immature resemble the male but lack the red face. Widespread but shy, quickly taking cover if disturbed. Occurs in pairs or family groups, in dry bush, *Acacia* bush and neglected cultivated land. The male Orange-winged Pytilia (*P. afra*) has a red face mask and orange-edged wings and is very finely barred below.
BEST VIEWING: widespread in suitable habitats

RED-BILLED FIREFINCH
Lagonosticta senegala bwerenda domojekundu (Swa)

Habitat: grasslands and gardens, sea level to 2 200 m **Length:** 10 cm **Status:** common resident

The male is pinkish-red with small, white dots on the chest. The wings and tail are brown, the vent is grey-brown and the bill is pinkish-red. The eyes are red, surrounded by a thin, yellow eye-ring. Female and immature are duller, with dark eyes surrounded by a pale eye-ring. Found in pairs or family groups. The male African Firefinch (*L. rubricata*) is very similar but has a blue-black bill and black vent. Female similar to female Red-billed, but has a pinkish wash on the chest and belly and a black vent. African Firefinch is shy and found in thickets and overgrown vegetation.
BEST VIEWING: widespread

CUT-THROAT FINCH
Amadina fasciata njiri koodamu (Swa)

Habitat: dry *Acacia* bush country, sea level to 1 300 m **Length:** 10 cm **Status:** locally common resident

A small, speckled, brown bird with a large, heavy bill. Male has a conspicuous, red, crescent-shaped band around the throat and a patch of rufous brown on the belly. Female and immature are paler than the male and lack the red throat and rufous-brown belly. Locally common, it is found mostly in dry *Acacia* bush country. When not breeding, occurs in flocks, often in association with waxbills, particularly at water holes. Although it normally builds its own nest, it often takes over those of other birds, such as Social Weaver.
BEST VIEWING: widespread in suitable habitats

BRONZE MANNIKIN
Spermestes cucullatus chigi madoa (Swa)

Habitat: savanna country, along forest edges, in cultivated land and gardens, sea level to 2 200 m **Length:** 9 cm **Status:** common resident

The head, throat and upper chest are black with a bronzy wash. The mantle and wings are ash-brown and the rump and tail coverts barred black and white. The white lower chest and belly and the barred black-and-white flanks are distinctive. Sexes similar; immature is brown with a black tail. Tame and gregarious. Black-and-white Mannikin (*Lonchura bicolor*) is similar – two distinct races occur in the region: in the west the male has a black head, back, wings and tail, contrasting with a white belly; eastern male has a distinctive bright chestnut back.
BEST VIEWING: widespread in suitable habitats

PIN-TAILED WHYDAH
Vidua macroura   **mzese mweupe, fumbwe (Swa)**

Habitat: grasslands, in cultivated land and gardens, sea level to 3 000 m **Length:** 30–31 cm (♂); 10 cm (♀) **Status:** common resident

The breeding male is unmistakable, with striking black-and-white plumage, a long, thin tail and a red bill. The female and immature are similar to non-breeding male; upperparts brown, with darker streaking and a buffy crown bordered with two black streaks. The female's bill is black when breeding and red when not breeding. The underparts are plain buffy with a blackish bill. Juvenile is plain grey-brown. The breeding male has a very distinctive, jerky display flight. The male Steel-blue Whydah (*V. hypocherina*) is all-blue-black, with a dark grey bill.

BEST VIEWING: widespread in suitable habitat during the rains

EASTERN PARADISE WHYDAH
Vidua paradisaea   **mzese mkiamrefu (Swa)**

Habitat: dry *Acacia* bush and grasslands, sea level to 2 200 m **Length:** 38–41 cm (♂); 13 cm (♀) **Status:** locally common resident

The breeding male is unmistakable, with a long, distinctively shaped, tapering black tail. The head and back are black, separated by a golden-buff collar, and the underparts are pale buffy with a rich chestnut breast. The female and immature are similar to the non-breeding male; buffy above with dark streaks, the top of the head is striped black and white and it is buffy-white below. Male very conspicuous when displaying. Broad-tailed Paradise Whydah (*V. obtusa*) differs in the tail being broader and not tapering to the tip, and has a rufous hindneck.

BEST VIEWING: widespread in suitable habitat during the rains

STRAW-TAILED WHYDAH
Vidua fischeri   **kitongo shingonyeusi (Swa)**

Habitat: dry bush and scrub country, sea level to 2 000 m **Length:** 28 cm (♂); 10 cm (♀) **Status:** locally common resident

The male, in breeding plumage, is unmistakable, with a creamy-coloured crown, breast and belly, which contrast with the rest of upperparts, which are black. It has a bright red bill and distinctive, long-and-thin, straw-coloured central tail feathers. The non-breeding male retains the red bill, is buff-coloured, streaked black and has a short, blackish tail. The female is similar to the non-breeding male; immature resembles the female but is duller and has a dark-coloured bill. Usually occurs in small groups in dry bush and scrub country. Parasitises the Purple Grenadier.

BEST VIEWING: widespread in suitable habitat during the rains

VILLAGE INDIGOBIRD
Vidua chalybeata   **kitongo domojekundu (Swa)**

Habitat: open woodlands, cultivated land and in gardens, sea level to 2 000 m **Length:** 10 cm **Status:** common resident

The breeding male is distinctive, with glossy, all-blue-black plumage, a white bill and bright orange-red legs. Males occurring along the East African coast differ in having red bills. The non-breeding male and female are similar, with dark-streaked upperparts, a broad buff stripe down the centre of the crown and a buffy streak over the eye. The underparts are whitish, with no streaking, and the bill is horn-coloured. Immature and juvenile are similar to non-breeding adults. Variable Indigobird (*V. funerea*) breeding male has purple, blue-black plumage, a white bill and pinkish-white legs.

BEST VIEWING: widespread during the rains

YELLOW WAGTAIL
Motacilla flava   **kiluwiluwi manjano (Swa)**

Habitat: short grasslands, lake shores, open cultivated land, sea level to 3 000 m **Length:** 17–18 cm **Status:** common Palaearctic migrant

A well-known, common, small wagtail. On arrival, its plumage is very variable but underparts usually yellowish. Many males attain their brighter yellow breeding plumage before departing northwards. Up to six races occur in East Africa, ranging from black-headed and blue-grey-headed individuals, to completely yellow-headed ones. All have yellow underparts, olive-green upperparts and a black tail, with white outer tail feathers. Often occur in their thousands, habitually accompanying herds of wildlife.

BEST VIEWING: widespread in suitable habitat; **Kenya:** Masai Mara NR (common); **Tanzania:** Serengeti NP (common)

AFRICAN PIED WAGTAIL
Motacilla aguimp   **kiluwiluwi majumba (Swa); en-kusini (Maa)**

Habitat: widespread in urban areas and countryside, sea level to 3 000 m **Length:** 20 cm **Status:** common resident

Distinctive, black-and-white, with a long tail. Head black, with a broad, white mark over the eye. The wings are black-and-white, and the tail is black, with white outer feathers. Below white, with a broad, black chest band. Sexes similar; immature shorter-tailed and brownish where adult is black. Similar Cape Wagtail (*M. capensis*) is smaller (15 cm), has olive-brown upperparts, a thin, greyish line over the eye and no white on the wings. Mountain Wagtail (*M. clara*) (17 cm) has a distinctively longer tail and a blue-grey back.

BEST VIEWING: widespread

YELLOW-THROATED LONGCLAW
Macronyx croceus   **tokeeo koomanjano (Swa)**

Habitat: grasslands, open country and cultivated land, sea level to 2 300 m **Length:** 20–22 cm **Status:** locally common resident

The bright yellow underparts and the bright yellow throat, encircled by a black band, are distinctive. The back is brown, with darker streaking. Sexes similar but the female is a little duller; immature paler and has a buffy throat and breast. Usually seen fluttering low over the grasslands, when its white-tipped outer tail feathers are conspicuous. The similar Pangani Longclaw (*M. aurantiigula*) has an orange-yellow throat, encircled by a less distinct band and the yellow colour is confined to the belly.

BEST VIEWING: Kenya: Masai Mara NR; **Tanzania:** Serengeti NP; **Uganda:** Queen Elizabeth NP

ROSY-BREASTED (PINK-THROATED) LONGCLAW
Macronyx ameliae   **tokeeo kifuachekundu (Swa)**

Habitat: damp grasslands, 600–2 200 m **Length:** 19–20 cm **Status:** locally common resident

Has salmon-pink-washed underparts and a bright salmon-pink throat, with a broad, black band across the chest. Upperparts are scalloped brown and black. Outer tail feathers are white, best seen in flight. Sexes similar, but the female is paler; the immature shows no pink colouring; both female and immature lack the black chest band. Gives a plaintive call, often when fluttering low over grassland; at this time the legs are often lowered.

BEST VIEWING: during the rain; **Kenya:** Masai Mara NR; **Tanzania:** Serengeti NP

GRASSLAND (AFRICAN) PIPIT
Anthus cinnamomeus   mnaana-mbuga (Swa)

Habitat: grasslands, sea level to 3 400 m **Length:** 15–17 cm
Status: common resident

This small and slender pipit has brown upperparts with darker streaking, particularly on the head and mantle. It has a bold face pattern, with a distinct, buffy line above the eyes and a dark malar stripe. The lower mandible and legs are pinkish. Below is buffy with dark brown streaks on chest, forming a necklace and, in flight, its white outer tail feathers are noticeable. Sexes similar; immature resembles adults. Long-billed Pipit (*A. similis*) is similar, but larger (18 cm); the outer tail feathers are buffy, not white.

BEST VIEWING: Kenya: Masai Mara NR; **Tanzania:** Serengeti NP; **Uganda:** Queen Elizabeth NP

PLAIN-BACKED PIPIT
Anthus leucophrys   mnaana mgongomweupe (Swa)

Habitat: savanna and grassland or other short grass areas, 700–2 200 m **Length:** 17 cm **Status:** locally common

Larger and more robust than the previous species. Upperparts usually uniformly brown but some birds have faint streaking on the back. Face pattern not as bold as Grassland Pipit and the lower mandible is pinkish-yellowish. Underparts paler, with indistinct darker streaking on the breast, and in flight its buffy, not white, outer tail feathers can be seen. Sexes similar; immature resembles adults. Found singly or in pairs, feeding on the ground and often seen sitting on a mound or rocks; has a habit of pumping its tail.

BEST VIEWING: widespread in suitable habitats

AFRICAN CITRIL
Crithagra citrinelloides   chiruku mdogo (Swa)

Habitat: forest edges, open scrub country, neglected cultivated land and gardens, 400–3 300 m **Length:** 11.5 cm **Status:** common resident

Several distinct races occur. The northern male has a black face and a small, yellow stripe above the eye. The western male has a black face, with a distinctive, bright yellow stripe above the eye. The southern male has a greyish face, with no eye stripe. All races have yellow upperparts, with dark streaking, while the rump and belly are yellow. Female lacks the black face of the male and has a yellow throat, with fine blackish streaks. Immature is similar to the female. Found in pairs or small parties in open scrub country, neglected cultivated land and gardens. The male has a sweet whistling song.

BEST VIEWING: widespread in suitable habitats

YELLOW-RUMPED (REICHENOW'S) SEEDEATER
Crithagra reichenowi   chiriku-kenya (Swa)

Habitat: open woodland, grasslands and cultivated land, sea level to 2 000 m **Length:** 11 cm **Status:** common resident

This small, dull seedeater is brown above, with dusky streaking and a distinct broad, pale stripe above the eye. The throat is whitish, the underparts are also whitish with streaks. The rump is bright lemon-yellow and very conspicuous in flight. Sexes similar; immature resembles adults but has a spotted breast. Occurs in pairs or small flocks in open woodland, grasslands and cultivated land. The similar Black-throated Seedeater (*C. atrogularis*) is darker, with a blackish throat and occurs in the west of the region.

BEST VIEWING: widespread in suitable habitats

YELLOW-FRONTED CANARY
Crithagra mozambica   chiruku usonjano (Swa); ol-tinyoie (Maa)

Habitat: open woodlands, scrub, cultivated land and gardens, sea level to 2 300 m **Length:** 11.5 cm **Status:** common resident

Small, brightly coloured, with green-yellow upperparts with dusky streaking. The forehead, throat, belly and rump are bright yellow. Face is yellow, with dark moustache stripes, and a dusky streak through the eyes. Sexes similar; immature resembles adults but is duller. Usually occurs in small flocks. Brimstone Canary (*C. sulphuratus*) is larger (14 cm), has a stouter bill and less distinct facial markings and the greenish rump does not contrast as sharply with the rest of upperparts.

BEST VIEWING: widespread in suitable habitats

WHITE-BELLIED CANARY
Crithagra dorsostriata   chiruku tumojeupe (Swa)

Habitat: dry bush and grasslands, 400–1 800 m, up to 2 650 m in northern Kenya **Length:** 11–12 cm **Status:** locally common resident

Replaces the Yellow-fronted Canary in the drier areas of the region. The upperparts are greenish-yellow, with darker streaking, the throat and chest are yellow and the belly is white. Birds occurring in southern Kenya and Tanzania have a much smaller area of white on the belly. The female and immature are similar to the male but generally duller. Like the Yellow-fronted Canary, has a bright yellow rump but face markings always less distinct. Usually occur in flocks.

BEST VIEWING: widespread in arid habitats

STREAKY SEEDEATER
Crithagra striolata   mpasuambega mchirizi (Swa)

Habitat: highlands, along forest edges, moorlands, scrub, cultivated land and gardens, 1 300–4 300 m **Length:** 14 cm **Status:** common resident

This common highland bird has brown upperparts, with heavy, dark streaking and a conspicuous, white stripe above the eyes. The underparts are buffy, with brown streaking on the throat, breast and flanks. Sexes similar; immature resembles adults but is duller. Occurs in pairs in the highlands. Has a sweet, pleasant song. In the highlands of southern Tanzania a distinctive race, Yellow-browed Seedeater (*C. whytii*), has a bright yellow face and edges to wings; the underparts are paler, with black streaking.

BEST VIEWING: widespread in the highlands

GOLDEN-BREASTED BUNTING
Emberiza flaviventris   kibarabara tumbonjano (Swa)

Habitat: open woodland, savanna and *Acacia* bush, sea level to 2 300 m **Length:** 15 cm **Status:** common resident

A small, long-tailed bird with a conspicuous, black-and-white-striped head, a rich golden breast and a yellow belly. The back is rufous-brown, there are distinctive white bars on the wings and white tips to outer tail feathers. Sexes similar; immature is paler. Usually found singly or in pairs. The similar Somali Golden-breasted Bunting (*E. poliopleura*) best separated by the mantle feathers, which are edged white, and by its white flanks. It also occurs in more arid habitats.

BEST VIEWING: widespread in suitable habitats

REPTILES AND AMPHIBIANS

East Africa is rich in reptiles and amphibians, with more than 420 species each of reptiles and amphibians recorded.

All reptiles are cold-blooded and, while many hibernate during the cool season, some aestivate during the hot dry season. Unfortunately, most reptiles are secretive and are therefore seldom seen but some, such as the agamas, are so brightly coloured and active that they cannot be missed. And, of course, there are few, if any, homes and premises that do not have geckos hunting for insects on the walls at night.

Most snakes are seldom seen: they are nocturnal and they hide in burrows and under rocks and vegetation, avoiding humans if possible. One exception is the highly venomous Puff Adder, which, although mainly nocturnal, can also be found lying curled up in the open. Puff Adders are well camouflaged and slow moving; because they freeze when approached, they are sometimes trodden on by walkers. The Boomslang is diurnal, lives in bushes and trees and can easily be overlooked by walkers in the bush. Luckily, it is not aggressive and will bite only in self-defence.

Always treat snakes with respect; although they don't make unprovoked attacks, they do react if cornered or threatened. If you encounter a snake, back slowly away from it. Be particularly wary of cobras: a Spitting Cobra, if threatened, will rear up and spit its venom into your eyes. If this should happen, quickly wash the eyes with plenty of water or milk and then seek medical help. Never try to kill or harm snakes; they are an indispensible part of the chain of life and help to control the numbers of rodents and other small animals.

Lizards come in many shapes and forms and are generally more easy to spot. The Nile Monitor, although often seen, is shy and usually dashes into the undergrowth or water. Tourists are always interested in chameleons and at many places local people will have captive ones on display; for a small fee one can photograph them. One of the most interesting-looking chameleons is the three-horned Jackson's Chameleon. At most safari lodges and camps agamas have become quite tame and can be easily observed.

Nile Crocodiles enjoy sunning themselves on the banks of rivers and lakes and can be spotted in most wildlife areas.

Only 44 of the more conspicuous reptiles and amphibians are illustrated in this chapter but, for anyone wanting to know more on this fascinating subject, I highly recommend the excellent, small and handy *Pocket Guide to the Reptiles and Amphibians of East Africa* by Stephen Spawls, Kim Howell and Robert C. Drewes (A&C Black Publishers, 2006).

Names used in this chapter follow those in *A Field Guide to the Reptiles of East Africa* by Stephen Spawls, Kim Howell, Robert C. Drewes and James Ash (Academic Press, 2002). Length measurements are taken from tip of nose to tip of tail. Where known, Kiswahili (Swa) and Maasai (Maa) names are included.

LEOPARD TORTOISE
Geochelone pardalis   **mzee kope (Swa); ol-oikuma (Maa)**

Habitat: semi-desert and savanna, 0–1 500 m **Length:** up to 72 cm
Weight: up to 40 kg **Status:** common

The largest land tortoise, it has a dome-shaped, steep-sided
shell. The shell has no serrations around the rim, is yellow with
various black radial patterns. The shells of large, older individuals
are often faded to a uniform brown or grey. The head is blunt-
shaped, with a hooked beak. The legs are very stout; the front
ones, which are covered in three or four rows of overlapping
scales, have five claws, while the rear ones have only four toes.
The undershield of the male is concave.

BEST VIEWING: Kenya: Masai Mara NR; **Tanzania:** Serengeti NP

PANCAKE (FLAT) TORTOISE
Malacochersus tornieri   **kobe, fur gobe (Swa)**

Habitat: rocky hills in savanna country **Length:** up to 22 cm
Status: vulnerable, threatened by collectors, particularly in Tanzania

A small, broad, flat, brown land tortoise with a soft, flexible shell
and a rounded snout. The front feet, which are covered in large
overlapping scales, have five claws, while the rear ones have only
four. Male has longer and thicker tail than female. Able to climb
up quite steep rock faces and hide in cracks, rock fissures and under
boulders. When threatened, able to wedge itself deep into cracks
and cling on with its claws, making it difficult to dislodge.

BEST VIEWING: widespread in suitable habitats

HAWKSBILL TURTLE
Eretmochelys imbricata   **kasa (Swa)**

Habitat: tropical and temperate marine waters, usually close to reefs
Length: up to 90 cm **Weight:** 130 kg **Status:** critically endangered

A small turtle, with a distinctive bird-like beak and an elongated
shell. The shell has beautiful markings; the scales are translucent
amber, marked with radiating red, honey, yellow, black and
brown streaks. The head is yellow, with black blotches in the
centre of the scales. The flippers are also black, with yellow-
edged scales. Male differs from female in having a longer,
narrower shell and a longer tail. Female lays clutches of 50–200
eggs at night, or during daytime if not disturbed; 2–4 clutches
are laid each season. Heavily persecuted for its shell.

BEST VIEWING: in the sea near many East African offshore islands

Reinhard Dirscher/FLPA

HELMETED TERRAPIN
Pelomedusa subrufa   **kasa (Swa)**

Habitat: dams, swamps and small rivers **Length:** up to 30 cm
Weight: up to 2.5 kg **Status:** common resident

A medium-sized, brown terrapin with a flattish shell, which is
is grey-brown but often stained. The head is broad with two
distinctive, pig-like nostrils. The feet are broad and webbed,
with sharp claws. Male has a longer, thicker tail than female,
and larger, narrower, flatter shell. Often found long distances
from water while moving in wet weather, especially after the
first rains of the season. A carnivore, eating insects, tadpoles
and sometimes birds, which it seizes as it drinks. If picked
up, produces foul-smelling liquid from glands on its flanks.

BEST VIEWING: widespread

SERRATED HINGED TERRAPIN

Pelusios sinuatus kasa (Swa)

Habitat: rivers, lakes and water holes **Length:** up to 55 cm
Weight: up to 20 kg **Status:** common resident

A large, dark-coloured, hinged terrapin with distinct serrations on the rear of its shell. Has a distinctive, long neck and a very broad head, with an elongated snout. The legs are broad and the feet are webbed, with sharp claws. Carnivorous, eating mostly molluscs, snails, fish and insects, but will also scavenge for carrion. Usually seen completely out of the water, basking in the sun, on the shoreline or on a rock or a partially submerged tree limb. If picked up, produces foul-smelling liquid from glands on its flanks.

BEST VIEWING: almost everywhere in suitable habitats;
Kenya: Nairobi NP

TROPICAL HOUSE GECKO

Hemidactylus mabouia olbaripo (Maa)

Habitat: almost everywhere, 0–1 700 m **Length:** up to 15 cm
Status: very common resident

The most commonly seen gecko. A medium to large gecko, colour varies from grey to light brown or brown, sometimes spotted; under electric lighting, can look tan or pale pinkish. The back has five wavy crossbars (not always easy to see) and the tail has 10 more distinct crossbars. Although well known around human habitation, it also occurs in loose-barked trees, palms, rock crevices and caves.

BEST VIEWING: close to lights, inside or outside homes

STRIPED SKINK

Trachylepis striata (Mabuya striata) mjusi (Swa)

Habitat: semi-desert, savanna and towns **Length:** up to 25 cm
Status: common resident

A common, medium-sized, mostly brown skink, with two conspicuous cream or yellow stripes from the head to the rear limbs, and white speckles on the flanks. Some individuals are olive or dull green. The length of the tail is just over half the skink's total length, helping to distinguish it from the Variable Skink *(T. varia)*. Female gives birth to up to nine live young. Can be found on buildings, walls and trees; becomes tame and confiding around homes and gardens.

BEST VIEWING: widespread in suitable habitat

JACKSON'S FOREST LIZARD

Adolfus jacksoni mjusi (Swa)

Habitat: highland forest
Length: 25 cm **Status:** common resident in the highlands of Kenya, Tanzania, Uganda, Burundi and Rwanda

A medium-sized lizard, with variable coloration (brown, olive or green) with distinctive spots on the flanks. There is often a brown band on the top of the head that extends along the back to the tail. When warming itself in the sun, often flattens its body and lifts its feet into the air, when its very long toes can be seen. Very active during the day in trees, mainly on the lower branches and the trunk, where it feeds on small insects. Often comes to the ground but never too far from the nearest tree so it can quickly return if disturbed. Lays eggs under bark or in leaf litter.

BEST VIEWING: widespread in suitable habitat

GREAT PLATED LIZARD
Gerrhosaurus major   mjusi (Swa)

Habitat: woodland savanna, 0–1 700 m   **Length:** up to 55 cm
Status: fairly common but shy and difficult to see

A stout, snub-nosed lizard with distinctive ear openings and square body scales. Its large size makes it unmistakable. It has a strong, thick tail, which is 50–60% of the lizard's total length, and short, strong, powerful legs. Colour variable, but mostly warm brown or tan. The western subspecies, *G. m. bottegoi*, is darker and spotted. Female lays a clutch of 2–6 eggs, usually beneath a rock or in a deep, damp hole. Terrestrial, often found on rocks and in rock crevices, at the base of rocky hills or in abandoned termite mounds, where it can often be seen warming itself in the early morning sun.

BEST VIEWING: Kenya: Samburu, Buffalo Springs NRs

BLUE-HEADED TREE AGAMA
Acanthocercus atricollis   balababa (Swa)

Habitat: savanna, woodlands, 0–2 400 m   **Length:** up to 37 cm
Status: common

All agamas have distinctive, large heads, prominent eyes, large ear openings, flattened bodies and long, thin tails. Displaying males of this species have a bright blue or turquoise head and throat. Female and juveniles are mottled brown-rufous, with a black mark on the neck and a line of pale blotches along the spine. Lives in small colonies with a dominant male. Very territorial, the dominant male will challenge and fight any intruding males. Female lays 4–15 eggs, usually in soft soil. Usually found on tree trunks but also occasionally on rocks and termite mounds.

BEST VIEWING: mainly in western Kenya and Uganda

RED-HEADED ROCK AGAMA
Agama agama   balababa (Swa)

Habitat: the coast, dry savanna and semi-desert, 0–2 000 m
Length: up to 35 cm   **Status:** common

A well-known agama. Male has a bright orange head (yellow in northern Kenya) and blue body. Non-displaying males are dull brown, often with a faint, darker marking across the body and speckles of green-yellow on the head. Female and immature are mottled brown with rufous patches, dark marks across the body and speckles of green on the head. Female lays 4–9 eggs. Like the Blue-headed Tree Agama, lives in small colonies with a dominant male. Males usually seen basking on rocks or displaying by bobbing the head up and down.

BEST VIEWING: widespread in suitable habitat

MWANZA FLAT-HEADED AGAMA
Agama mwanzae   balababa (Swa)

Habitat: rocky outcrops in savanna and grassland
Length: up to 32 cm   **Status:** common

Often confused with the Red-headed Rock Agama, but dominant breeding male has pink on the head, back and chest, and a violet or blue-white line along the back. The front legs are blue while the rear ones are green. Non-breeding male is mottled grey with a blue line along the back. Female and juvenile are brown with darker crossbars across the body and a line of paler spots along the back. Legs and tail usually blue. Frequently seen basking on rocks, often a whole colony together with a dominant male.

BEST VIEWING: Kenya: Masai Mara NR; **Tanzania:** Serengeti NP

FLAP-NECKED CHAMELEON
Chamaeleo dilepis   kinyongo (Swa)

Habitat: coastal forest, woodland, savanna and semi-desert
Length: up to 43 cm **Status:** common

A large chameleon with distinctive, small to large ear flaps. Colour very variable, usually green, but can be brown or grey, with a distinctive, white stripe along the flanks. Under the chin and along the back is a line of spiky scales; the orange or yellow colour of the skin between the scales is best seen when the creature is agitated. When it is angry, its body colour darkens and black spots appear. The prehensile tail is usually curled. Usually found in bushes or trees. Female smaller and lays 20–65 eggs in damp soil.

BEST VIEWING: widespread in suitable habitat, particularly in Tanzania

JACKSON'S CHAMELEON
Chamaeleo jacksoni (*Trioceros jacksoni*)   kinyongo (Swa)

Habitat: woodland, forests and gardens, 1 600–2 300 m
Length: up to 38 cm **Status:** common

A distinctive-looking chameleon. Male has three long horns. Female smaller (average 25 cm), with 1–3 short horns, sometimes none. Colour variable; male mostly green, female generally a darker green with darker mottling. Males use horns when fighting other males. Female gives birth to 7–28 live young. Usually found in trees and bushes in central Kenya highlands. The easily confused Usambara Three-horned Chameleon (*C. deremensis*) is smaller, green and has a distinctive sail-like dorsal ridge.

BEST VIEWING: Kenya: forests and gardens around Nairobi;
Tanzania: Meru NP

WHITE-THROATED SAVANNA MONITOR
Varanus albigularis   mburukenge, kenge (Swa)

Habitat: coastal woodland, savanna and semi-desert, 0–1 500 m
Length: up to 1.6 m **Status:** common but shy

Monitor lizards are the world's largest lizards. This species is smaller than the better-known Nile Monitor and usually occurs far from water. It is heavily built, dull grey or brownish, with a distinct blunt, roundish snout. The body has bands of pale spots and the tail is banded. Although mostly terrestrial, will climb trees and rocks. During the dry season may aestivate in a hole and occasionally along a tree branch. Preys on birds and their eggs, small mammals, smaller lizards and tortoises and will eat carrion. Female lays 8–50 eggs in a hole or termite mound.

BEST VIEWING: Kenya: Samburu NR; **Tanzania:** Tarangire NP

NILE MONITOR
Varanus niloticus   mburukenge, kenge (Swa)

Habitat: near fresh-water rivers and lakes, 0–1 600 m
Length: up to 2.5 m **Status:** very common

Not as shy as the White-throated Savanna Monitor, so more readily seen. Mostly grey-green with yellow stripes and spots. Runs fast, climbs trees and is an outstanding swimmer. Uses its tail, not legs, when swimming; can stay underwater for up to 20 minutes. Hunts on the ground or in trees, along the water's edge and in water for a variety of food items such as crabs, slugs, water beetles, frogs, lizards, birds and birds' eggs. Also raids unattended crocodile nests and eats carrion. Female lays 20–60 eggs, often in active termite mounds. Usually seen lying around on rocks or along the water's edge.

BEST VIEWING: Kenya: Lake Baringo, along the shores of Lake Victoria

NILE CROCODILE
Crocodylus niloticus   mamba (Swa)

Habitat: rivers, lakes and dams, 0–1 600 m **Length:** up to 5.5 m
Weight: up to 1 000 kg **Status:** common

Unmistakable, large, some may exceed 5 m in length. Usually brown but can look green if recently emerged from water. A swift swimmer, but can move fast on land too. Large males are territorial. Female smaller than male, excavates nest on elevated sandbanks, above flood level. Lays 20–95 white, hard-shelled eggs, covering them in sand. Carnivorous, hunting fish and mammals in the water, but will also snatch humans and other mammals on the water's edge. Able to stay underwater for up to 45 minutes.

BEST VIEWING: Kenya: Masai Mara NR (Mara River); **Tanzania:** Serengeti NP (Grumeti River); **Uganda:** Murchison Falls NP (River Nile)

SOUTHERN AFRICAN ROCK PYTHON
Python natalensis   chatu (Swa)

Habitat: savanna, grassland and woodlands, 0–2 200 m
Length: up to 5.5 m **Status:** widespread, probably more
common than is generally thought

Large, thickset, powerful snake with a large, triangular head. Has no fangs, so kills by constriction. Colour is a mixture of browns, tan and yellows, with a dark, arrow-shaped mark on the crown. Most common near rivers, lakes and swamps at lower altitudes. Mostly nocturnal; usually in or near water, sometimes in trees. Feeds on mammals as large as Impala. Female lays up to 100 eggs in a pile in an animal burrow and then coils around them for protection until they hatch, 60–85 days later.

BEST VIEWING: widespread, mostly in southern Kenya and Tanzania

CENTRAL AFRICAN ROCK PYTHON
Python sebae   chatu (Swa)

Habitat: savanna, grassland and woodlands, 0–2 200 m
Length: up to 6 m **Status:** common and widespread

Similar to Southern African Rock Python but generally paler, with an arrow-shaped, darker mark on the crown, a yellow stripe through the eye and dark patches in front of and behind the eye. The top of the head is covered in medium to large scales while the Southern African Rock Python has small smooth, scales. This species occurs mostly in Uganda, western areas of Kenya and lower areas of coastal Kenya and Tanzania, while the previous species occurs mostly in Tanzania and southern Kenya.

BEST VIEWING: widespread, mostly occurring in Uganda, Lake Victoria region and coastal Kenya

BROWN HOUSE SNAKE
Lamprophis fuliginosus   nyoka (Swa)

Habitat: forest, woodland and savanna, 0–2 400 m
Length: 50–80 cm but up to 1.2 m **Status:** common

A harmless snake with a triangular head, rather like a python. The colour varies considerably from shades of brown, grey and black to olive. Usually with a pair of pale lines on each side of the head, which sometimes extends down the length of the body. Juvenile occasionally has spotted neck that eventually fades with age. Nocturnal, hunting at night for lizards and small mammals (beneficial to man as it helps to control rodents). Although harmless to humans, it has needle-sharp teeth and can bite if handled. Female lays 2–16 eggs.

BEST VIEWING: almost everywhere apart from northeast Kenya

Leonard Hoffman/IOA

CAPE WOLF SNAKE
Lycophidion capensis nyoka (Swa)

Habitat: grassland and savanna, 0–2 400 m **Length:** up to 60 cm
Status: common

A small snake with a flat head. Colour variable, from brown to grey with distinctive paler-edged scales. Has long teeth, hence its common name. Harmless to humans. Nocturnal, feeding on lizards and other small snakes. Female lays 3–8 eggs.

BEST VIEWING: widespread in suitable habitat

BATTERSBY'S GREEN SNAKE
Philothamnus battersbyi nyoka (Swa)

Habitat: moist savanna and woodland, usually near water
Length: up to 90 cm **Status:** widely distributed

A long, thin, green tree snake with large distinctive, golden-brown eyes. Body bright emerald-green or a duller grey-green. Active during the day, usually in bushes or trees near water, where it waits for prey. Swims well and can hunt underwater. Although harmless to humans, has sharp teeth; when biting, it jerks its head from side to side, causing lacerations. Preys mainly on frogs but also chameleons and lizards. Sometimes confused with the Green Mamba, which has a larger head and is a duller green, with smooth scales and a smaller eye. Female lays 3–11 eggs.

BEST VIEWING: widespread in suitable habitat

SPOTTED BUSH SNAKE
Philothamnus semivariegatus nyoka (Swa)

Habitat: coastal forests, woodlands and thickets, 0–1 500 m
Length: up to 1.3 m **Status:** widely distributed

A large, slim snake with a green body and distinctive black crossbars spaced along its body and black spots on the flanks. Its eyes are large, with a golden-brown iris and a distinctive appearance of a raised eyebrow. Various shades of green; those occurring in southern Tanzania are bronzy towards the tail. Active during the day and, unlike other green snakes, not tied to water. Harmless to humans. Preys mainly on lizards and geckos. Female lays 3–12 eggs.

BEST VIEWING: widespread in suitable habitat

Johan Marais

BOOMSLANG
Dispholidus typus ngole (Swa)

Habitat: semi-desert, savanna and woodland, 0–2 200 m
Length: up to 1.85 m **Status:** fairly common

Although non-aggressive towards humans, this large, back-fanged green tree snake is highly venomous. It has a distinctive, large, egg-shaped head, with very large, yellow, black-veined eyes. Colour variable, male mostly bright green, female grey-brown. Juvenile has a pale stripe along the back, light grey flanks, the head is dark brown above, white below, the eyes are emerald-green. Hunts during the day in trees and bushes, but will descend to the ground to cross open areas. Most common prey are chameleons and agamas. Female lays up to 25 eggs in a tree hollow or in damp vegetation.

BEST VIEWING: widespread in suitable habitat

Johan Marais

OLIVE (HISSING) SAND SNAKE
Psammophis mossambicus   nyoka (Swa)

Habitat: savanna, woodland and riverine areas in semi-desert,
0–1 300 m **Length:** up to 1.7 m **Status:** common

Although a back-fanged venomous snake, its bite is not life-
threatening to humans. A large, brown snake with a rounded
snout, big eyes and black-edged scales. Hunts by day, mainly on
the ground but also in trees, preying on lizards, small snakes,
rodents, frogs and birds. Female lays up to 30 eggs in a tree
hole or damp vegetation.

BEST VIEWING: widespread in suitable habitat

Johan Marais

COMMON EGG-EATER
Dasypeltis scabra   nyoka (Swa)

Habitat: semi-desert, savanna, woodlands and forests, 0–2 600 m
Length: up to 1.1 m **Status:** widely distributed

A harmless, slim snake with a blunt, bullet-shaped head and small
but prominent eyes with vertical slits. Usually brown or grey,
with dark or pale, distinctive markings along the back; the inside
of the mouth is black. Nocturnal, searching on the ground or in
trees and bushes for birds' eggs. When threatened, moves body in
a series of C-shaped coils, rubbing the coils together to produce a
hissing sound. Similar in appearance to the smaller (up to 70 cm),
dangerous Northeast African Carpet Viper (*Echis pyramidum*),
which also has the C-coil threat display. Lays up to 28 eggs.

BEST VIEWING: widespread in suitable habitat

Chris & Mathilde Stuart

EAST AFRICAN GARTER SNAKE
Elapsoidea loveridgei   nyoka (Swa)

Habitat: moist grassland, savanna and woodland, 600–2 200 m
Length: up to 65 cm **Status:** widely distributed

A short-headed, glossy black, distinctive snake with 19–36
narrow, white, yellow or white-edged pink bands. Sometimes
the centre of the bands is dark, the bands becoming white
rings. Nocturnal, hunts for other snakes, lizards, frogs and small
rodents. Non-aggressive and its bite is not lethal.

BEST VIEWING: widespread in suitable habitat

Steve Spawls

EGYPTIAN COBRA
Naja haje   swila, ita, kimbubu (Swa)

Habitat: grassland, savanna and woodland, 1 000–1 600 m
Length: up to 2.5 m **Status:** widely distributed

A very large, broad-headed, thick-bodied, venomous snake.
Colour, brown-rufous above, creamy-yellow below, with dark
bar across the throat; juvenile is paler. Hunts both during the
day and at night for small mammals, frogs, toads, eggs, as well
as other snakes. Hides in termite mounds and among rocks. If
molested, will rear up and spread its hood, may rush forward and
strike. This cobra does not spit venom but a bite can be fatal. The
female lays up to 20 eggs.

BEST VIEWING: widespread in suitable habitat

Steve Spawls

BLACK-NECKED SPITTING COBRA
Naja nigricollis   swila, ita, kimbubu (Swa)

Habitat: coastal thickets, savanna and open woodland, 0–1 800 m
Length: up to 2.7 m **Status:** common

This large, thick-bodied cobra occurs in two distinct forms. One is brown-olive or grey, usually with a dark bar across the throat, and can grow up to 2.7 m. The other is smaller, up to 2 m in length, and darker, usually black, grey or coppery, with a pinkish bar across the throat. All black forms occur in western Kenya. Although mainly terrestrial, does climb trees. Hunts for frogs, birds, small rodents, snakes and lizards. If molested, rears up, spreads its hood and spits venom accurately, up to 3 m, into the eyes of the aggressor. The bite from this cobra can be fatal. Female lays up to 22 eggs.

BEST VIEWING: widespread in suitable habitat

Chris & Mathilde Stuart

BLACK MAMBA
Dendroaspis polylepis   nyoka (Swa)

Habitat: forest, savanna and woodland, 0–1 600 m
Length: up to 3.2 m **Status:** widely distributed

A very large, slender snake with a 'coffin-shaped' head. Colour not black, despite its name, but varies from brown, to olive and dark grey; sometimes has black speckles towards the end of the tail. Its name probably comes from the fact that the inside of its mouth is black. Can be found on the ground, among rocks, or climbing trees, where it hunts for small mammals, birds and other snakes. Males often wrestle with one another. A bite from this snake can be fatal. Female lays up to 17 eggs.

BEST VIEWING: widespread in suitable habitat

Steve Spawls

VELVETY-GREEN NIGHT ADDER
Causus resimus   nyoka (Swa)

Habitat: coastal thickets, savanna and woodland, 0–2 000 m
Length: up to 75 cm **Status:** widely distributed

A small, bright green snake with a short head and round, yellow eyes. Some individuals have a black, V-shaped mark on the head and scattered black blotches on the body. In spite of its name, active by day and night, hunting for frogs and toads. If molested, may rear up, inflate its body and make hissing and puffing sounds. Strangely, there are no recorded bites by this snake. Venom of other night adders painful but not deadly. Female lays up to 11 eggs.

BEST VIEWING: widespread in suitable habitat

Leonard Hoffman/IOA

PUFF ADDER
Bitis arietans   bafu, moma (Swa)

Habitat: all habitats, 0–2 400 m **Length:** 0.7–1 m, but can be up to 1.9 m **Status:** common

Africa's most dangerous snake. A big, squat snake with a broad, triangular head, which has a distinctive pale line between the eyes. Colour very variable: brown, green, grey or orange, with chevron patterns on its back. Nocturnal, usually hiding in thick vegetation during the daytime. Hunts by ambushing small mammals. Because of its remarkable camouflage, it is often trodden on by herders and their stock. A bite from this snake can be fatal. An angry Puff Adder inflates its body and hisses loudly, hence its name. Female gives birth to 10–50 live young.

BEST VIEWING: semi-desert where there is less cover

GUTTURAL (AFRICAN COMMON) TOAD
Amietophrynus gutturalis   chura (Swa)

Habitat: savanna **Length:** up to 90 mm (♂); up to 120 mm (♀)
Status: common in Tanzania and southern Kenya

A stocky, brown or grey toad with dark-edged blotches on its back.
Has large, obvious glands behind the eyes. Often found feeding on
insects attracted to house lights. If molested, can release a thick,
sticky, white secretion, which is lethal to most predators, although
Civet and some snakes seem to be immune. Males gather around
the edges of ponds, where they make loud and reverberating calls.
They mate as the females enter the water. Many eggs are deposited
in long strings of jelly. Tadpoles are small and black.

BEST VIEWING: widespread in suitable habitat

RED-BACKED TOAD
Schismaderma careens   chura (Swa)

Habitat: savanna and miombo woodland **Length:** up to 90 mm (♀)
Status: common

An unmistakable large toad with a rusty-coloured back, with two
small, dark, rounded marks on it. The rest of the body is creamy-
white or grey. Breeds in seasonal pools, even those that have been
fouled by large animals. The male, which is slightly smaller than
the female, makes loud, cow-like mooing sounds, which can be
heard a long distance away. The tadpoles are black and form large
masses in the water.

BEST VIEWING: widespread in suitable habitat

Louis du Preez

MARBLED SNOUT-BURROWER
Hemisus marmoratus   chura (Swa)

Habitat: grassland savanna and woodland **Length:** 22 mm (♂);
34 mm (♀) **Status:** common

An unmistakable frog with a flat, triangular snout, which is
used for digging. The round, squat body is grey or brown with
darker spots. Some individuals have a pale line running down
the back. The female digs a burrow, where it mates and deposits
its eggs. The burrow may be some distance from water and, if
rising waters fail to reach it, the female carries the tadpoles to
the nearest water.

BEST VIEWING: widespread in suitable habitat

Louis du Preez

BOCAGE'S BURROWING TREE FROG
Leptopelis bocagii   chura (Swa)

Habitat: grassland and savanna **Length:** 50 mm (♂); 58 mm (♀)
Status: widely distributed

A large, stout frog with distinctive cat-like vertical pupils and
enlarged toe tips. Pale brown with an M-shaped mark on its back.
Breeding pairs dig a hole near water or in a depression, which will
become flooded, where the female lays her eggs.

BEST VIEWING: widespread in suitable habitat

Alan Channing

Alan Channing

SHARP-NOSED TREE FROG
Hyperolius nasutus   chura (Swa)

Habitat: reeds and grassy open areas in savanna **Length:** c. 25 mm
Status: common

A tiny reed frog with a distinctive, sharp, elongated nose. A light, translucent green, with two narrow, darker-edged pale stripes running along both sides of the body, from the nose to rear leg. Some have a dark stripe running down the middle of the back. The call of this tree frog is described as '*ziiip ziiip ziiip*'. Female lays about 200 eggs, which are attached to submerged vegetation.

BEST VIEWING: widespread in suitable habitat

Leonard Hoffman/IOA

COMMON REED FROG
Hyperolius viridiflavus   chura (Swa)

Habitat: pools and marshes in savanna **Length:** up to 33 mm
Status: very common

A very common reed frog with distinctively variable colours in the region. *H. glandicolor ferniquei*, occurring in the Masai Mara and Serengeti, is pale with tiny dots all over the body and pink toes. *H. mariae*, which occurs along the East African coast, is pale brown with yellow markings on the back. All make the distinctive, well-known metallic '*tink tink*' call. Female lays eggs on submerged vegetation in the water.

BEST VIEWING: widespread in suitable habitat

Steve Turner

SENEGAL KASSINA
Kassina senegalensis   chura (Swa)

Habitat: wet areas in savanna **Length:** c. 42 mm **Status:** common

Sometimes called Running Frog after its habit of running rather than leaping. It is terrestrial. Colour silver-grey to gold-brown, with dark, pale-edged blotches. Males make their wonderful, musical, liquid '*boink*' call from overhanging vegetation or on the ground near the water's edge. Female lays up to 200 eggs attached to floating vegetation.

BEST VIEWING: widespread in suitable habitat

David Elsworthy

SOUTHERN FOAM-NEST FROG
Chiromantis xerampelina   chura (Swa)

Habitat: coastal woodland **Length:** up to 42 mm (♂); up to 65 mm (♀)
Status: locally common

A grey or tan-coloured frog with distinctive webbing between its toes. Turns chalky white in sunlight. Often found sitting exposed in the hot sun, which no other African frog can do. Female deposits its eggs in foam nests, which it constructs in vegetation overhanging water. The foam hardens overnight and 6–8 days later the foam decomposes and the tadpoles drop into the water below. The Northern Foam-nest Frog (*C. petersi*) is larger, female up to 92 mm, and inhabits more arid areas.

BEST VIEWING: East African Coast; **Kenya:** Tsavo East, Tsavo West NPs

GALAM WHITE-LIPPED FROG
Hylarana galamensis (Amnirana galamensis)   chura (Swa)

Habitat: permanent ponds and pools in woodland and savanna
Length: c. 77 mm (♂); c. 85 mm (♀) **Status:** locally common

A large frog with distinctive, long, unwebbed front toes. The rear toes are also long, but webbed. Pale brown with a broad, golden stripe along the body; this stripe may sometimes be speckled black. The contrasting pale lips are diagnostic. The Forest White-lipped Frog (*H. albolabris*) is darker brown above with darker blotches, has distinctive longitudinal skin folds and the toe tips are large and round. Occurs in moist forest in western Kenya and Uganda.

BEST VIEWING: widespread in suitable habitat

Alan Channing

MASCARENE ROCKET FROG
Ptychadena mascareniensis   chura (Swa)

Habitat: near water in savanna and woodland **Length:** 43–57 mm (♂); 43–68 mm (♀) **Status:** common

Rocket frogs get their name from their jumping ability: they can jump 3 m or more in one jump. This species is brown or greyish-brown, usually with a green, yellow or brown line running down the centre of the back. There is also a pale line on the rear legs. Males make a duck-like clucking call. Has the distinction of being the only frog species that occurs both on Madagascar (which has perhaps twice as many frog species as Africa) and on the African mainland.

BEST VIEWING: widespread in suitable habitat

Louis du Preez

EDIBLE BULLFROG
Pyxicphalus edulis   chura (Swa)

Habitat: low-altitude woodland and grassland **Length:** up to 105 mm (♂); up to 120 mm (♀) **Status:** common

A large, fat, broad-headed frog with large, prominent eyes and a wide mouth. Colour usually olive to dark green, occasionally brown; the back has short folds and bumps. Breeding male brighter than female. Active during the day. Bullfrogs bury themselves during the dry season and secrete a cocoon around themselves (they have been reputed to emerge as much as seven years later). After rainstorms, they emerge and immediately start calling and breeding in temporary pools. As the name *edulis* implies, they are eaten in parts of the region.

BEST VIEWING: eastern areas of the region

Louis du Preez

LAKE VICTORIA CLAWED FROG
Xenopus victorianus   chura (Swa)

Habitat: dry woodland and forests **Length:** 78 mm (♂); 60 mm (♀) **Status:** locally common

A large, unmistakable, dark frog with long, clawed feet. Colour variable, olive-green to yellowish-green with small dark spots and blotches on the back. The eyes are distinctive: they are small and on the top of the head. Spends virtually its whole life in water but can survive droughts by burrowing into the mud. Often found in very dirty water such as watering holes. Males make a series of '*drick drick drick*' calls.

BEST VIEWING: areas east of Lake Victoria

Alan Channing

INSECTS

There are roughly one million known insect species on Earth, with more being discovered all the time. This wealth of insect life is under constant threat, however, due to habitat destruction and other interferences by humans. These threats to our planet's insect species are unfortunate, given the vital roles that many play in different ecosystems. Many insects are important pollinators of plants; most species are harmless and beneficial. However, some, such as mosquitoes, are harmful as they transmit diseases both to man and other animals, while others, such as locusts and termites, destroy crops.

Some of the better-known insects, and possibly the most beautiful, are butterflies. There are more than 3 000 butterfly species in Africa, which is eight times more than in Europe and, of these, at least 900 occur in East Africa. There are four stages in the life cycle of a butterfly: egg, caterpillar, chrysalis and adult. The duration of each stage varies according to species and location. In Africa, a species might be in the egg stage for a mere three days, caterpillar stage for eight and a chrysalis for seven days. Its lifespan as an adult butterfly depends on the species; some can live a whole year and will aestivate during the hot dry season. Although there are no moths featured in this book, some are just as beautiful as butterflies and can easily be confused with them. While most moths fly at night, some also fly during the daytime. Most moths have fat, furry bodies, but so do some butterflies. The safest way to distinguish between them is by their antennae: a moth's antennae are generally feathered and have pointed or blunt ends, while butterflies have antennae with thickened or clubbed ends.

Unfortunately, there are no guidebooks available on East African insects, but Mike Picker, Charles Griffiths and Alan Weaving's *Field Guide to Insects of South Africa* and Steve Woodhall's *Field Guide to Butterflies of South Africa* are useful reference works for this region too.

DRAGONFLIES/DAMSELFLIES
Order Odonata

Habitat: near fresh water **Size:** wingspan 2–6 cm **Status:** common

Members of a very large and varied order. Dragonflies and damselflies are both carnivorous predators, preying on other insects, such as mosquitoes and flies. They have large eyes and short antennae. Dragonflies are more strongly built and fast flying; damselflies are smaller and more slender. At rest, dragonflies hold their wings at right angles to their bodies, while damselflies fold their wings along their bodies. Both breed in water. Eggs are laid in slits in green trees or bushes hanging over water. When the eggs hatch, tiny nymphs drop in the water, where they stay until they are ready to change into winged adults.

BEST VIEWING: at almost all fresh-water sites

PRAYING MANTIDS
Family Mantidae

Habitat: bushes, trees and gardens **Size:** 1.5–15 cm **Status:** common

Mantids have hardened forewings; the hind legs are not developed for jumping. They are usually green, brown or brightly coloured, with frilly protuberances to blend in with their surroundings, and large, distinctive eyes. Brightly coloured ones are normally found in flowers. Carnivorous mantids, with their good camouflage, lie in wait for their prey (insects and small vertebrates). They use their front legs to capture and hold prey while they devour it. This is often the fate of male mantids, which are often eaten by the females. Females lay around 60 eggs in a foamy mass, on grasses and plants.

BEST VIEWING: almost everywhere in vegetation

Leonard Hoffman/IOA

GRASSHOPPERS/LOCUSTS
Order Orthoptera

Habitat: grasslands **Size:** 7 mm–10 cm **Status:** at times very common, especially during rains

Members of a huge order, these insects usually have two pairs of wings, the forepair of which are thickened and protective; in some forms the wings are much reduced or even absent. The hindlegs are well developed and are used for jumping. Makes a distinctive noise by rubbing the hindlegs against the wings. These insects form three groups: short-horned grasshoppers (including locusts), long-horned grasshoppers (which have long antennae and are usually leaf-like) and crickets and mole-crickets (which live underground).

BEST VIEWING: almost anywhere

STICK INSECTS
Order Phasmatodea

Habitat: mostly found in grasslands **Size:** 1–25 cm **Status:** common but can be difficult to spot

Another large order, its members are mostly small and resemble twigs or dry grass stems. Most have inconspicuous wings. Although very similar to Mantids, they are not related. Most cannot fly or jump, so rely on their camouflage for safety, remaining motionless if disturbed. Some species have wings that can be used for flight or in a defensive display if threatened, and some perform a rocking movement when disturbed. Nocturnal vegetarians.

BEST VIEWING: almost anywhere where there is vegetation

AFRICAN MONARCH/COMMON TIGER
Danaus chrysippus

Habitat: throughout the region, except forest interiors
Size: wingspan 8–10 cm **Status:** common

Very conspicuous butterfly with orange-brown wings bordered with black and white. The black body is covered in distinctive, white spots. Sexes similar; male differs only in having a black spot in the middle of each hindwing. This butterfly is closely associated with plants such as Milkweed (*Gomphocarpus fruticosus*); its larva feeds on it, making the larva and the butterfly poisonous and unpalatable. Other butterflies, such as the female Diadem, mimic the Monarch to keep them safe from predation. A slow, lazy flyer. Roosts in long grass, often in clusters.

BEST VIEWING: widespread in suitable habitat

AFRICAN BLUE TIGER
Tirumala petiverana

Habitat: widespread **Size:** wingspan 6–8 cm **Status:** common

A large, unmistakable butterfly. Wings dark blue, with numerous pale spots, body black with white spots. Sexes are alike. Like the monarchs, this butterfly is poisonous, so safe from predation. Sometimes seen at damp mud or mammal droppings. Males often found at food plants containing toxic alkaloids, which are often poisonous to animals and are used as a defence against predators. At times, large numbers gather on flowering *Acacia* trees. Takes part in mixed migrations.

BEST VIEWING: widespread in suitable habitat

LAYMAN
Amauris albimaculata

Habitat: forests but occasionally found in open country
Size: wingspan 7.8–8.2 cm **Status:** common

The forewings are blackish with white spots, while the hindwing has a pale buffish patch and a row of small white dots. Body is black with distinct white spots. Female is similar to and mimics the female Mocker Swallowtail. Although primarily a forest-dwelling butterfly, it often can be found in open country when attracted to flowers. In forests, usually flies high, with a slow, floating flight but comes down lower when feeding on flowers, animal dung and damp patches.

BEST VIEWING: widespread in suitable habitat

FRIAR
Amauris niavius

Habitat: open forests and neglected cultivated land
Size: wingspan 7.8–8.5 cm **Status:** common

A large butterfly with black wings with distinctive, white markings. The black body has white spots. Female duller than male. This butterfly is mimicked by a number of other species, such as Mocker Swallowtail. Although a forest species, it can be found along riverine vegetation in savannas. One of the plants it feeds on is *Heliotropium indicum*, which contains pyrrolizidine alkaloids, making the butterfly poisonous and bitter tasting. Also feeds on flowers and visits mammal droppings and carrion. Flight slow and lazy, relying on its toxicity for protection.

BEST VIEWING: widespread in suitable habitat

WANDERING DONKEY
Acraea neobule

Habitat: widespread but avoids forests **Size:** wingspan 4.8–5.6 cm
Status: common

The most common and widespread member of the *Acraea* genus. *Acraea* butterflies are toxic and, when attacked or handled, they release a honey-coloured liquid that contains cyanide. The extensive transparent areas in the forewing of this species are distinctive, as is the black, white-spotted body. The hindwing is orange with black dots and is edged with a black band with orange dots. Female similar, usually paler. This butterfly has adapted well to habitats changed by man. Low-flying, usually found feeding on flowers, particularly on flowering *Acacia* trees.

BEST VIEWING: widespread in suitable habitat

WHITE-BARRED CHARAXES
Charaxes brutus

Habitat: forests and forest edges **Size:** wingspan 6–9 cm
Status: common

A dark butterfly with a distinctive, white band that crosses both pairs of wings. Sexes similar but female has broader white band. There are two pointed tails on each hindwing. A strong flyer, usually occurring in treetops, but descends to the ground to settle on muddy patches, animal droppings, carrion or rotting fruit; rarely visits flowers. Aggressive, will chase other butterflies, flying insects and even birds out of its area.

BEST VIEWING: widespread in suitable habitat

Dino Martins

GREEN-VEINED EMPEROR
Charaxes candiope

Habitat: occurs almost everywhere except arid areas in the north of the region **Size:** wingspan 6.5–9.5 cm **Status:** one of the most common *Charaxes*

A large honey-coloured butterfly with green veins and green leading edge of the wings. Sexes similar. Hindwings have two tails; the female's are both the same length, while the male's upper tail is shorter than the lower one. Like other *Charaxes*, strongly territorial, frequently chasing intruders. Males spend most of the time in treetops or forest canopies, while females are usually found closer to food. At times a long-distance migrant.

BEST VIEWING: widespread in suitable habitat

Dino Martins

GUINEAFOWL
Hamanumida daedalus

Habitat: savanna and forests, up to 3 000 m **Size:** wingspan 5.5–7.8 cm
Status: common

A distinctive and unmistakable butterfly. Brownish, with tiny, black-edged white spots. Sexes similar. Its flight is always just above ground level, hugging the contours of the land. Although found mainly in savannas, it also occurs in forests, where it keeps to pathways, often settling with wings open. In dry savannas it can be seen drinking at water holes.

BEST VIEWING: widespread in suitable habitat

Brian Finch

DIADEM
Hypolimnas misippus

Habitat: widespread **Size:** wingspan 6–8 cm; female larger than male
Status: common

A black butterfly with two bold, pale blotches on the upperwing and a large, pale patch on the underwing. These blotches are edged blue-purple. The female is very different, being an almost perfect mimic of the common African Monarch, only differing by lacking the hindwing spots. Males are pugnacious with a strong, fast flight; female's flight is more leisurely. Feeds on flowers, mammal droppings and is often found at damp patches. A common butterfly in Africa and India. Has been recorded almost 1 000 km off the coast of Angola.

BEST VIEWING: widespread in suitable habitat

FOREST MOTHER-OF-PEARL
Protogoniomorpha parhassus (*Salamis parhassus*)

Habitat: forests but occasionally savanna **Size:** wingspan 6.5–9 cm
Status: common

A large, distinctive, spectacular forest butterfly. Its shining mother-of-pearl colour changes from white to rose to pearl in different lights. Wings have dark spots, tips of forewings are dark tips, hindwings have small eyespots. Sexes similar but female less shiny and sometimes yellowish. Its flight is light and dancing, often high. Frequently found at damp patches in the forest. Can also be found resting among foliage. The similar Clouded Mother-of-Pearl (*Protogoniomorpha anacardii*) is smaller and less shiny and has black wing tips.

BEST VIEWING: most East African forests

YELLOW PANSY
Junonia hierta (*Precis hierta*)

Habitat: dry country grasslands and gardens **Size:** wingspan 4–5 cm
Status: fairly common

This family of small butterflies is very active and has a powerful flight. An attractive small, straw-coloured and black butterfly, with bright blue spots on the hindwings; females similarly coloured, but darker, and some lack the blue spots. It cannot be confused with any other species. Migratory, often a member of mixed species migrating during the rainy season. Attracted to flowers, particularly *Lantana* and flowering *Acacia* trees, and often found on damp earth. Often settles on the ground with open wings.

BEST VIEWING: in the Rift Valley when *Acacia* trees in flower

DARK BLUE PANSY
Junonia oenone (*Precis oenone*)

Habitat: highlands, savanna and forests **Size:** wingspan 4–5.2 cm
Status: common

A dark, mainly velvety-black butterfly with large, distinctive, blue patches on the hindwings and a broken white line along the outer edge. There are white spots on the dark forewings. Both forewings and hindwings have two eyespots. Female similar, but generally paler, and some may lack the blue spots. Attracted to flowers, particularly flowering *Acacia* trees, and often found in gardens feeding on flowers.

BEST VIEWING: gardens and flowering *Acacia* trees

SOLDIER PANSY
Junonia terea (Precis terea)

Habitat: widely distributed, prefers forest edges
Size: wingspan 5–6 cm **Status:** common

A widely distributed and common butterfly in East Africa, with two subspecies. Brown with a yellowish-brown band across all wings. In the western subspecies these bands are broad, while in the eastern subspecies the bands are much narrower. There are a number of small eyespots in the hindwing. Often feeds on garden flowers, settling on low foliage. Males patrol forest paths and clearings, often feeding on dung.

BEST VIEWING: flower gardens in the region

PAINTED LADY
Cynthia cardui (Vanessa cardui)

Habitat: almost any habitat **Size:** wingspan 4–5 cm
Status: at times very common

Should not be confused with any other East African butterfly. Wings are orange with black markings and white spots. At the outer edge of both wings is a narrow black-and-white band; the hindwing also has three rows of black spots. When the wings are closed a row of eyespots are visible on the hindwing. With wings closed this butterfly is well camouflaged. Sexes similar. Basks with the wings held open. A very common butterfly, found all over the world. In other parts of the world it is migratory, but this is rarely observed in Africa.

BEST VIEWING: flower gardens in the region

DIMORPHIC ADMIRAL
Antanartia dimorphica

Habitat: highland forest edges **Size:** wingspan 4.4–5 cm
Status: common

Very similar to the European Admiral. Forewings blackish with a dark orange band and a few small, pale orange spots on the outer forewing. Fast-flying, likes to feed on flowers but also attracted to dung and other bad-smelling items. The outer edges of the hindwings have dark orange bands, also a false eye and a short tail.

BEST VIEWING: highland glades, grasslands and forest edges

LARGE ORANGE TIP
Colotis antevippe

Habitat: savanna **Size:** wingspan 4–4.5 cm **Status:** common

The various Orange Tips are the most common butterflies in East Africa. Most are white, with distinctive orange/red-marked tips on the forewing. Many show seasonal variation, in the dry season being duller above and more camouflaged on the underside. Male white, with black-edged, orange wing tips. There is a small distinctive white spot on the forewing. Hindwings are white with black markings along the edges. Female similarly marked, but much duller, and some individuals lack orange wing tips. Large numbers live in colonies but males are known to travel long distances.

BEST VIEWING: widespread in suitable habitat

Brian Finch

SCARLET TIP
Colotis danae

Habitat: throughout region, except forests **Size:** wingspan 3.5–5.5 cm
Status: common

The most common and widespread *Colotis* butterfly. A beautiful white butterfly, with black-edged, bright-scarlet wing tips. A small, distinctive, black spot on the forewing. Hindwings are white with black markings along the edges. Female lacks the scarlet tips and has darker markings. In the dry season many are reddish-brown below and often settle among dry grasses and leaves. A nectar feeder, rarely found at damp patches. It has a lively, dancing flight. During hot days many can be found resting in the shade.

BEST VIEWING: widespread and common in suitable habitat

MIGRATORY BUTTERFLY/BROWN-VEINED WHITE
Belenois aurota

Habitat: savanna and open forests **Size:** wingspan 4–5 cm
Status: common

A small, white butterfly with blackish-brown wing markings. Hindwings have a yellow-orange tinge. Female similar to male but duller, with less defined markings. Veins on the underside of hindwings are underlined in black. Often migrates in large numbers, has a fast, direct flight. Very fond of flowers, particularly Cornflower (*Vernonia glabra*), and is attracted to damp places and buffalo droppings.

BEST VIEWING: almost anywhere

AFRICAN MIGRANT
Catopsilia florella

Habitat: forest edges, gardens and savanna **Size:** wingspan 5.4–6.6 cm
Status: common throughout the region

A migratory white butterfly. Strong-flying, with a distinctive wing shape. Male white with a thin black edging on the forewing, female duller white but may be bright yellow with pale brown spots. Its flight is fast, often above the ground, visits flowers; males are mud-puddlers. Attracted by flowers. Migrates in large numbers, often with other butterflies.

BEST VIEWING: common and widespread in suitable habitat

COMMON GRASS YELLOW
Eurema hecabe

Habitat: found in most habitats apart from forests
Size: wingspan 3.2–4.2 cm **Status:** common

Grass Yellows are common small butterflies, of which there are nine species in Africa; all have a weak flight. Male of this species deep yellow with blackish forewing tips. Female more variable, with paler and less distinct markings. Usually found fluttering among the undergrowth, often roosts in small clusters at night. Attracted to flowers and damp patches.

BEST VIEWING: almost anywhere

MOCKER SWALLOWTAIL/FLYING HANDKERCHIEF
Papilio dardanus

Habitat: forests, along riverine vegetation in savannas, and gardens
Size: wingspan 8–11 cm **Status:** common

One of Africa's most abundant and widespread Swallowtails. A large species, male mainly cream-coloured with black markings and distinctly tailed. Sometimes known as Flying Handkerchief as it is usually seen flying swiftly along forest edges. Female very different, with no tails, and mimics other butterflies, such as Friar and African Monarch; these butterflies are toxic to birds and lizards, protecting them from attack, especially during egg-laying, when they are vulnerable. This species often migrates with other species. Hovers over flowers with quivering wings when feeding.
BEST VIEWING: widespread in suitable habitat

CITRUS BUTTERFLY (SWALLOWTAIL)
Papilio demodocus

Habitat: widespread in the region, often in gardens
Size: wingspan 10–13 cm **Status:** common

A member of the Swallowtail family, although it has no tail. Swallowtails are common large impressive butterflies. The Citrus Butterfly is perhaps Africa's best-known butterfly. Dark brown, with yellow markings and two colourful eyes on the hindwing. Sexes alike, but males often has deeper-coloured spots. Visits gardens, where it feeds on flowers and regularly visits damp patches and elephant dung. Often takes part in migrations with other species. The larvae feed on cultivated citrus trees, hence the common name.
BEST VIEWING: any flower garden in the region

NOBLE SWALLOWTAIL
Papilio nobilis

Habitat: forests and forest edges, occasionally gardens
Size: wingspan 8–11 cm **Status:** common

An unmistakable, striking-looking, golden-yellow butterfly with a pale brown wing marking. Sexes very similar. Flight is usually high but does visit flowers, especially in the early morning. At times males disperse from their forest habitats and can be found far away, including gardens in Nairobi.
BEST VIEWING: Kenya: Masai Mara NR (along the Mara River)

GREEN BANDED SWALLOWTAIL
Papilio phorcas

Habitat: forests **Size:** wingspan 7.5–9.5 cm
Status: widespread and common

A blue-green and black swallowtail. Female has two forms: the more common is similar to the male; the other is dark brown with yellow markings. Often visits mammal dung and decomposing vegetation and, in the cool highlands, often found sitting on low vegetation in the morning, with wings open until it is warm enough to fly.
BEST VIEWING: widespread in suitable habitat

TREES AND SHRUBS

East Africa has well over 1 000 tree species, including shrubs and lianas. This chapter features only 92 of the more common ones but also includes 11 exotic species. The exotic species such as Jacaranda and Flamboyant are common and often planted because they are attractive but some, such as the many *Eucalyptus* species, are planted for timber.

A tree can be loosely defined as a perennial woody plant with a single trunk growing taller than 2 m and branches that continue to grow during the life of the plant. Although most of our trees conform to that description, there are many, mostly in arid areas, that branch at almost ground level but are still considered trees. Trees are under attack from many fronts: the ever-increasing rural population needs trees for cooking, large areas of forests are being destroyed for timber and/or development, and climate change is affecting their well-being. Trees are a national heritage and belong to everyone and their protection and conservation should have the highest priority with the region's governments.

The photographs of each species mostly show their leaves and/or flowers, unless the tree has a unique shape, such as the Baobab. In the description, the bark, leaves, flowers and fruits are described, as is the habitat, the altitude and height of the tree. The measurements given are only guidelines because there are many variations, for example, if the tree is close to water it will be taller than one growing in a more arid area. Identifying trees can be very difficult, but bear in mind that climate, altitude, aspect and soil all govern the distribution of trees; look carefully at the shape and size of the leaves and any flowers or seedpods; the colour and texture of the bark can often be a clue.

The trees are presented in systematic order. Many do not have English common names. The scientific name is very important, as many English common names are confusing. Flame Tree is a good example: some people know it as an *Erythrina*, others as a *Spathodea* or Nandi Flame, and others as the Australian Flame Tree *Brachychiton*. The Pencil Cedar is not a cedar and the Meru Oak is not an oak.

I have followed Henk Beentje's *Kenya Trees, Shrubs and Lianas* (National Museums of Kenya, 1994) in the naming and classification of tree species. In some cases a botanical name has been updated since its publication, e.g. *Cordia ovalis* is now *Cordia monoica* and is written as *Cordia monoica* (*C. ovalis*).

Where possible, I have included local names: Swahili (Swa), Kikuyu (Kik), Maasai (Maa), Luganda (Lug), Chagga (Chag), Turkana (Turk), Kamba (Kam), Arusha (Aru), Luo (Luo) and Teso (Teso).

SPINY TREE FERN
Cyathea manniana rusirusiru (Kik)

Habitat: highland forests, particularly valley bottoms and alongside forest streams and waterfalls, 1 350–2 500 m **Height:** up to 10 m
Status: locally common

A large evergreen fern with large fronds, up to 3.5 m long, arching from the crown, whose stems are spiny. The presence of spines on leaf bases and stalks distinguishes this species from other tree ferns.
BEST VIEWING: throughout East Africa's mountains and highland areas

CYCAD
Encephalartos hildebrandtii msapo, mkwanga (Swa)

Habitat: coastal belt and *Brachystegia* woodland below 300 m
Height: up to 6 m **Status:** not uncommon, a protected species

Palm-like with a thick trunk, leaves up to 2.5 m in length, made up of about 80 pairs of stiff, rough leaflets, which often have spines about 20 cm long. Female cones contain orange-red seeds, are dull yellow, up to 50 cm long, growing from the base of the leaves. Male cones, which are borne on a separate tree, are dull red, shorter and slimmer.
BEST VIEWING: Kenya: Kaya Kinondo Sacred Forest, Diani, Shimba Hills NP

AFRICAN PENCIL CEDAR
Juniperus procera oltarakwai (Maa); mutarakwa (Kik)

Habitat: dryer highland forest, 1 800–2 950 m **Height:** up to 40 m
Status: locally common

A large (largest *Juniperus* in the world), distinctive evergreen tree, with a tall, straight trunk. Bark is pale brown with vertical cracking and peeling in long strips. Two types of leaves: young leaves needle-like and prickly, growing in threes; older leaves, pressed tightly over stems in tight rows, feel smoother and smell strongly when crushed. Male cones are tiny, 2 mm across, rounded, and yellowish; female cones are larger, up to 8 mm across, and purple-blue when ripe.
BEST VIEWING: Kenya: Rift Valley Escarpment, Mount Kenya NP; **Tanzania:** Arusha NP, Kilimanjaro, Mount Meru; **Uganda:** Rwenzori Mountains

PODO/EAST AFRICAN YELLOWWOOD
Podocarpus falcatus muthengera (Kik); ol-biribiri (Maa)

Habitat: dry highland forests, 1 250–2 700 m **Height:** up to 30 m
Status: widespread in suitable habitat

A tall evergreen tree with a broad (up to 2 m in diameter), straight trunk with cracking, pale, greyish-brown bark that flakes into irregular rectangles. Often festooned with Old Man's Beard (*Usnea* sp.). Stiff, long, shiny, green leaves on the ends of branchlets, up to 5 cm long, younger leaves longer and paler. Separate male and female trees; male cones resemble catkins, up to 2 cm long, and are pinkish. Female trees produce small, round seeds.
BEST VIEWING: Kenya: Aberdare, Mount Kenya NPs; **Tanzania:** Arusha (Mount Meru), Kilimanjaro NPs

BOSCIA
Boscia augustifolia mnafisi (Swa); oloireroi (Maa)

Habitat: arid bushland, up to 1 200 m **Height:** 1–6 m **Status:** common

An evergreen shrub or tree with smooth, silvery-grey bark. Olive-green elliptical leathery leaves, up to 6 cm long. Strongly scented, white or yellowish flowers with 6–20 conspicuous stamens and in dense heads. Round fruits attract birds and baboons when ripe.

BEST VIEWING: Kenya: Lake Turkana, Tsavo East, Tsavo West NPs, Masai Mara NR; **Tanzania:** Serengeti NP; **Uganda:** Kidepo Valley NP

SILKY OAK
Grevillea robusta mgrivea (Swa); meresi (Chag)

Habitat: widely planted above 1 200 m **Height:** up to 20 m
Status: common; exotic

A tall, semi-deciduous tree with a straight trunk, dark grey, rough bark, which is vertically furrowed. Distinctive, fern-like, leathery, green leaves are silky silver-grey below and up to 30 cm long. Numerous orange flowers in spikes, up to 12 cm long, often drip nectar, attracting sunbirds and bees. Frequently planted as a windbreak in coffee plantations.

BEST VIEWING: Kenya: Embu, Meru districts; **Tanzania:** Arusha District

FRIED EGG TREE/SNUFF-BOX TREE
Oncoba spinosa mwage (Kik); saa (Luo)

Habitat: riverine forest or bush, up to 1 800 m **Height:** up to 9 m
Status: fairly common

A spiny, much-branched shrub or tree with smooth, light grey or brown bark. Branches with slender, sharp axillary spines, up to 7 cm long. Oval, shiny, green leaves, about 8 cm long, solitary fragrant flowers, up to 8 cm across, with waxy, white petals and a conspicuous mass of orange-yellow stamens. Shiny, hard, red-brown fruits, about 5 cm across.

BEST VIEWING: Kenya: Kakamega Forest

EAST AFRICAN GREENHEART/PEPPER-BARK TREE
Warburgia ugandensis ol-songonoi (Maa); muthiga (Kik);
mukuzanume (Lug)

Habitat: riverine forests and drier upland forests, 1 600–2 400 m
Height: up to 25 m **Status:** locally common

A large, evergreen tree, with a dense, rounded crown. Distinctive, rough, dark brown bark, cracking into rectangular pieces; sap sticky. Leaves alternate, dark green above, whitish below, with a prominent centre rib, edge wavy, up to 10 cm long. Small, inconspicuous, cream-coloured flowers, about 1 cm across. Fruits hard, rounded, up to 5 cm in diameter, green to purple-black with a waxy, white surface. Fruits taste peppery, liked by Elephant, green pigeons, baboons and monkeys. Heavily debarked for medicinal purposes.

BEST VIEWING: Kenya: Masai Mara NR; **Uganda:** Maramagambo Forest

GIANT CACTUS
Cereus peruvianus

Habitat: gardens and public parks **Height:** 4–7 m
Status: common in some areas; exotic

A sturdy-looking, tall-growing cactus, with 5–7-sided branches, covered in spines, which are up to 4 cm long. Occasionally bears large, beautiful white flowers that open at night.

BEST VIEWING: gardens and tourist lodges in the region

SPOTTED GUM
Eucalyptus maculata   mkaratusi (Swa); kalitunsi (Lug)

Habitat: widely planted **Height:** up to 40 m **Status:** locally common; exotic

A very tall tree, with a distinctive, dimpled trunk. Bark is jigsaw-patterned, with grey, brown and yellowish flaking patches. Leaves long and narrow and the flowers on stalks are white. Seedpods like woody capsules, cup-shaped, about 2 cm across, in bunches. The very similar, Lemon-scented Gum (*E. citriodora*) differs in having pale, smooth bark and lemon-scented leaves.

BEST VIEWING: widespread

GREY IRON BARK GUM
Eucalyptus paniculata

Habitat: prefers higher altitudes on black cotton soils
Height: up to 55 m **Status:** locally common; exotic

A very tall gum tree, with distinctive, deeply fissured, dark brown bark and narrow leaves, up to 17 cm long. Fluffy, small, white flowers in clusters; small seedpods, up to 7 mm long. Timber very hard and resistant to decay.

BEST VIEWING: Kenya: Nairobi area

VELVET-LEAVED COMBRETUM
Combretum molle   murema (Kik); ol-mororoi (Maa)

Habitat: dry, wooded grassland, 150–2 100 m **Height:** 10 m
Status: locally common

A deciduous, spreading tree, with a crooked trunk. Bark rough, grey-brown, becoming darker and deeply fissured with age. Broad, oval leaves, up to 17 cm long, on short stalks; a distinctive feature is the undersurface, which is densely furry and conspicuously net-veined. Distinctively shaped seedpods have four wings; when ripe seedpods are reddish-brown and resemble blossoms.

BEST VIEWING: Kenya: Ol Donyo Sabuk, Tsavo East, Tsavo West NPs

RED POD TERMINALIA
Terminalia brownii   mbarao (Swa); mpoke (Chag)

Habitat: dry savanna woodland, 700–2 000 m **Height:** 4–5 m,
occasionally higher **Status:** widely distributed

A deciduous shrub, with smooth, grey-brown bark and an
attractive, layered appearance. Leaves oval, 7–10 cm long,
with white hairs on the underside; grow in spirals, turn bright
red before falling. Flowers are white or cream, in spikes up to
12 cm long. The characteristic, broadly elliptical, two-winged
seedpods turn red-purple.

BEST VIEWING: Kenya: Nairobi Botanic Gardens

GIANT ST JOHN'S WORT/CURRY BUSH
Hypericum revolutum   susimua (Kik); osasimwa (Maa)

Habitat: dry evergreen montane forests, 1 930–3 800 m
Height: up to 12 m **Status:** common

A shrub or tree, with distinctive, yellow flowers and red-brown,
scaly bark. The flowers, 4–5 cm across, have numerous, bright
yellow stamens and are borne on the end of branches. Leaves
are narrow, elliptical, up to 3 cm long. This species gives off a
smell similar to curry, hence its common name. In Europe during
medieval times the genus was dedicated to St John the Baptist.

BEST VIEWING: widespread in the highland areas

GREWIA
Grewia tephrodermis (*G. bicolor*)   mkone (Swa); ositeti (Maa)

Habitat: dry bush and grasslands, up to 1 800 m **Height:** up to 9 m
Status: widespread and common

A shrub or small tree, with distinctive, jagged-edged leaves. Bark
grey-brown and deeply fissured, often peeling. Leaves, up to 9 cm
long, are shiny, dark green above and silvery-white below. There
is a form recorded in Kenya (Taita and Ukambani) with coarsely
serrated leaves. Attractive clusters of fragrant, bright yellow flowers,
up to 1.5 cm across. Small, round, green, hairy fruits, 6 mm in
diameter, turn orange-brown when ripe.

BEST VIEWING: widespread and common in suitable habitats

GREWIA
Grewia similis   mkole (Swa); ol-neligwat (Maa)

Habitat: evergreen bush and grasslands, 600–2 200 m **Height:** 3 m,
occasionally higher **Status:** widespread in areas of East Africa with
rainfall above 750 mm

A straggling bush or small tree, and also occasionally a climber.
Bark grey and smooth, becoming rougher with age. Shiny, green,
almost rounded leaves, about 5 cm across. The flowers, in groups
of 3–6, are bright mauve, pink or magenta, about 2 cm across,
with yellow anthers and mauve filaments. Fruits 2–4-lobed,
orange to golden-brown when ripe. Small sunbirds feed on the
flowers. Does not occur in dry areas.

BEST VIEWING: widespread and common in suitable habitats

BAOBAB
Adansonia digitata   mbuyu (Swa); ol-mesera (Maa)

Habitat: coastal and dry savanna east of the Rift Valley, up to 1 000 m
Height 25 m **Status:** common east of Rift Valley

A majestic tree with a colossal, wide trunk. Bark silvery-grey, smooth
and fibrous, often pock-marked, or damaged by Elephant. Leaves
compound, divided into 5–7 dark green and shiny leaflets; branches
leafless for large periods of the year. Flowers large, waxy and white,
with a ball of fine stamens in the centre, open at night, attracting
bushbabies and fruit bats, which pollinate them. Fruits large, hard-
shelled, up to 24 cm long, covered in greyish hairs, hanging on
stalks, contain brown seeds enclosed in a whitish, edible pulp.

BEST VIEWING: Kenya: Tsavo East, Tsavo West, Meru NPs;
Tanzania: Tarangire, Lake Manyara, Mikumi, Ruaha NPs

KAPOK TREE
Ceiba pentandra (*Bombax ceiba*)   msufi (Swa)

Habitat: sea level up to 2 000 m **Height:** 30 m **Status:** common; exotic

A tall, distinctive tree, with prominent, horizontal, layered branches,
and its trunk covered in sharp, conical spines. The bark is grey but
greenish on the branches. Leaves made up of 5–10 narrow leaflets
radiating from long, narrow stalks, up to 20 cm long. Has small,
colourful, white to pinkish flowers, up to 3 cm across, which are
pollinated by bats. The seedpods are large, hard, woody capsules,
up to 30 cm long, and very conspicuous when the tree is bare. The
seeds are covered in long, silky fibres known as kapok, which was
used for various purposes, e.g. as stuffing for life-jackets and pillows,
and as insulation. Often confused with the Bombax tree.

BEST VIEWING: coastal strip but planted inland

BOMBAX/CHORISIA
Ceiba speciosa (*Chorisia speciosa*)

Habitat: Widely planted as an ornamental tree, up to 2 000 m
Height: up to 25 m **Status:** quite common in towns; exotic

Often confused with the Kapok Tree, this deciduous tree has a
smooth, green-grey trunk covered in hard, distinctive, woody
spines, and a distinguishing rounded crown. Leaves compound,
made up of 5–7 leaflets radiating from stalks (up to 15 cm long).
Large, strikingly conspicuous, pink flowers have five petals,
yellowish-white, streaked with pink towards the centre, with
protruding style and stigma. The seedpods, which split open on
the tree, are grey to pale brown, oval-shaped and up to 15 cm
across. The seeds are embedded in a silky mass of fine white fibres.

BEST VIEWING: gardens in cities and towns

AUSTRALIAN FLAME TREE
Brachychiton acerifolius (*Sterculia acerifolia*)

Habitat: widely planted in the highlands, 1 600–2 660 m
Height: 15–30 m **Status:** common; exotic

A stunning-looking, easily recognisable tree when in flower. A
native of Australia, it has smooth, grey bark, which bears scars
where branches have become detached. Large, up to 30 cm across,
pawpaw-like, glossy, green leaves with long, slender stalks. The
flowers are bright red and made up of five joined, bell-shaped
segments, up to 2.5 cm long. Fruits smooth, black capsules, up to
10 cm long, which split while still on the tree.

BEST VIEWING: gardens in cities and towns

ORANGE-LEAVED CROTON
Croton dichogamus   ol-logerdangai (Maa); kereru (Kik)

Habitat: dry bush and rocky outcrops, up to 2 200 m **Height:** up to 3 m
Status: locally common in dry savanna

Usually forming thickets, but occasionally a shrub or small tree.
Narrow aromatic leaves, silvery below turning orange, up to
6 cm long, spaced alternately along slender branches. Small,
inconspicuous, yellowish flowers. Fruits three small-lobed capsules,
up to 1 cm across. Thickets are favoured by Lion and Cheetah;
apart from shade, the aromatic leaves are thought to provide
them with some protection from biting flies.
BEST VIEWING: Kenya: Masai Mara NR, Nairobi NP;
Tanzania: Serengeti NP

BROAD-LEAVED CROTON
Croton macrostachyus   ol-keparlu (Maa); mutundu (Kik)

Habitat: forests, forest margins and wooded grassland, 600–2 000 m
Height: up to 25 m **Status:** widespread

A tree with large, spreading branches and a grey trunk. Large,
heart-shaped, grey-green leaves turn orange before falling. Yellow-
white, sweet-smelling flowers borne on long, dense, erect spikes.
BEST VIEWING: Kenya: Masai Mara NR; **Tanzania:** Arusha, Lake Manyara
NPs, Ngorongoro CA; **Uganda:** Queen Elizabeth NP

CROTON
Croton megalocarpus   mukinduri (Kik); nkulumire (Lug);
ol-mergoit (Maa)

Habitat: evergreen highland and riverine forests, 900–2 100 m
Height: up to 35 m **Status:** locally common

A large, spreading upper-storey tree with layered branches. The
bark is rough, dark grey, usually cracking. Long oval leaves, up to
12 cm long, dull green above and silvery below. A very distinctive
tree when in flower; flowers are pale yellow, hanging in spikes up
to 25 cm long. Fruits are grey, woody capsules, about 2.5 cm in
diameter, which contain three seeds.
BEST VIEWING: widespread in highland areas; **Kenya:** Nairobi area;
Tanzania: Arusha NP

KIBWEZI EUPHORBIA
Euphorbia bussei var. *kibwezensis*   kithui (Kam)

Habitat: dry arid bushland up to 2 000 m **Height:** up to 12 m
Status: uncommon

A tall tree-like euphorbia with a crown of rising 2–5-winged,
segmented branches. Clusters of golden-yellow flowers appear near
the end of branches; small, three-angled fruits are red when ripe.
BEST VIEWING: Kenya: Kibwezi Forest; **Tanzania:** Serengeti NP,
Ngorongoro CA

CANDELABRA EUPHORBIA/TREE EUPHORBIA
Euphorbia candelabrum   **mtupa (Swa); ol-bobongo (Maa)**

Habitat: dry thornbush and wooded grassland, up to 1 800 m
Height: up to 18 m **Status:** locally common

A large, distinctively shaped, spiny, tree-like euphorbia; has a short, thick trunk with a crown of characteristic, erect, spiny braches. Greenish-yellow flowers in small groups above upper spines, fruits small, green-red capsules.
BEST VIEWING: Kenya: Mai Mahui; **Tanzania:** Serengeti, Lake Manyara NPs; **Uganda:** Queen Elizabeth NP (very common)

FINGER EUPHORBIA
Euphorbia tirucalli   **mtupa mwitu (Swa); ol-oile, manyara (Maa)**

Habitat: dry bush country, up to 1 600 m **Height:** up to 6 m
Status: locally common

A thick bush or a small tree with a straight trunk and a bushy crown. Branches smooth and spineless, flowers creamy-white, growing in terminal clusters. Small, three-lobed, dark green fruits, up to 6 mm across. The latex is extremely poisonous and is used as a fish poison. Often grown as a hedge around cattle bomas, particularly in dry areas. The Maasai who live in the area near Lake Manyara in Tanzania call this tree manyara, presumably the origin of the names of the lake and the national park.
BEST VIEWING: Kenya: Tsavo East, Tsavo West NPs; **Tanzania:** Lake Manyara NP

HAGENIA/EAST AFRICAN ROSEWOOD
Hagenia abyssinica   **mumondo (Kik); mlanga (Chag);**
                                kisichetwa (Lug)

Habitat: mountain forests, 2 400–3 600 m, but occasionally lower in high-rainfall areas **Height:** up to 20 m **Status:** common

An attractive, mountain forest tree, tall with a round crown, usually found above the bamboo zone. The bark is red-brown, flaking and deeply fissured. Soft compound leaves, up to 40 cm long, are bright green with silvery hairs on the underside, reddish when young. Unmistakable when flowering, with masses of flowers in hanging sprays up to 60 cm in length, giving the tree a distinctive two-toned effect.
BEST VIEWING: any East African mountain, usually above 3 000 m;
Kenya: Aberdare NP; **Tanzania:** Ngorongoro CA; **Rwanda:** Nyungwe NP

ORCHID TREE/CAMEL'S FOOT TREE
Bauhinia variegata var. *variegata*

Habitat: gardens, up to 2 200 m **Height:** 6 m but occasionally taller
Status: common; exotic

A small tree with smooth, grey bark; leaves two-lobed, resembling a camel's foot. Its pink flowers somewhat resemble those of an orchid. Brown, flat seedpods, up to 20 cm long, hang in untidy bunches. Releases seeds while still on the tree.
BEST VIEWING: most tourist lodges throughout East Africa;
Kenya: Nairobi City Park

DELONIX/WHITE POINCIANA
Delonix elata ol-derkersi (Maa); muangi (Kam)

Habitat: hot, dry thornbush country, 100–1 000 m **Height:** 5–8 m, occasionally up to 15 m **Status:** locally common

A spreading deciduous tree with smooth, shiny, grey bark. Leaves have 2–12 pairs of pinnae further divided into leaflets, each leaflet oval-shaped, about 4 cm long. Beautiful, distinctive, white flowers, with four white petals, one smaller yellow petal and long, protruding, orange-brown stamens. Reddish-brown seedpods are thin and long, up to 20 cm, containing oblong seeds in horizontal rows.

BEST VIEWING: Kenya: Samburu NR, Tsavo East, Tsavo West NPs; **Tanzania:** Lake Natron

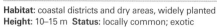

FLAMBOYANT
Delonix regia mjohoro (Swa)

Habitat: coastal districts and dry areas, widely planted **Height:** 10–15 m **Status:** locally common; exotic

A striking, deciduous tree with a flat, umbrella-shaped crown. Leaves compound, with 2–12 pairs of pinnae, each pinna oval-shaped, less than 1 cm long. Its distinctive, scarlet flowers are in clusters and often appear before the leaves. Each flower, up to 10 cm in diameter, consists of five wavy petals, the top one paler splashed with scarlet. Bears characteristic, 75 cm-long, brown seedpods, honeycombed with horizontal seed chambers; pods remain on the tree for many months. A native of Madagascar, where it is now apparently rare.

BEST VIEWING: East African coastal strip; Kenya: Lake Baringo Lodge (good example)

TAMARIND
Tamarindus indica mkwaju, msisi (Swa); moya (Cha); mukoge (Lug); olmasambrai (Maa)

Habitat: dry savanna, woodland and riverine areas, up to 1 500 m **Height:** up to 30 m **Status:** widely distributed

A large dense, distinctly rounded, deciduous tree with drooping branches. Bark is grey-brown, roughly grooved and flaking. Leaves are up to 15 cm long, made up of 9–21 leaflets, each about 3 cm, with rounded tips that fold at night. Orchid-like flowers, occurring in small bunches, are yellow with red veins, about 2.5 cm across. Seedpods are sausage-shaped, hairy pale brown, up to 15 cm long, containing shiny brown seeds surrounded by a sweet sticky pulp.

BEST VIEWING: East African coastal strip; Kenya: Tsavo East, Tsavo West NPs; **Tanzania:** Lake Manyara, Tarangire, Ruaha NPs

FLAT-TOP ACACIA
Acacia abyssinica subsp. calophylla njora rahisi (Swa); mugaa (Kik)

Habitat: wooded grasslands and forest edges, 1 800–2 400 m **Height:** 20 m **Status:** locally common

A large *Acacia*, with a flattish crown. Feathery leaves with 10–40 pinna pairs, each pinna with 20–30 pairs of small (3 × 0.5 mm) leaflets. Bark rough and fissured, brown to almost black. Thorns in pairs, length varies, usually less than 2 cm, sometimes absent. Round, white flowers; reddish in bud. Seedpods, up to 12 cm long, dark with darker spots, mostly straight, splitting on the tree or on the ground.

BEST VIEWING: Kenya: Lake Nakuru NP, Nyanza province; **Tanzania:** Ngorongoro CA, Serengeti, Lake Manyara, Arusha NPs; **Uganda:** Mbale, Karamoja districts, Mount Elgon NP

APPLE-RING ACACIA
Faidherbia albida (*Acacia albida*)   olasiti (Maa)

Habitat: mostly in dry riparian areas, 550–1 800 m **Height:** 30 m
Status: common

A very tall *Acacia*, with a wide, spreading crown. Leaves grey-green, with 3 10 pairs of pinnae, each pinna with 6–23 leaflet pairs, 3.5–6 × 0.7–2.3 mm. Bark dull grey and fissured, thorns straight and in pairs, up to 2 cm long, often pointing downwards. Creamy-white flowers on spikes, up to 14 cm long. Pods very distinctive, bright orange, thick and usually twisted into hoops and spirals. Both pods and leaves used by herders for fodder.

BEST VIEWING: Kenya: Nakuru, Taita Hills; **Tanzania:** Lake Manyara, Ruaha NPs, Ngorongoro CA; **Uganda:** Masaka, Karamoja, Ankole districts

WAIT-A-BIT THORN
Acacia brevispica   mwarara (Swa); olgirgiri (Maa)

Habitat: dry scrub, thickets and forest edges, up to 1 800 m
Height: 1–1.5 m **Status:** common

Usually a scandent low shrub, or small tree. Leaves with 6–18 pairs of pinnae, each pinna with 20–40 leaflet pairs, 2–6 × 0.5–1 mm. Bark grey, but new stems are brown, growing in a distinctive zigzag. Spines mostly hooked, spreading along the stem. Flowers small, 3 cm, creamy-white on branching stalks, up to 10 cm long. Seedpods are straight, 15 cm long and purple-brown when mature, splitting while still on the tree.

BEST VIEWING: Kenya: Baringo, Laikipia, Kajiado, Meru districts; **Tanzania:** Shinyanga, Pare districts; **Uganda:** Karamoja District

WHISTLING THORN ACACIA/ANT-GALLED ACACIA
Acacia drepanolobium   mbalibali (Swa); eluai (Maa)

Habitat: poorly drained black cotton and clay soils and stony ground, 700–2 500 m **Height:** up to 6 m **Status:** widespread and common in suitable areas

Usually a small bush or tree, occasionally grows up to 6 m. Easily recognised by the swollen galls at the base of the larger spines; the galls are reddish when young, slowly turning black, inhabited by Cocktail Ants (*Crematogaster* sp.). Leaves 6–18 pairs of pinnae, each pinna with 20–40 pairs of leaflets, 6 × 2 mm.

BEST VIEWING: Kenya: Nairobi NP; **Tanzania:** Moshi, Dodoma districts, Serengeti NP; **Uganda:** Karamoja, Mbale districts

RIVER ACACIA
Acacia elatior   ol-lerai (Maa)

Habitat: along river banks and dry watercourses in arid areas, 180–1 100 m **Height:** 40 m **Status:** common

A distinctive tall *Acacia* tree with dark, almost black, bark, which is deeply fissured. Leaves with 5–13 pairs of pinnae, leaflets in 13–25 pairs, narrow, glabrous, 1.2–4 × 0.5–4 mm. Distinctive large white spines, up to 9 cm long, with swollen bases interspersed with smaller, brown spines. Flowers round, white or pale yellow. Purplish-brown seedpods, 3–12 cm long.

BEST VIEWING: Kenya: Samburu, Buffalo Springs NRs; **Tanzania:** Ruaha NP; **Uganda:** Karamoja District

WHITE THORN ACACIA
Acacia hockii   mgunga (Swa); oljarboani (Maa)

Habitat: widespread in dry bush and wooded grassland, 750–2 250 m
Height: 6–9 m **Status:** widespread

A shrub or small tree, often with a flattened crown. Bark green-yellow, with characteristic peeling, exposing new yellow bark. Leaves with 2–11 pairs of pinnae, each pinna with 9–29 pairs of small leaflets, 2–6.5 × 0.5–1.3 mm. Small, straight white spines, up to 4 cm long, in pairs, and bright yellow flowers that slowly turn brown. Seedpods turn reddish-brown and are up to 12 cm long.

BEST VIEWING: Kenya: Sultan Hamud, Loita Hills; **Tanzania:** Serengeti NP; **Uganda:** Lake Mburu NP, Ankoli, Masaka districts

RED THORN ACACIA
Acacia lahai   ol-tepessi (Maa); mugaa (Kik); melelek (Aru)

Habitat: cool highland areas, 1 500–1 900 m **Height:** 15 m
Status: locally common

A very distinctive, flat-topped tree with rough, fissured, dark coloured bark. Usually grow close to each other, but individuals often preserved for shade in wheat-growing areas. Straight, pale grey spines in pairs, up to 7 cm long. Pinnate leaves, 6–15 pairs of pinnae, leaflets in 10–28 pairs, 1.5–4.5 × 0.3–0.8 mm. White-cream flowers in spikes up to 7 cm long, flower branchlets covered with red glands. The seedpods, straight or curved, 4–7 cm long, split while still on the tree.

BEST VIEWING: Kenya: Lake Nakuru NP; **Tanzania:** Ngorongoro CA; **Uganda:** Mbali, Karamoja districts

BLACK WATTLE
Acacia mearnsii   muwati (Swa)

Habitat: commercial plantations but widely naturalised, in the highlands up to 2 300 m **Height:** 12 m **Status:** common; exotic

A fast-growing, medium-sized, thornless tree. Has small, dull green, feathery leaves, with small leaflets, up to 4 mm long. Bark black and fissured, often dripping with resinous gum. Small, round, fragrant flowers in clusters, seedpods flattened, up to 10 cm long, constricted between the seeds. The bark is used commercially for the production of tannin.

BEST VIEWING: Kenya: large plantations near Eldoret

HOOK-THORN/BLACK THORN ACACIA
Acacia mellifera   kikwata (Swa); muthia (Kam); oiti orok (Maa)

Habitat: dry bush country, up to 1 800 m **Height:** 2 m, occasionally up to 8 m **Status:** common

A widespread bush, occasionally a tree, in dry bush and wooded grasslands or on lava, often forming impenetrable thickets. Bark brown and smooth, the spines are small, dark tipped, hooked and in pairs. Leaves with 2 or 3 pinna pairs, leaflets 1 or 2 pairs per pinna, 22 × 16 mm. Flowers, closely packed, white or cream with a pinkish core, attract sunbirds and bees. Seedpods thin, almost papery, pale brown to straw-coloured, broad and flat, containing 2–4 seeds.

BEST VIEWING: Kenya: Kitui, Baringo districts, Tsavo East, Tsavo West NPs; **Tanzania:** Serengeti, Pare, Handani districts; **Uganda:** Mbale, Karamoja districts

THREE-THORNED ACACIA/GUM ARABIC TREE
Acacia senegal   kikwata (Swa); ekonoit (Teso); ol-derkosi (Maa)

Habitat: *Acacia-Commiphora* bush and woodland, up to 1 900 m
Height: up to 12 m **Status:** common

A low-branched shrub or tree, rounded when young, often forming
thickets. Bark waxy, usually peeling, yellow- to red-brown. Distinctive
hooked thorns, up to 7 cm long, in threes, centre one hooked downwards, outer two curving upwards. Leaves with 3–6 pinna pairs, leaflets
8–18 pairs per pinna, 1–7 × 0.5–1.8 mm. Creamy-white, fragrant
flowers in spikes, up to 10 cm long, usually appear before leaves. Flat
seedpods, up to 15 cm long, furry grey-yellow, turning papery brown
with prominent veins, contain few seeds.

BEST VIEWING: Kenya: Isiolo, Samburu, Magadi districts; **Tanzania:**
Dodoma, Iringa districts, Serengeti NP; **Uganda:** Kitgum, Mbale districts

WHITE THORN/WHITE-GALLED ACACIA
Acacia seyal   mgunga (Swa); ol-lerai (Maa)

Habitat: dry bush and wooded grasslands, 550–2 200 m **Height:** up
to 12 m **Status:** common

A small tree often with a flat crown, usually in colonies. Distinctive
bark covered in greenish-yellow or orange-red powder, which comes
off when rubbed. Straight, white, stout spines diverging in pairs, up
to 8 cm long, sometimes smaller or absent. Leaves with 3–8 pinna
pairs, 11 or 12 pairs of narrow elliptical leaflets per pinna. Bright
yellow,fragrant, round flowers, 12 mm in diameter, often appear
before leaves. Seedpods shiny, red-brown when ripe, narrow and
curved, up to 20 cm long. Can be mistaken for *A. xanthophloea*.

BEST VIEWING: Kenya: coastal areas, Magadi, Baringo, Narok districts;
Tanzania: Lake Manyara, Serengeti NPs; **Uganda:** Karamoja District

UMBRELLA THORN
Acacia tortilis   mgunga (Swa); oltepesi (Maa)

Habitat: widespread in savanna woodlands and semi-desert,
600–2 000 m **Height:** 18 m **Status:** common

A familiar, flat-topped or umbrella-shaped tree. Bark grey to almost
black and deeply fissured. Spines in pairs, two types: straight and
long, 3–8 cm, and shorter and hooked, up to 7 cm. Leaves with 2–10
pinna pairs, with 6–19 pairs of leaflets per pinna, 0.5–3 × 0.5–1 mm.
Round flowers, white or cream, attract insects, birds, baboons and
monkeys. The brown pods are distinctive, twisted and often curled
into rings. Pods are much favoured by wildlife; Maasai herdsmen use
long hooked sticks to knock them off for their livestock.

BEST VIEWING: Kenya: Amboseli NP; **Tanzania:** Lake Manyara, Tarangire,
Serengeti NPs; **Uganda:** Karamoja District

FEVER TREE/YELLOW-BARKED ACACIA
Acacia xanthophloea   mgunga (Swa); ol-lerai (Maa)

Habitat: beside lakes and rivers, often in black cotton soil, 600–2 000 m
Height: 25 m **Status:** common

As this well-known tree grows in low-lying swampy areas, the early
pioneer settlers associated it with malaria. Straight, white spines are
in diverging pairs, 10 cm long. Feathery pinnate leaves, 3–6 pinna
pairs, with 8–17 pairs of leaflets per pinna, 2.5–6.5 × 0.7–1.8 mm.
Flowers are small, round heads, white tinged pink, yellow in
southern Tanzania. Pods mostly straight, 13 cm long, constricted
between the seeds.

BEST VIEWING: Kenya: Lake Naivasha; **Tanzania:** Arusha, Lake Manyara
NPs, Ngorongoro Crater (Lerai Forest is named after the Maasai name)

LARGE-LEAVED ALBIZIA
Albizia grandibracteata   awak (Luo); mulongo (Luganda)

Habitat: wet evergreen forests and riverine forests, 1 200–1 800 m
Height: 20 m **Status:** common

A large, deciduous tree with a flattish or round crown. Bark smooth, grey or brownish. Leaves in pairs, distinctive, broadly oval but unequal-sided, increasing in size, the topmost pair being the largest. The flowers are colourful, mostly pink with red anthers. Seeds glossy, reddish-brown, 12 cm long, very obvious when tree is bare.

BEST VIEWING: Kenya: Kakamega Forest; **Tanzania:** western part of country; **Uganda:** common

PEACOCK FLOWER
Albizia gummifera   mcani mbao (Swa); ol-osepakupes (Maa)

Habitat: widespread, 1 000–2 300 m **Height:** 15 m (can grow larger in wet forests) **Status:** locally common

A spreading, deciduous shade tree, usually flat topped. Smooth, grey bark. Leaves are glossy, dark green; leaflets can be up to 12 pairs, 1–2 cm long. Flowers are pale pink-and-white clusters, with pale stamens topped with bright red anthers. The glossy, pale brown pods, up to 17 × 3 cm, often in clusters, are thin and papery. Used traditionally by some locals as a ceremonial meeting point.

BEST VIEWING: Kenya: Kakamega Forest; **Tanzania:** Ngorongoro CA

SICKLE BUSH
Dichrostachys cinerea   mkingiri (Swa); ol-merumuri (Maa)

Habitat: wooded grasslands, up to 1 500 m **Height:** up to 5 m
Status: widespread in wooded grassland, sea level to 1 700 m

A small spiny acacia-like shrub or tree, often forming thickets, with distinctive flowering spikes, which are divided into two parts: one bears long, thin, sterile filaments that are pale pinkish, the second has a short, yellow catkin. Flower droops so that the pinkish part is above the yellow, fertile flower. Feathery leaves, with 2–19 pairs of pinnae, long and narrow leaflets in 9–41 pairs per pinna. The seedpods are flat and contorted into strangely shaped clusters.

BEST VIEWING: Kenya: Tsavo East, Tsavo West NPs;
Tanzania: Serengeti NP

AFRICAN BLACKWOOD/AFRICAN EBONY
Dalbergia melanoxylon   mpingo (Swa); muingo (Kam)

Habitat: savanna and deciduous woodland, up to 1 300 m **Height:** up to 11 m **Status:** threatened

A semi-deciduous, much-branched, straggly shrub or small, spiny tree, with an irregular-shaped crown. Bark is pale grey becoming darker and rougher with age. Dark green leaflets, 8–12 per leaf, about 1.5 cm long, clustered on branches. Flowers are white and small, in short-branched sprays. Seedpods thin and flat, about 7 cm long. The heartwood is purplish-black and is exported to make musical instruments. It is also widely used by the famous Makonde and Kamba carvers.

BEST VIEWING: Kenya: Chulu, Tsavo East, Tsavo West NPs;
Tanzania: Serengeti, Tarangire NPs

Sue Allan

RED-HOT POKER TREE/FLAME TREE/LUCKY BEAN TREE
Erythrina abyssinica   **mwamba-ngoma (Swa); ol-opongi (Maa)**

Habitat: rocky bush country, up to 2 000 m **Height:** up to 12 m
Status: widely distributed

An attractive, deciduous, flowering tree, with a short trunk and
stout, spreading branches. Distinctive, corky bark, with thick
spines. Leaves on long stalks consist of three rounded leaflets,
the terminal one the largest. Usually leafless when it produces its
spectacular orange-red flowers. The flowers are in erect heads up to
15 cm long. Distinctively shaped, furry, brown seedpods contain
poisonous, shiny red-and-black seeds, used for making necklaces.
BEST VIEWING: Kenya: National Museum of Kenya (Nairobi),
Mount Elgon NP

LUCKY BEAN TREE
Erythrina burtii   **mboosi (Kam); engaroji (Maa)**

Habitat: wooded grassland and *Acacia-Commiphora* bush,
950–1 800 m **Height:** up to 17 m **Status:** rare

A flat-topped, deciduous tree with spiny branches and deeply
fissured bark, with thick spines. Rounded leaves on short stalks.
Trifoliolate, broadly oval or rounded leaves on short shoots,
with round, oval leaflets, 1–5 × 1–5 cm. Usually leafless when
flowering; its deep red flowers, 6–9 cm long, are in dense masses.
Brown papery seedpods hang in clusters containing bright
orange-red seeds.
BEST VIEWING: Kenya: Amboseli NP

FLAME TREE/LUCKY BEAN TREE
Erythrina lysistemon

Habitat: gardens **Height:** 5–8 m **Status:** common; exotic

Originally from South Africa, this *Erythrina* differs from
E. abyssinica in the shape of its flowers and leaves. Bark is grey-
brown dotted with brown, hooked thorns on its trunk. Spectacular
when leafless; the conspicuous bright red flowers are tubular
and grow horizontally from its stems. Leaves are trifoliolate with
triangular leaflets. Black seedpods hang in clusters, bursting open
to release bright red-and-black seeds (lucky beans).
BEST VIEWING: gardens and parks

CASUARINA
Casuarina cunninghamiana   **mvinje (Swa)**

Habitat: highlands **Height:** up to 23 m **Status:** common; exotic

Casuarina trees are specially adapted to hot, dry climates. Their
leaves are replaced by grey-green branchlets, which are more
drought resistant than soft leaves. Their extensive root system
allows them to thrive in poor soils. This species has a dark,
deeply fissured trunk, which is thick at the base. Its short, thin,
soft branchlets are 9–20 cm long, with 7–9 white-tipped scales in
each whorl. Male flowers are greenish and small, at the ends of
branches, female flowers are in clusters. The fruits are small, 1 cm
long. Often planted as a windbreak in the highlands.
BEST VIEWING: widespread in suitable habitats

CASUARINA/WHISTLING PINE
Casuarina equisetifolia   mvinje, moinga (Swa)

Habitat: coastal woodland and beaches near high-tide mark on sand or coral **Height:** 7–25 m **Status:** common

Common name derived from characteristic sound of the wind in the trees. The rough bark is grey-brown, cracked with age and contains tannin. Leaves, at the joints of branchlets, are minute, in whorls of 6 or 7, up to 30 cm long. Branchlets hang down in tight, crowded tufts along branches. Male flowers small on the ends of some branchlets, female flowers tiny with red stigmas. Seedpods are cone-like, up to 2.5 cm long, in dense clusters, which release hundreds of small, winged seeds. Fast-growing, hardy, often planted as a soil stabiliser: roots have nodules containing nitrogen-fixing bacteria.
BEST VIEWING: East African coast

GIANT-LEAVED FIG
Ficus lutea   mumbu (Kik)

Habitat: riverine forests, up to 2 000 m **Height:** up to 16 m
Status: locally common

A tall, spreading evergreen, but occasionally deciduous tree. Often grows on rocks, occasionally has aerial roots. The bark is grey-brown. The elliptical leaves, about 20 cm long, are in dense spirals from stout branches. The soft, hairy figs, about 2 cm across, are borne just below each leaf; when young, they have a brown cap that falls off as the fruits mature. Like other figs, much loved by birds and monkeys.
BEST VIEWING: Kenya: Kakamega Forest NR; **Kenya/Tanzania and Uganda:** shores of Lake Victoria

SYCAMORE FIG
Ficus sycomorus   mukuyu (Swa); orng'aboli (Maa)

Habitat: riverine and woodland, up to 1 850 m **Height:** up to 25 m
Status: common, widely distributed

A large spreading, sometimes buttressed tree with distinctive, yellowish bark and round, rough leaves, 2.5–13 × 2–10 cm, on hairy stalks, up to 3 cm long. The figs, up to 3 cm across, are distinctive as they grow in bunches directly from the trunk and branches. The flowers are tiny and, as in all figs, occur inside the fruits. The fruits are much loved by baboons, monkeys and fruit-eating birds and insects, which attract many insect-eating birds.
BEST VIEWING: Kenya: Nairobi NP; **Tanzania:** Lake Manyara, Serengeti NPs; **Uganda:** widespread

STRANGLER FIG/WILD FIG
Ficus dekelekane   oreteti (Maa); mugumo (Kik); mkuu (Chag)

Habitat: highland forests and grasslands, 1 050–2 400 m **Height:** up to 25 m **Status:** widespread and common

A large, deciduous, wide-spreading tree, often buttressed with characteristic multi-stemmed aerial roots that crisscross the trunk and often look like frayed rope. Bark is grey and smooth. Leaves, up to 12 cm long, are generally oval. Small fruits, up to 1.5 cm in diameter, occur in clusters next to leaves. Seedlings can often be seen growing in other trees. A good example is on the track to Mount Meru in Arusha NP, where a tree has formed an arch over the road. Sacred to many people, its Maasai name means 'sacred place'.
BEST VIEWING: Kenya: common in the Nairobi area; **Tanzania:** Arusha, Lake Manyara NPs, Ngorongoro CA

RED-LEAVED ROCK FIG
Ficus ingens   onogoret (Maa)

Habitat: rocky riverine gorges and on lava in dry country
Height: 1–7 m **Status:** locally common

A spreading tree, occasionally with aerial roots, often growing
on rocks. Bark grey-brown. The leaves are ovate or elliptical,
5–17 cm × 2–8 cm. Round, reddish/purple figs, 6–12 cm across,
usually just below the leaves on stalks, up to 5 mm long.

BEST VIEWING: Kenya: Masai Mara NR; **Tanzania:** Serengeti NP

MIRAA/SOMALI TEA/KHAT
Catha edulis   mailungi, muirungi (Kik); ol-meraa (Maa)

Habitat: evergreen and riverine forests, 1 500–2 500 m **Height:** up
to 7 m, occasionally up to 25 m **Status:** common where cultivated

A fast-growing, much-branched tree, with distinctive, drooping
foliage. In areas where cultivated, the trees become twisted and
gnarled from pruning. Narrow, elliptical, wedge-shaped serrated
leaves, up to 11 cm long, usually sharply pointed. Small, pale
yellow or white flowers, in branched, axillary clusters. The leaves
contain a powerful stimulant and are packed into tight bundles
and sold in Kenya, Somalia, the Arabian Peninsula and even
Europe. It is reported that Kenya earns over US$ 150 000 000
from the sale of Miraa leaves.

BEST VIEWING: Kenya: Chyulu NP, Meru, Kericho areas

TOOTHBRUSH TREE
Salvadora persica   mswaki (Swa); ol-remit (Maa)

Habitat: dry *Acacia* woodland up to 1 500 m **Height:** up to 9 m
Status: widespread and common

A small evergreen tree or scrambling bush, with rough, grey-
brown bark, sometimes forming thickets. Fleshy, elliptical leaves,
up to 5 cm long, and very small, creamy-green flowers in loose
heads, up to 10 cm long. The fruits are small, 6 mm across,
translucent-white turning pink or red.

BEST VIEWING: Kenya: Samburu NR, Tsavo East, Tsavo West NPs;
Tanzania: Serengeti, Tarangire NPs

CAPE CHESTNUT
Calodendrum capense   murarachi (Kik); ol-larashi (Maa)

Habitat: dry highland forests, but widely planted in towns,
1 600–2 300 m **Height:** up to 20 m **Status:** common

A spectacularly beautiful, deciduous, domed-shaped flowering tree,
bare for much of the year, but it stands out in the forest when
covered in pink, scented flowers. The bark is smooth and pale grey.
Large, oval, dark green leaves, up to 14 cm long. Shiny, black seeds
contained in small capsules, 4 cm across, which are covered in soft,
woody spines; they split open while still on the tree.

BEST VIEWING: Kenya: Rift Valley escarpment; **Tanzania:** Ngorongoro
Crater ascent road; **Uganda:** western areas

TECLEA
Teclea simplicifolia   **munderendu (Kik); olgelai (Maa)**

Habitat: dry forests and evergreen rocky bushland, 850–2 300 m
Height: up to 9 m **Status:** common

A shrub or a much-branched evergreen tree, with smooth, dark grey bark. Simple, long, tapering leaves with blunt tips, up to 15 cm long, and dark green on upper surface. Small, fragrant, greenish-yellow flowers, in axillary clusters. The fruits, orange-red when ripe, are small and smooth, about 1 cm in diameter.

BEST VIEWING: widespread in suitable habitats

DESERT DATE
Balanites aegyptiaca   **mjunju (Swa); olng'oswa (Maa)**

Habitat: dry, savanna grassland, up to 2 000 m **Height:** 6–10 m
Status: common

A small, rounded, evergreen tree, with green thorns and dark brown, deeply fissured bark. Leaves, often on short stalks, in pairs, up to 5 cm long. Fragrant, yellow-green flowers in clusters. Date-like fruits, about 5 cm long, yellow when ripe. The fruits and leaves are heavily browsed by camels, goats and giraffes.

BEST VIEWING: Kenya: Masai Mara NR; **Tanzania:** Lake Manyara, Serengeti, Tarangire NPs

COMMIPHORA
Commiphora africana   **mbambara (Swa); iguu (Kam); osilalei (Maa)**

Habitat: dry savanna and bush grasslands, from sea level to 1 780 m
Height: 5–10 m **Status:** locally common

A deciduous, spiny shrub or tree, with distinctive, peeling bark. The underbark, which is green, peeling into reddish-brown scrolls, exudes pale sap. Branchlets are tipped with spines. The leaves have three leaflets, the terminal one the largest. Small, up to 5 cm, red flowers, in tight clusters. Fruits tiny, pinkish-red, round or oval, containing one hard seed.

BEST VIEWING: East African coastal strip; **Kenya:** Lake Magadi, Tsavo East, Tsavo West NPs

HONEYSUCKLE TREE
Turraea robusta   **muringa (Kik); ol-burobinik (Maa)**

Habitat: wooded grassland and riverine forest, to 2 000 m **Height:** up to 9 m **Status:** widely distributed

A shrub or small tree with rough, brown bark and oval, shiny, dark green leaves, up to 15 cm long. Fragrant creamy-white flowers, 2.5 cm across, with narrow petals and a prominent, orange stamen, in dense clusters, turning yellow with age. Small, rounded fruits, about 1.5 cm across, turning dark brown or black when ripe, are very distinctive when split open on the ground, resembling small stars.

BEST VIEWING: Kenya: Masai Mara NR, Kakamega Forest; **Tanzania:** Serengeti NP

MANGO TREE
Mangifera indica mwembe (Swa)

Habitat: up to 2 000 m **Height:** 10–15 m, occasionally taller
Status: common, widely planted; exotic

A dense evergreen tree with a short, thick trunk and a rounded crown. The dark green leaves long, up to 30 cm, crowded at the end of the branches. Young leaves are soft and copper-coloured. Small, creamy-brown to white flowers on pyramidal heads, up to 60 cm long. Fruits round or oval, up to 15 cm long, green slowly ripening to yellow. Thought to have been introduced from India.

BEST VIEWING: coastal districts

RHUS
Rhus natalensis mtishangwe (Swa); olmisigiyoi (Maa)

Habitat: forest margins, thickets and wooded savanna, up to 2 700 m
Height: up to 6 m **Status:** widespread

Mostly a many-branched bushy shrub; occasionally a tree. Bark dark grey-brown, branchlets paler, dotted with breathing pores. Leaves elliptical, with prominent midribs, with three leaflets, the terminal one the largest, up to 9 cm long. Greenish or yellowish-white, very small flowers, up to 1.5 mm across, in loose clusters, up to 15 mm long. Fruits edible, small, kidney-shaped, orange. Giraffes, goats and monkeys eat the leaves; fruits are popular with children.

BEST VIEWING: Kenya: Nairobi NP, Masai Mara NR;
Tanzania: Serengeti NP

GIANT HEATH
Erica arborea ol-kibejus (Maa); muthithinda (Kik)

Habitat: rocky high-altitude moorlands, 2 100–4 500 m **Height:** up to 7.5 m **Status:** common

A much-branched, upright shrub or tree, with needle-like, bright green leaves. Scented, bell-shaped, white or pink flowers, 1.5–3 mm long, borne in large terminal heads. Fruits are red, in small capsules, 3 mm long.

BEST VIEWING: all East African mountains

GIANT DIOSPYROS
Diospyros abyssinica mdaa-mwitu (Swa); muiruthi (Kik);
ol-chartuyan orok (Maa)

Habitat: dry and riverine and highland forests, up to 2 100 m
Height: 9–30 m **Status:** locally common

A tall forest tree, with a tall, dark coloured, slender trunk. The dark, rough bark cracking into narrow purplish strips is distinctive. Long elliptical leaves, up to 12 cm long, glossy, dark green above. Small, white, fragrant flowers in axillary clusters. The fruits are small, round, red-yellow, turning black when ripe, and look like dried currants when on the ground. The fruits are much liked by birds, particularly orioles and turacos. Elephant and giraffes browse the leaves.

BEST VIEWING: Kenya: riverine forests, Masai Mara NR, Kakamega Forest; **Tanzania:** Arusha, Lake Manyara NPs

EUCLEA
Euclea divinorum **mdaa (Swa); mukinyai (Kik); mkenye (Chag); ol kinyei (Maa)**

Habitat: dry, rocky woodland and grassland in highland areas, up to 2 100 m **Height:** up to 10 m **Status:** widespread, often the dominant species

An evergreen shrub, but occasionally a tree with dark, dull green leaves. Bark grey becoming darker and cracking with age. Small, creamy-white flowers in small sprays are very conspicuous. Fruits are small, up to 5 cm, and purple-black when ripe. Dye from its roots used to colour sisal baskets.

BEST VIEWING: Kenya: Laikipia Plateau, Rift Valley escarpment

BUDDLEJA
Buddleja polystachya **ol-biran (Maa)**

Habitat: montane forest and bushland, 2 000–3 000 m **Height:** 6 m **Status:** common

A straggly bush, but occasionally a tree, with pale brown bark. Leaves grey-green above, undersides and stems covered in soft, white hairs. Small, tubular, orange-yellow flowers in groups of 3 or 4 along spikes, up to 20 cm long. Fruits are small, dry capsules. When in flower, attracts butterflies and insects.

BEST VIEWING: Kenya: Aberdare, Mount Kenya NPs; **Tanzania:** Ngorongoro CA

WILD OLIVE
Olea europaea subsp. *cuspidata* **mutamaiyu (Kik); ol-orien (Maa)**

Habitat: evergreen woodland and dry highland forests, 950–2 400 m **Height:** up to 15 m **Status:** common

A much-branched, spreading tree or shrub, trunk gnarled, with characteristic pockets and dark brown, rough bark. Stiff, pointed, oval leaves, 3–8 cm long, on short stalks, dark green above, paler below, with silvery or gold scales. Small, white flowers, up to 5 cm across, in branched sprays. Fruits purple when ripe, oval, up to 1 cm long and very attractive to birds, e.g. African Olive Pigeon (*Columba arquatrix*).

BEST VIEWING: Kenya: Aberdare, Mount Kenya NPs; **Tanzania:** Mount Kilimanjaro NP

EAST AFRICAN OLIVE
Olea capensis subsp. *hochstetteri* **musharagi (Kik); ol-loliondo (Maa)**

Habitat: prefers higher-rainfall areas than previous species, 1 150–2 550 m **Height:** up to 20 m **Status:** common

A tall, evergreen tree with pale, almost white, rough bark and steeply ascending branches. Stiff leaves, up to 10 cm long, dark green above, on 3 cm-long stalks. Small white flowers in branched terminal sprays, up to 10 cm in length. Oval fruits up to 2 cm long, purple when ripe, attractive to hornbills.

BEST VIEWING: Kenya: Mount Kenya NP; **Tanzania:** Arusha NP

QUININE TREE
Rauvolfia caffra olemudongo'o (Maa)

Habitat: riverine forests and watercourses, 650–1 900 m **Height:** up to 20 m **Status:** common

An evergreen shrub or tree with a dense, round crown. Distinctive, long, leathery leaves in whorls of 3–5 on short, grooved stalks. Small, scented, white flowers. Fruits round, two-lobed, fleshy, green turning black when ripe. Much loved by birds, particularly turacos.

BEST VIEWING: Kenya: Masai Mara NR; **Tanzania:** Arusha, Lake Manyara NPs

WILD MANGO
Tabernaemontana ventricosa muerere (Kik)

Habitat: riverine and ground-water forests, 700–1 650 m **Height:** up to 10 m **Status:** widespread

A leafy, evergreen shrub with dark green, elliptical leaves. Sweet-scented, white flowers. Green, rounded, ridged fruits are in pairs; when mature they split, exposing bright orange pulp that contains brown seeds. Not related to the true Mango.

BEST VIEWING: Tanzania: Lake Manyara NP

LARGE-LEAVED GARDENIA
Gardenia ternifolia var. *jovis-tonantis* kimwemwe (Swa); ol'dagurguriet (Maa)

Habitat: savanna grassland, up to 2 100 m **Height:** up to 6 m **Status:** common

A shrub or tree, often with a distinctive, stunted look, particularly in wildlife areas where it is heavily browsed by giraffes. The bark is greenish grey, spotted with breathing pores. Long, dark green leaves, up to 12 cm long, in whorls of three. Fragrant, creamy-white flowers, up to 10 cm across, with a conspicuous corolla. Grey-brown fruits are woody, ovoid, and crowned with a permanent calyx.

BEST VIEWING: Kenya: Masai Mara NR; **Tanzania:** Serengeti NP; **Uganda:** throughout

GARDENIA
Gardenia volkensii mpoto-wa-ndovu (Swa); munyawa (Kik); ol'dagurguriet (Maa)

Habitat: wooded grasslands, up to 1 800 m **Height:** up to 7 m **Status:** common

A shrub or small tree with pale grey bark. Hairless leaves in pairs are broadly spoon-shaped. Masses of white, fragrant flowers, 10–11 cm across, quickly fade to yellow. Fruits round and warty, about 10 cm in diameter.

BEST VIEWING: Kenya: Arabuko Sokoke Forest, Samburu NR; **Uganda:** Gulu District

GIANT GROUNDSEL/TREE SENECIO
Dendrosenecio johnstonii (*Senecio johnstonii*)

Habitat: 2 750–3 350 m **Height:** up to 9 m **Status:** locally common

A spectacular mountain shrub or small tree, usually with 2 or 3 branches that end in a dense rosette of large, cabbage-like leaves, 1 m in diameter. The leaves close at night, forming an insulation blanket. As the branches grow, the lower leaves turn yellow and die but remain attached, creating a thick lagging around the trunk. The bark is corky and deeply furrowed. Produces bright yellow flowers at 10–20-year intervals. There are a number of subspecies, all very similar, each occurring on different mountains in East Africa, e.g. *D. kilimanjari* (*S. kilimanjari*) occurs only on Kilimanjaro.

BEST VIEWING: alpine zone of the East African mountains

LELESHWA BUSH
Tarchonanthus camphoratus   mkalambati (Swa); ol-leleshwa (Maa)

Habitat: dry bush and grassland especially on stony ground, 1 500–2 300 m **Height:** up to 7.5 m **Status:** common

A much-branched shrub or tree, bark brown-grey, rough and fissured, peeling into long strips. Narrow, soft, long leaves, up to 10 cm long, are camphor-scented; upper surface green, undersurface and new shoots covered in creamy-white hairs giving the tree a silvery appearance. Male and female flowers in sprays on different trees; male flowers are creamy-brown, female flowers paler, developing into woolly, fruiting heads. The seeds are tiny, covered in dense, woolly, cotton-like white hairs.

BEST VIEWING: Kenya: Lake Nakuru NP

GIANT LOBELIA
Lobelia telekii   muhehe (Kik)

Habitat: open wet rocky areas, around 3 000 m **Height:** up to 4 m **Status:** common

Characteristic of African mountains, lobelias grow on dry, rocky slopes. They can shut their leaves close to the core, insulating the dense bracts at night. This species resembles a tree but is a tall, tree-like, rosette-forming plant. Its long, narrow leaves secrete a slimy solution, thought to have antifreeze qualities. Hundreds of delicate, small, blue flowers (1 mm across), neatly arranged, spiral up and around a central pillar, which can be up to 30 cm across. Scarlet-tufted Sunbird (*Nectarinia johnstoni*) feeds on and pollinates the flowers.

BEST VIEWING: Kenya: Mount Elgon, Aberdare, Mount Kenya NPs; **Uganda:** Mount Elgon NP (Mount Elgon is on Kenya-Uganda border)

LARGE-LEAVED CORDIA
Cordia africana   makobokobo (Swa); muringa (Kik)

Habitat: forests and savanna in higher-rainfall areas, 1 200–2 000 m **Height:** up to 10 m, occasionally higher **Status:** locally common

An attractive, tall, deciduous forest tree with a rounded crown, easily recognised when in flower. Trunk often crooked. Leaves broad, oval, leathery and rough, up to 16 cm long, dull, dark green above, paler below, veins and midrib very prominent below. The scented flowers, in dense clusters, are white and funnel-shaped, with crinkly edges. The fruits are small, round, 1 cm in diameter, and contain seeds embedded in sticky, sweet flesh.

BEST VIEWING: Kenya: Kakamega Forest; **Tanzania:** Lake Manyara NP

SANDPAPER CORDIA
Cordia monoica (C. ovalis)   msasa (Swa); mukua (Kik); o-seki (Maa)

Habitat: widespread in dry areas, up to 1 800 m **Height:** 6–12 m
Status: common

A rounded, evergreen shrub or tree, with thin, peeling, blue-grey, smooth bark. Oval leaves, 5–8 cm across, have the texture of sandpaper above and are soft and hairy below, with three prominent veins; they are used as sandpaper by the Maasai. Branchlets, leaf and flower stalks all densely covered in rusty hairs. Small, white to dull yellow, fragrant flowers in terminal clusters.
BEST VIEWING: Kenya: Masai Mara NR; **Tanzania:** Serengeti NP

SAUSAGE TREE
Kigelia africana   mwegea (Swa); ol-darpoi (Maa)

Habitat: wooded grasslands, forest edges and riverine forests, up to 1 850 m **Height:** up to 15 m **Status:** common, widespread

A wide-spreading, low-branched tree, with a rounded, dense crown and pale grey-brown bark. Its compound, elliptical, rough leaves, up to 10 cm long, consist of 3–5 leaflet pairs plus a terminal one. Deep-maroon, large tubular flowers hanging on rope-like stalks, usually up to 3 m long. Flowers are rich in nectar, attracting birds during the daytime and bats at night. Fruits, which hang on long stalks, are like large grey sausages, up to 1 m long and weighing up to 10 kg. The stalks remain on the tree after the flowers and fruits have fallen.
BEST VIEWING: Kenya: Samburu NR; **Tanzania:** Lake Manyara, Tarangire, Serengeti NPs; **Uganda:** Queen Elizabeth, Kidepo Valley NPs

JACARANDA
Jacaranda mimosifolia   mucakaranda (Kik)

Habitat: widespread, up to 2 200 m **Height:** up to 20 m
Status: common; exotic

A large, well-known, deciduous tree, spectacular when in flower. The bark is smooth and grey-brown, becoming rougher and darker with age. The leaves, bright green when young, turning darker with age, are feathery and fern-like. The delicate, bell-shaped, mauve-blue flowers, about 4 cm long, open mostly while the tree is leafless. The woody seedpods are flat with a wavy edge, up to 7 cm in diameter. One edge opens to release numerous, transparent, winged seeds.
BEST VIEWING: most towns and cities in the region

MARKHAMIA
Markhamia lutea   muho (Kik); nsambya (Lug); mabet (Maa)

Habitat: open woodland, 700–1 900 m **Height:** up to 15 m
Status: common, widely planted

A tall, evergreen tree, with reddish-brown, finely cracked bark. Compound leaves in terminal groups, up to 30 cm long, with 3–5 pairs of dark green, wavy leaflets, plus a terminal one, up to 10 cm wide. Often covered in bright yellow, trumpet-shaped, 6 cm-long flowers, striped orange-red inside. The very distinctive seedpods, up to 75 cm long, split while still on the tree, and hang in spiral clusters.
BEST VIEWING: Kenya: Kakamega Forest, Mount Kenya NP

AFRICAN TULIP TREE/NANDI FLAME
Spathodea campanulata   kibobakasi (Swa)

Habitat: riverine and highland forests, 1 500–2 000 m **Height:** up to 18 m **Status:** common, widely planted in cities and towns

A striking, deciduous, flowering tree with a rounded crown. Large leaves with 9–13 leaflets are velvety underneath. Stunning, dense clusters of trumpet-shaped, bright orange or yellow flowers with yellow edges and throat (some trees with yellow flowers occur). The buds are densely covered in soft, brown hair and contain large amounts of water. The oblong seedpods are black, containing winged seeds.

BEST VIEWING: tourist lodges in the region; **Kenya:** Aberdare NP

KEDONG DRACAENA
Dracaena ellenbeckiana   olekidong (Maa)

Habitat: dry, rocky hill slopes, 1 050–2 000 m **Height:** 3–7.5 m **Status:** locally common

A spindly shrub or an almost palm-like tree with thin branches. The bark is pale grey and marked with leaf scars. Leaves blue-green, lance-shaped and narrow, about 50 cm long, and in dense, spreading terminal tufts. Small, yellow-green flowers in terminal heads, up to 75 cm long. Fruits are small, three-lobed and orange when ripe. The hollowed-out stems are used as arrow quivers.

BEST VIEWING: Kenya: Rift Valley escarpment (Nairobi–Naivasha road)

STEUDNER'S DRACAENA
Dracaena steudneri   msanaka (Swa); muthari (Kik);
                              olebenyan (Maa)

Habitat: most highland forests, 1 250–2 100 m **Height:** 3–12 m **Status:** locally common

A very distinctive tree, with large, dark green, fibrous leaves, around 1 m long, in large, terminal rosettes. The flowers are pale yellow-green, in terminal clusters, forming a large flowering head, about 1 m in height. The sweet-scented flowers open at night and fade during the day. Fruits, initially green, slowly turning red and then black, are juicy and much liked by birds.

BEST VIEWING: Kenya: common in parks and gardens in Nairobi

BORASSUS PALM/AFRICAN FAN PALM
Borassus aethiopum   mvumo (Swa); katunda (Lug)

Habitat: along watercourses in grasslands and along the coastal belt, up to 400 m **Height:** 30 m **Status:** common in suitable habitat

The tallest indigenous palm in the area, with a distinctive swelling above the middle of its smooth, grey trunk. Large, fan-shaped leaves, up to 4 m long and 3 m broad, are divided into many segments. Male and female flowers on separate trees; male flowers in large, branched, pollen-producing catkins; female flowers larger, in longer, unbranched heads.. The fruits, which are loved by Elephant, are large, 15 cm long, orange-brown, round and shiny.

BEST VIEWING: Tanzania: Selous GR; **Uganda:** Kidepo Valley NP

DOUM PALM
Hyphaene compressa mkoma (Swa); eng'oli (Turk)

Habitat: coastal belt and arid inland areas, sea level to 1 400 m
Height: up to 15 m **Status:** common, but threatened by unsustainable
commercial harvesting in Turkanaland

A distinctive-looking and unusual palm, with up to four branches.
Young palms form dense thickets. The leaves are fan-shaped on
long, spiny stalks in sparse clusters. The orange-brown, pear-
shaped fruits, about 8–10 cm, occur in clusters and are much liked
by baboons and Elephant, which disperse the seeds. The fruits are
also eaten by coastal people and the Turkana.

BEST VIEWING: East African coastal strip; **Kenya:** Samburu, Buffalo
Springs NRs

AFRICAN WILD DATE PALM
Phoenix reclinata mkindu (Swa); ol-tukai (Maa)

Habitat: along watercourses and swamps, up to 3 000 m **Height:** up
to 10 m **Status:** common

A tall, slender palm when mature; forms into low thickets when
young. The large compound leaves, up to 3 m long, are made up
of many leaflets. Male and female flowers are borne on different
trees; male creamy, female greenish and smaller. Fruits are
yellow-brown, turning dull red.

BEST VIEWING: Kenya: Amboseli NP (Ol Tukai); **Tanzania:** Arusha, Lake
Manyara, Serengeti NPs; **Uganda:** Queen Elizabeth NP

MOUNTAIN BAMBOO
Oldeana alpina mwanzi (Swa); ol-ndiani (Maa)

Habitat: moist slopes of East African mountains, 2 400–3 000 m
Height: 15 m **Status:** common where suitable habitat exists

Unmistakable, forming a thick and, in some places, almost
impenetrable zone between the montane forests and the *Hagenia-
Hypericum* belt above. On Kilimanjaro it occurs only in small
patches on the northern slopes. Narrow elliptical leaves taper to a
thread-like tip, 5–20 × 0.6–1.5 cm. The new shoots are particularly
liked by Mountain Gorilla and Golden Monkey.

BEST VIEWING: Kenya: Aberdare, Mount Kenya NPs;
Tanzania: Kilimanjaro, Arusha NP (Mount Meru); **Uganda:** Rwenzori
Mountains, Bwindi, Mgahinga Gorilla NPs; **Rwanda:** Volcanoes NP

WHITE DOMBEYA
Dombeya rotundifolia mtorobwe (Swa); olawuo (Maa)

Habitat: dry wooded grassland, 900–2 250 m **Height:** 3–4.5 m
Status: locally common

A shrub or tree, with dark brown, corky, rough bark, often
flowering while leafless. Dark green, broadly rounded, almost
heart-shaped leaves, 6–19 cm across, are sandpapery above. The
leaves are also finely serrated and have five veins radiating from
the leaf stalk. Sweet-scented, white or pinkish flowers, 2 cm across,
in clusters, resemble cherry blossoms. Flower petals persist for
months, becoming brownish. The small, round fruits are hairy.

BEST VIEWING: Lake Magadi road

WILD FLOWERS

It is not clear exactly how many different flowering plants grow in East Africa. However, the wide range of ecological and climatic conditions has certainly given the area a rich heritage of wild flowers, and there may well be in excess of 11 000 species in the region. Included in this guidebook are 36 of the more common flowers that can be seen in East Africa, which should give an indication of the diversity and beauty of the region's wildflowers.

When driving in the bush, stop for a moment, get out of your vehicle (if it is safe to do so) and look around, particularly on the ground. (Note: in some wildlife areas you are not allowed out of your vehicle, so ask your guide first.) You will be surprised how many flowers you will find. Many of them will be tiny, only a few millimetres across, but all of them will be quite beautiful. If you wish to identify the flower later, take a photograph of it and its leaves – often the size or shape of the leaf helps with identification. When taking a photograph, include something for perspective that will indicate the size of the flower. A good method is to take a number of photographs of the flower from different positions and then take one with your thumb close to the flower. To facilitate recording measurements of flowers and leaves, a ruler has been printed on the back cover of this guidebook.

Although it is often tempting to dig up an attractive flower and take it home, it is best not to do so, as the plant will probably die, and it is illegal to do so in any of the national parks and reserves. Unless the plant is about to be destroyed, by development, for instance, it is best left where it has grown naturally and where it can be enjoyed by other people.

The flowers are arranged in systematic order and, as is the case with trees and shrubs, often there is no common name. All names are taken from Michael Blundell's *Collins Guide to the Wild Flowers of East Africa* (William Collins Sons & Co. Ltd, 1987). In some cases the botanical names have been updated since publication of that book, e.g. *Carissa edulis* is now *Carissa spinarum* and is written as *Carissa spinarum* (*C. edulis*).

The habitat and the altitude where a flowering plant is found can often help in identification. These are included in the text, as well as the approximate height or length (in the case of climbing plants) of the plant, where relevant, and a description of the flower and the leaves.

Where possible, local names have been included and are abbreviated as follows: Swahili (Swa), Maasai (Maa), Samburu (Sam).

WATER LILY
Nymphaea caerulea   myungiyungi, makula (Swa); orpaleki (Maa)

Habitat: fresh-water lakes and ponds, quiet backwaters of rivers, sea level to 2 700 m **Status:** locally common

Strikingly beautiful blue flowers, up to 11 cm across, with pale yellow centres. Heart-shaped leaves, with a V-notch, up to 25 cm across. The leaves, which float on the water's surface, are on long stalks and are green above and maroon below. The submerged seedpods are much liked by Purple Gallinule (*Porphyrio martinica*), African Jacana and even Olive Baboon, which wade into the water to harvest them.

BEST VIEWING: widespread throughout the region, except northern Uganda

STONECROPPER
Kalanchoe lanceolata   mkilua nungu (Swa)

Habitat: dry country, sea level to 2 500 m **Height:** up to 1 m
Status: locally common

An erect succulent with yellow or orange-red flowers clustered together in flower heads. The flowers have four petals and are 8 mm across. Upper leaves oblong, leaves with irregular serrated edges, lower leaves are boat shaped. Found singly or in large communities growing in the shade of trees. Blooms after the rains.

BEST VIEWING: widespread in suitable habitats in the region

BUSY LIZZY/PINK BALSAM
Impatiens hochstetteri

Habitat: shady places beside streams in lowland and highland forests, 800–3 350 m **Height:** 20–50 cm **Status:** common

Small, pale mauve or pink flowers, in clusters of 1–3. Leaves vary in size and shape, which is attributed to different habitat conditions; those growing in damper, shadier places have longer, thinner-textured leaves. Seedpods explode when ripe, shooting the seeds quite far. Sometimes forms large colonies.

BEST VIEWING: widespread in suitable habitats

BEGONIA
Begonia meyeri-johannis

Habitat: wet highland forests, 1 550–2 400 m **Length:** up to 10 m
Status: locally common

There are 18 species of *Begonia* in East Africa. This one, a woody climbing plant, is common in the wet highland forests and is often found near waterfalls. It bears beautiful, waxy, pink-tinged, white flowers with bright yellow sepals, on pinkish fleshy stems. The leaves are broad, ovate, with prominent veins.

BEST VIEWING: Kenya: Aberdare, Mount Kenya NPs;
Tanzania: Kilimanjaro NP; **Uganda:** Rwenzori Mountains NP;
Rwanda: Nyungwe NP

BUTTERCUP BUSH
Ochna ovata   mtamboo mwitu (Swa); onkorukoti (Maa)

Habitat: arid bushlands and forest margins, 600–1 900 m
Height: 1–2 m, occasionally up to 5 m   **Status:** locally common

There are 16 species of *Ochna* in East Africa. This one is a hairless shrub, sometimes a small tree, with bright yellow-green, scented flowers, 1.2 cm across, grouped together usually in fives, on short axillary stems. The flowers are quick to fall, revealing red sepals, similar to petals. Fruits purple-black, 1.1 × 0.6 cm across, surrounded by red sepals, 1.9 × 0.6 cm. The fruits are favoured by birds. Leaves long and narrow, with net-like veins, especially when aged, edges serrated.

BEST VIEWING: Kenya: common in Nairobi area, central areas;
Tanzania: around Lake Victoria, Tabora, Kondoa Districts

ABUTILON
Abutilon mauritianum   mbeha, mjamanda (Swa)

Habitat: sea level to 2 000 m   **Height:** up to 1.5 m   **Status:** common

There are about 30 species of *Abutilon* in Africa, of which this is the most common in East Africa. An evergreen, woody, shrub with solitary, bright gold-yellow flowers, about 4 cm across. The flowers, which usually flower after midday, have more than 20 carpels, which are topped with hairy bristles. The leaves are velvety, rounded or heart-shaped.

BEST VIEWING: widespread in suitable habitats

WILD HIBISCUS
Hibiscus cannabinus   mchachano (Swa); engaranyi naibor (Maa)

Habitat: dry grassland and semi-arid areas, 600–2 100 m
Height: 50 cm   **Status:** locally common

There are about 64 species of *Hibiscus* in East Africa. This common species is a small, erect, woody plant with distinctive hairy stems covered in small spikes. Flowers are maroon-purple or yellow, with purple centres, about 6 cm across. All have characteristic stamens, which are united to form a tubular column. *H. flavifolius*, which occurs in dry, rocky grassland, has small (about 2.2 cm) cream or white flowers with bright orange stamens. *H. vitifolius*, which occurs along forest edges in low-rainfall areas, has deep yellow flowers with a purple centre.

BEST VIEWING: widespread in suitable habitats

PAVONIA
Pavonia urens   mchokochore (Swa); osupukioi-orok (Maa)

Habitat: edges of highland forests and along watercourses in drier areas, 1 220–2 700 m   **Height:** 1 m   **Status:** common

A soft, hairy shrub with clusters of single pink, mauve or white flowers, 2–4 cm across, with long, darker stamens. The mauve variety can look very similar to *Hibiscus cannabinus*. Velvety, oblong leaves have coarsely serrated edges, with 3–5 lobes, except the upper ones, which have no lobes. The stems are used by rural people for making twine.

BEST VIEWING: widespread in suitable habitats in the region

LION'S CLAW
Crotalaria agatiflora　　　mchekecheke (Swa); olontwalan (Maa)

Habitat: upland grasslands especially near forest edges, 1 600–3 000 m
Height: up to 3 m, occasionally up to 10 m　**Status:** common

A woody shrub with striking, yellow-green, beak-like flowers. The flowers' keels are boat-shaped, 4.5–5.5 cm long, with black tips, and are borne in clusters on stout stalks. When dry, the seedpods rattle ('*crotala*' is the Greek for 'rattle'), before exploding with a loud crack. Much liked by sunbirds, particularly the Golden-winged Sunbird (*Nectarinia reichenowi*), which has a long, curved bill that appears to be specially adapted to feed on this flower.
BEST VIEWING: Kenya: Aberdare NP; **Tanzania:** Ngorongoro Crater rim; **Uganda:** widespread

DESERT ROSE
Adenium obesum　　　mdagu (Swa); oloteti (Maa)

Habitat: rocky areas in dry bush, 50–1 230 m　**Height:** up to 3 m
Status: locally common

A thickset, often bulbous shrub or small tree with a smooth grey-green bark; resembles a small baobab tree. Striking, funnel-shaped, showy, bright deep-pink flowers, about 15 cm across, which appear before the leaves. The leaves are obovate, shiny, dark green above, paler below, with a prominent midrib, crowded at the ends of branches. Seedpods in pairs, grey-brown, tapering at both ends, about 24 cm long.
BEST VIEWING: Kenya: Samburu, Buffalo Springs NRs, Lake Bogoria; **Tanzania:** Olduvai (Oldupai) Gorge; **Uganda:** northern regions

CARISSA
Carissa spinarum (*C. edulis*)　　　mtanda mboo (Swa); olmiraa (Maa)

Habitat: sea level to 2 000 m　**Height:** up to 4 m
Status: locally common

A large, thorny bush, attractive when flowering, with terminal clusters of sweet-scented, pink-white Jasmine-like flowers. The flowers, 1 × 1.5–2 cm across, are arranged in terminal clusters and are red on the outside. Large spines can be single or forked. The leathery leaves are shiny, dark green above, paler below. The mature purple-black fruits are eaten by humans and birds, and Hartlaub's Turaco feeds its young on these berries.
BEST VIEWING: widespread and common in suitable habitats

DEAD SEA FRUIT
Calotropis procera　　　mpamba mwitu (Swa)

Habitat: dry, stony ground, often in disturbed places, 300–1 200 m
Height: up to 4 m　**Status:** locally common

A tall, stout, woody shrub with a close mass of purple-white flowers, 2–2.4 cm across. The ovate, veined, stalkless leaves are spaced at intervals along the stem. Distinctive, green seedpods look like inflated bladders, 10–25 cm in diameter. Common on disturbed ground, especially in arid country that is occasionally flooded.
BEST VIEWING: widespread and common in suitable habitats

CARALLUMA
Caralluma speciosa

Habitat: arid, stony areas, 100–1 680 m **Height:** up to 45 cm
Status: uncommon

A perennial succulent with clusters of erect, four-angled, grey-green stems. The dense flowering head, up to 6 cm across, consists of numerous purplish to dark violet flowers, 2–2.5 cm across, with yellow centres. The flowers have a strong fetid odour that attracts flies for pollination. *C. russelliana* is very similar, but its flower head is larger, 8.5 cm, although individual flowers are smaller, 1.5 cm.

BEST VIEWING: Kenya: Buffalo Springs, Samburu NRs;
Tanzania: Maasai, Tanga Districts; **Uganda:** northern regions

DAISY/WILD MARIGOLD
Aspilia mossambicensis   onkoyabase (Maa)

Habitat: bush and grassland, sea level to 2 150 m **Height:** 1.5 m
Status: common, except in drier areas

A much-branched, woody, perennial shrub with rough, elliptical, lance-shaped, opposite leaves. Bright yellow flowers up to 3.5 cm across, usually solitary but sometimes in clusters. Occasionally rampant, covering neighbouring vegetation if not controlled. One of 13 species occurring in East Africa. The less common *A. pluriseta* is very similar and widespread.

BEST VIEWING: Kenya: throughout; **Tanzania:** most areas apart from the west; **Uganda:** throughout

GUTENBERGIA
Gutenbergia cordifolia   nain'gong'u in-dero (Maa)

Habitat: rocky, eroded, poor grassland, 1 200–2 400 m **Height:** up to 50 cm **Status:** locally common

A small, erect herb with elliptical, tapering leaves, which usually have soft white hairs underneath. The deep purple flowers, about 1.4 cm across, can be solitary or in bunched heads. At times can become invasive. In 2001, which was a very wet year, *G. cordifolia* and *Bidens* sp. encroached over large areas of the floor of the Ngorongoro Crater, causing a major loss of indigenous vegetation, which resulted in a number of Black Rhinoceros dying of starvation.

BEST VIEWING: widespread in suitable habitats

EVERLASTING FLOWER
Helichrysum formosissimum

Habitat: open, tussocky grassland in the bamboo zone, 2 700–4 100 m
Height: up to 3 m **Status:** common

There are 80 species of *Helichrysum* in East Africa; all but two occur above 1 500 m. Their flowers are characteristic of East Africa's mountains. This species has a much-branched stem, woody at the base, with dense heads of pretty, soft pink-white flowers, about 2 cm across, with yellow centres. These daisy-like flowers become dry as the plant matures; the dried flowers retain their colour for years. The leaves are narrow, elliptical, stalkless and crowded.

BEST VIEWING: Kenya: Aberdare NP; **Tanzania:** Kilimanjaro NP;
Uganda: Rwenzori Mountains NP

POM-POM
Kleinia abyssinica (*Notonia abyssinica*) emasiligi (Maa)

Habitat: rocky soils, 760–2 400 m **Height:** up to 1 m
Status: locally common

There are 21 species in East Africa, of which 14 were originally classified in the genus *Notonia*. A tall, perennial herb with 1–7 showy, bright red flower heads, 3.5 cm across. The leaves are oval, pointed and fleshy. A variant, *K. abyssinica* var. *hildebrandtii*, found in eastern, northern and central Kenya, is smaller and the flower heads are only 2 cm across.

BEST VIEWING: Kenya: western areas; **Tanzania:** around Lake Victoria, Maasai, Tanga, Iringa districts; **Uganda:** widespread

GIANT MORNING GLORY
Ipomoea kituensis mlayoka, mruo (Swa)

Habitat: *Acacia-Combretum* bushland, 800–2 040 m **Length:** up to 6 m
Status: common after rains

A rampant, woody shrub with long, twining, soft, hairy stems. Large, showy, funnel-shaped flowers in white, cream or yellow, with purple centres. The leaves are large, heart-shaped, 3.5–14.5 cm long and 3–16 cm wide. The well-known Morning Glory (*I. cairica*), a prolific, twining climber, has pale mauve-pink flowers, occasionally white with darker centres, about 5.5 cm across. *I. cairica* is found in forest clearings, damp grassland, on waste and cultivated land at 750–1 890 m.

BEST VIEWING: Kenya: Tsavo East, Tsavo West NPs; **Tanzania:** Kondoa, Tanga districts

RESURRECTION PLANT
Craterostigma pumilum

Habitat: dry grassland areas, 1 000–3 000 m **Height:** 3 cm
Status: common

These small herbs all but disappear during the dry season but suddenly became apparent soon after rain, when they flower profusely. The tiny violet-like, blue-violet flowers, 7 mm across, are borne at the end of a single stem. The broad, veined, often serrated leaves form a distinctive rosette.

BEST VIEWING: Kenya: Nairobi area; **Tanzania:** Maasai District; **Uganda:** Jinja District

WASTE PAPER FLOWER
Cycnium tubulosum kiwavi (Swa)

Habitat: black cotton soils, grassland, marshy areas, 600–3 000 m
Height: up to 75 cm **Status:** common

Semi-parasitic on grass roots to which it is attached. The flowers, 4–5 cm across, on long stalks, vary from white, shades of pink to mauve. Common after rain, it can look like paper tissues dotted across the plains, hence its common name (it is also called Kleenex Flower). Its leaves, up to 8 cm long, are narrow, slightly oval and pointed. *C. tubulosum* subsp. *montanum* is the common Waste Paper Flower in the Serengeti and Masai Mara.

BEST VIEWING: Kenya: Masai Mara NR; **Tanzania:** Serengeti NP; **Uganda:** all regions

CROSSANDRA
Crossandra subacaulis   egegeiye (Maa)

Habitat: savanna country and rocky slopes, up to 1 690 m
Height: up to 30 cm **Status:** common

An erect, scrambling, shrubby plant with small, upright spikes of orange or red, lobed flowers, up to 5 cm across, which grow upwards from the centre of the leaves. It is an almost stemless, low-growing herb with tight rosettes of leaves. The similar *C. mucronata* differs in having small, apricot-orange, lobed flowers, 1.8–2.6 cm across.

BEST VIEWING: widespread

BLACK-EYED SUSAN
Thunbergia alata   kijako-gura (Swa); oltamiloi (Maa)

Habitat: damp areas, forest edges, sea level to 2 740 m
Height: up to 3 m **Status:** common

A perennial, vigorous creeper with soft, dark green, heart-shaped leaves. The five-petalled flowers, up to 4 cm across, are bright orange with deep violet to black centres. Occasionally white flowers occur. Its relative *T. gregorii* has larger, all-yellow flowers, 4.5 cm across, and without a dark centre; the flower bracts are much hairier.

BEST VIEWING: widespread in suitable habitats

SUNBIRD FLOWER/LION'S EAR
Leonotis nepetifolia   mlisha kunga (Swa); ol-bibi (Maa)

Habitat: mostly disturbed places, sea level to 2 100 m
Height: up to 2 m **Status:** common

An erect, woody annual with spherical flower heads, up to 7 cm across. The heads of orange-red flowers occur at evenly spaced intervals on the angled (square) stem. The velvety flowers, 2.5 cm long, grow out of rigid, spiky, protective sheaths. Below each flower ball are pairs of elongated, drooping leaves, 10 cm long. The flower heads remain long after the flowers have died. This member of the mint family is very popular with sunbirds.

BEST VIEWING: widespread in suitable habitats

BLUE BUTTERFLY BUSH
Rotheca myricoides (*Clerodendrum myricoides*)   mkua-usiku (Swa);
                                      olmakutukut, ol-magotogot (Maa)

Habitat: bushland and forest edges, 1 200–2 400 m
Height: up to 2.5 m **Status:** common

A climbing shrub with oval, almost stalkless leaves, arranged in whorls around the stem. The flowers, 1.5 cm across, have five petals, which are white to pale blue, with a dark blue lower petal, which is longer than the others. The flowers look a little like dainty blue butterflies, hence its common name.

BEST VIEWING: Kenya: widespread in all but the drier areas;
Tanzania and Uganda: widespread

DAY FLOWER
Commelina benghalensis engaiteteyai (Maa)

Habitat: damper areas and disturbed land, sea level to 2 500 m
Height: up to 20 cm **Status:** common

There are 50 species of *Commelina* in East Africa. This species is a low-growing, creeping herb with bright sky-blue flowers, which open during the morning and are usually closed during the afternoon, except in overcast weather. The flowers, 2 cm across, are produced from within a folded bract. The leaves are long, narrow and pointed. The similar *C. latifolia* has darker blue flowers.
BEST VIEWING: widespread in suitable habitats in the region

ALOE
Aloe volkensii kismamleo (Swa); olomborgishi (Maa)

Habitat: dry, rocky bushland, 900–2 300 m **Height:** 5 m or more
Status: locally common

A tall, usually single-stemmed but occasionally branched *Aloe* with olive-green, tooth-edged leaves that secrete a clear latex when cut, the medicinal properties of which are well known. The attractive, orange-red flowers are produced in much-branched heads and attract sunbirds. Flowers after the rain.
BEST VIEWING: Kenya: Narok, Kajiado districts; **Tanzania:** Olduvai (Oldupai) Gorge, Serengeti NP; **Uganda:** western regions

FLAME LILY
Gloriosa superba mkalau (Swa); sagotai (Maa); sakutari (Sam)

Habitat: widespread, up to 2 530 m **Height:** 3 m or more
Status: locally common

A scrambling, climbing plant, which appears with the rains. The lance-shaped leaves have tips that act as tendrils, hooking themselves onto any support. Large, 7.5 cm across, spectacular-looking, brilliant scarlet flowers, with long, protruding stamens. Flowers have six wavy-edged petals marked at the base with yellow and green. There are also yellow-flowered varieties.
BEST VIEWING: widespread

RED-HOT POKER
Kniphofia thomsonii

Habitat: alongside streams and marshy areas, 1 000–1 600 m
Height: up to 1 m **Status:** locally common

An upright herb with a dense, poker-shaped head of hanging flowers, 16 × 6.5 cm, tapering to the tip, on a stout stem. Each trumpet-shaped flower is up to 3 cm long, ranging in colour from yellow to red. The flowers are much liked by sunbirds. The leaves are narrow, grass-like, tough, up to 100 cm long.
BEST VIEWING: Kenya: Mount Elgon, Aberdare NPs; **Tanzania:** Maasai, Mbeya districts; **Uganda:** eastern districts

GROUND LILY
Ammocharis tinneana   olesila (Maa)

Habitat: dry bushland or wooded grassland, 350–1 400 m
Height: up to 30 cm **Status:** locally common

A striking plant when flowering, with a round head of pink to dark red flowers; the head consists of 20 flowers on stems up to 34 cm long. The leaves are thick, dark green, and spread in a fan from the base. Often found in large communities, flowering after the first rains.

BEST VIEWING: Kenya: Masai Mara NR, Tsavo East, Tsavo West NPs; **Tanzania:** Mpwapwa, Kondoa, Morogoro, Iringa districts; **Uganda:** northern regions

TUMBLEWEED/POM-POM LILY
Boöphone disticha   olang'ung'wei (Maa)

Habitat: rocky grassland, 1 500–2 500 m **Height:** 60–90 cm
Status: locally common

The large head of dense, pink-red flowers, up to 20 cm across, appears annually before the rains, from a bulb protruding well above ground. Flower stalks lengthen to up to 30 cm and stiffen when fruiting, eventually breaking away and tumbling with the wind, so dispersing seeds. Differs from similar Fire-ball Lily by having leaves arranged in a fan; leaves are up to 30 cm long, appearing after the flowers. Bulb is highly poisonous to cattle; its name is derived from the Greek words for 'ox-killer'.

BEST VIEWING: Kenya: Masai Mara NR; **Tanzania:** Serengeti NP; **Uganda:** northern regions

PYJAMA LILY
Crinum macowanii   nyonyoro (Swa)

Habitat: grassland and marshy areas, 500–2 700 m **Height:** up to 80 cm **Status:** locally common

A bulbous plant with thin, dull green leaves. Its distinctive funnel-shaped, white flowers are striped pink, giving it its common name. Flowers 10–15 ,on long stalks, up to 20 cm long, appearing before the rains and emitting a heavy perfume in the evening. An all-white form occurs in the Samburu and Shaba NRs, Kenya.

BEST VIEWING: Kenya: widespread; **Tanzania:** Ngorongoro Crater rim; **Uganda:** northern and eastern regions

FIRE-BALL LILY/BLOOD LILY
Scadoxus multiflorus   osila (Maa)

Habitat: open grassland, rocky places and semi-arid areas, sea level to 2 500 m **Height:** up to 30 cm **Status:** widespread and common

A striking red ball of flowers, up to 20 cm across (composed of about 150 small, narrow-petalled individual flowers), on a single stout stem. The flower stem has maroonish spots at the base. Flowers appear with the first rains, before the shiny, bright green leaves, and last for about 10 days. Produces bright red, fleshy berries, about 8 mm across. Grows from a bulb deep in the ground, often found in the shade of trees.

BEST VIEWING: widespread except in the drier areas

PARROT'S BEAK GLADIOLUS
Gladiolus natalensis

Habitat: grasslands, 1 200–3 050 m **Height:** 25–40 cm
Status: common and widespread

Has large, showy, hooded flowers, about 2 cm across, borne on long, erect stems. Coloration varies from bright orange to yellow, often streaked or flecked brown. A variety with yellow flowers streaked with orange occurs in rocky areas of western Kenya. The leaves are long, thin and sword-shaped (an old name for *Gladiolus* was *Xiphium*, from the Greek word *xiphos*, which means 'sword'). This flower is one of the ancestors of the cultivated gladiolus.

BEST VIEWING: widespread in suitable habitats

MOUNTAIN GLADIOLUS
Gladiolus watsonioides

Habitat: stony soils, 3 050 m or higher **Height:** 5.5–10 cm
Status: locally common

The most beautiful member of this family. A striking plant with bright scarlet-red flowers with a long, curved tube. Flowers are borne on a single spike on a leafy stem. Leaves, 5–7 × 0.5–1.4 cm wide, are ribbed, flat and sword-shaped. Plants vary in size and flower colour in different areas: Kilimanjaro plants are slightly taller; flowers of Mount Kenya plants are deeper red; those on the Aberdares are somewhere between the two.

BEST VIEWING: Kenya: Aberdare, Mount Kenya NPs;
Tanzania: Kilimanjaro, Arusha (Mount Meru) NPs

TREE ORCHID
Aerangis thomsonii

Habitat: shady places in highland forests, 1 500–3 000 m
Status: common

An epiphytic orchid with stout woody stems. Found low down on tree trunks and branches, with thick aerial roots and dark green, bilobed, hard, leathery leaves. Pure white flowers, 4–10, on long stalks, with tubular spurs, 10–15 cm long. Flowers are sweetly scented, especially after dark. Blooms March–April and October–November. The similar *A. brachycarpa* differs in having egg-shaped leaves, which are borne together in a fan, 2–12 white flowers, 4–6 cm across, with a spur 4–6 cm long.

BEST VIEWING: Kenya and Tanzania: highland forests;
Uganda: Mount Elgon NP

LEOPARD ORCHID
Ansellia africana

Habitat: wooded grasslands, sea level to 2 200 m **Height:** up to 1.5 m
Status: locally common

The largest of the epiphytic (not parasitic) orchids, spectacular when in flower. Usually found in large clumps in trees, especially baobabs and coastal palms, but occasionally also on rocks. Leaves, 80–100, 30 × 4 cm, branching from the upper ends of thick, papery stems, which are up to 1 m long. Lightly scented, yellow flowers, 10–100, up to 4 cm across, are heavily blotched reddish-brown, on stalks up to 1 m long.

BEST VIEWING: Kenya: Shimba Hills NR; **Tanzania:** on baobabs, Lake Manyara NP; **Uganda:** Mount Elgon NP

BIBLIOGRAPHY AND FURTHER READING

MAMMALS

Dorst, Jean & Dandelot, Pierre. 1970. *A Field Guide to Larger Mammals of Africa*. Collins, London.

Estes, R. 1991. *Behavior Guide to African Mammals*. University of California Press, California.

Kingdon, J. 1997. *The Kingdon Field Guide to African Mammals*. Academic Press, London.

Maloiy, G.M.O. & Eley, R.M. 1992. *The Hyrax*. Regal Press, Nairobi, Kenya.

McColaugh, Doreen Wolfsen. 1989. *Wild Lives – Profiles of East African Mammals*. African Wildlife Foundation.

Walker, C. 1996. *Signs of the Wild – A field guide to the spoor and signs of the mammals of Southern Africa*. 5th edition. Struik Publishers, Cape Town.

BIRDS

Bennun, Leon & Njoroge, Peter. 1999. *Important Bird Areas in Kenya*. Nature Kenya, Nairobi.

Britton, P.L. 1980. *Birds of East Africa, Their Habit, Status and Distribution*. East African Natural History Society, Nairobi.

Dickinson, E.C. (ed.) 2003. *The Howard & Moore Complete Checklist of the Birds of the World* (revised and enlarged 3rd edition). A&C Black/Croom Helm, London.

Lewis, A. & Pomeroy, D. 1989. *A Bird Atlas of Kenya*. A.A. Balkema, Rotterdam.

Oberprieler, Ulrich & Cillié, Burger. 2009. *The Raptor Guide of Southern Africa*. Game Parks Publishing, Pretoria.

Richards, Dave. 1995. *A Photographic Guide to Birds of East Africa*. 3rd edition. New Holland, London.

Stevenson, Terry & Fanshawe, John. 2002. *Field Guide to the Birds of East Africa*. T & AD Poyser, London.

Zimmerman, Dale A., Turner, Donald A. & Pearson, David J. 1996. *Birds of Kenya and Northern Tanzania*. Russel Friedman Books, South Africa.

REPTILES AND AMPHIBIANS

Spawls, Stephen, Howell, Kim, Drewes, Robert & Ash, James. 2002. *A Field Guide to the Reptiles of East Africa*. Academic Press, London.

Spawls, Stephen, Howell, Kim M. & Drewes, Robert C. 2006. *Pocket Guide to the Reptiles and Amphibians of East Africa*. A&C Black Publishers, London.

INSECTS

Carder, Nanny & Tindimubona, Laura. 2002. *Butterflies of Uganda*. Uganda Society.

Goodden, Robert. 1971. *Butterflies*. Hamlyn, London.

Larsen, Torben B. 1991, 1996, 2000. *The Butterflies of Kenya and their Natural History*. Oxford University Press.

McGavin, George C. 2000. *Insects, Spiders and Other Terrestrial Arthropods*. Dorling Kindersley, London.

Picker, Mike, Griffiths, Charles & Weaving, Alan. 2004. *Field Guide to Insects of South Africa*. Random House Struik, Cape Town.

Skaife, S.H. 1979 (revised edition). *African Insect Life*. Country Life, UK.

Woodhall, Steve. 2005. *Field Guide to Butterflies of South Africa*. Struik Publishers, Cape Town.

TREES AND SHRUBS

Beentje, Henk. 1994. *Kenya Trees, Shrubs, and Lianas*. National Museums of Kenya.

Dale, I.R. & Greenway, P. 1961. *Kenya Trees and Shrubs*. Buchanan's Kenya Estates Ltd, Kenya.

Dharani, Najma. 2002. *Field Guide to Common Trees & Shrubs of East Africa*. Struik Publishers, Cape Town.

Dharani, Najma. 2006. *Field Guide to Acacias of East Africa*. Struik Publishers, Cape Town.

Noad, Tim & Birnie, Ann. 1989. *Trees of Kenya*. T.C. Noad and A. Birnie, Nairobi, Kenya.

FLOWERS

Allen, David J. 2007. *A Traveller's Guide to the Wildflowers and Common Trees of East Africa*. 2nd edition. Camerapix Publishers International, Nairobi.

Blundell, Michael. 1987. *Collins Guide to the Wild Flowers of East Africa*. William Collins Sons & Co. Ltd., London.

Sapieha, Teresa. 1989. *Wayside Flowers of East Africa*. Teresa Sapieha, Nairobi, Kenya.

Wedekind, Joan & Sutton, Angela. 2009. *Some Wild Flowers of the Ngong Hills*. Jaws, Kenya.

GENERAL

Alden, Peter C., Estes, Richard D., Schlitter, Duane & McBride, Bunny. 1995. *National Audubon Society Field Guide to African Wildlife*. Alfred A. Knopf Inc., New York.

Erickson Wilson, Sandra. 1995. *Bird and Mammal Checklists for Ten National Parks in Uganda*. National Biodiversity Data Bank, Kampala, Uganda.

Loon, Rael & Loon, Hélène. 2005. *Birds – the Inside Story*. Struik Publishers, Cape Town.

Richards, Dave. 2007. *Safari Guide Kenya*. New Holland, London.

Roodt, Veronica. 2005. *The Tourist Travel and Field Guide of the Serengeti National Park*. Papyrus Publications, South Africa.

Williams, John G. 1970. *A Field Guide to the National Parks of East Africa*. Collins, London.

GLOSSARY

aestivation – a state of dormancy or torpor during hot weather

arboreal – living in trees

axillary cluster – a bud borne at the axil of a leaf, capable of developing into a branch shoot or flower cluster

bract – modified leaf

browser – a mammal that feeds predominantly on the growing shoots and buds of certain woody shrubs and trees

buttress – the flared base of certain trees

carpel – the female reproductive organ of a flower, consisting of an ovary, a stigma and usually a style

cere – the area on the upper part of the beak that contains the bird's nostrils

colonial – living in a colony

compound leaf – a leaf consisting of several or many distinct parts (leaflets) joined to a single axis, the rachis

coral rag – rubbly limestone composed of ancient coral reef material

covert feathers – a set of feathers that cover other feathers and help to smooth airflow over the wings and tail

crepuscular – active primarily at dawn and dusk

critically endangered – the highest risk category assigned by the IUCN Red List of Threatened Species

decurved (of a bill) – curved downward

diurnal – active during the daytime, rather than at night

elliptical leaf – simple, oval-shaped leaf

endangered (of species) – having numbers so small that it is at risk of extinction

epiphytic (of a plant) – deriving moisture and nutrients from the air and rain; usually growing on another plant but not parasitically

fissure – a long, narrow opening or line of breakage made by cracking or splitting

flight feathers – the primaries, secondaries and tertials on the wing, and major tail feathers

gall – an abnormal growth formed in response to the presence of insect larvae, mites or fungi on plants and trees

gape – the region where the two mandibles join, at the base of the beak

glabrous – free from hair or down; smooth

gorget – a band or patch of distinctive colour on the throat of an animal, especially an area of brightly coloured feathers on the throat of a bird

grazer – a mammal that predominantly feeds on non-woody vegetation such as grasses

immature (of a bird) – young, in plumage between juvenile and adult

juvenile (of a bird) – young, in its first fully feathered plumage

keels – two lower petals that are usually fused, enclosing the stamens and pistil of a flower

lek – a long-established area where mammals and birds gather for courtship and mating

lore – the surface on each side of a bird's head between the eye and the upper base of the beak, or between the eye and nostril in snakes

lyrate (of horns) – shaped like a lyre, roughly U-shaped

malar stripes – the area of the face below the eyes and between the nose and ears

mandible – the jawbone in vertebrates

melanistic – having unusually dark colouring, resulting from high levels of pigments

mud-puddling – an activity mostly seen in butterflies, which gather on wet soil, dung and carrion to obtain nutrients such as salts and amino acids

nocturnal – active at night

non-breeding plumage – the plumage some adult birds acquire when not breeding

non-passerines – non-perching birds

obovate (of a leaf) – ovate, with the narrower end at the base

opposite (of leaves) – growing in pairs from opposite sides of the twig at the same level

ovate (of a leaf) – having an oval outline or ovoid shape, like an egg

Palaearctic – of a subregion that includes Europe, Asia north of the Himalayas, northern Arabia, and Africa north of the Sahara

parasite – an organism that grows, feeds and is sheltered on or in a different organism, contributing nothing to the survival of its host

passerines – perching birds, including all songbirds

pinnate (of a compound leaf) – having leaflets arranged on either side of the stem, typically in pairs opposite each other

primaries – the largest feathers on the edge of a bird's wing

race – a geographically distinct population of a species

raptor – a bird of prey

resident (of a bird) – non-migratory

riparian – living along streams, ponds and lakes or any watercourses

scandent – characterised by a climbing mode of growth

secondaries – large feathers between the primaries and the tertials of a bird's wing

sepal – one of the separate, usually green, parts forming the calyx of a flower

simple leaf – a leaf having a single blade on its stalk, which is attached to a woody twig; when the stalk is removed from the twig a distinct scar is left on the twig

spathe – a large sheathing bract enclosing the flower cluster of certain plants, especially the spadix of arums and palms

speculum – an iridescent patch of colour on the wings of some ducks and other birds

stamen – the pollen-producing reproductive organ of a flower

tertials – the innermost flight feathers of the wing, attached to the humerus bone in the bird's upper arm; there are usually 3–4 tertials

trifoliolate – having three leaflets

vermiculations – a dense, irregular pattern of lines, as though made by worm-tracks

vulnerable (of species) – species likely to become threatened unless its circumstances change

wattle – a coloured, fleshy lobe hanging from the head or neck of domestic chickens, turkeys and some other birds

whorl – the attachment of sepals, petals, leaves or branches at a single point on a plant

INDEX

REPTILES AND AMPHIBIANS

WILD FLOWERS